FUTURISTIC GEOGRAPHY
The Chandigarh Periphery Zone : 2020

FUTURISTIC GEOGRAPHY

The Chandigarh Periphery Zone : 2020

PAWAN KUMAR SHARMA

DEEP & DEEP PUBLICATIONS PVT. LTD.
F-159, Rajouri Garden, New Delhi - 110 027

FUTURISTIC GEOGRAPHY
The Chandigarh Periphery Zone : 2020

ISBN 978-81-8450-353-1

Typeset by RAHUL COMPOSERS
358, Pocket-B, Phase-2, Sector-16B, Dwarka, New Delhi - 110 075

Printed in India at MAYUR ENTERPRISES
WZ Plot No. 3, Gujjar Market, Tihar Village, New Delhi - 110 018

Published by DEEP & DEEP PUBLICATIONS PVT. LTD.
F-159, Rajouri Garden, New Delhi - 110 027 • Phone : 25435369, 25440916
E-mail : ddpubs@gmail.com • ddpbooks@yahoo.co.in
Showroom :
2/13, Ansari Road, Daryaganj, New Delhi - 110 002 • Telefax : 23245122

Contents

Foreword

Peripheries are often described as neglected, marginalised and exploited entities. Not so in the case of Periphery Zone of Chandigarh. It underwent an experience to the contrary. While the Periphery Control Act was devised to retain it as an open, green, rural countryside, the political and economic interests have gradually been turning it into an extensive, modern, urban sprawl. This is the research story which Dr. Pawan Kumar Sharma narrates for our sensitisation to this anomaly.

When approached by Dr. Sharma to write a Foreword to his book, Futuristic Geography (The Chandigarh Periphery Zone: 2020), the response was in a spontaneous affirmative. The feeling was that the periphery he dealt with was a special kind of territory and he had ventured to test his skill in area of research in which a few in Indian Geography had tested the waters. It was an exercise in Futuristic Geography, a theme dear to my intellectual inclination. Also through a long association, I was familiar with the authentic quality of any research Dr. Sharma undertakes. There was a temptation to respond to all this by way of occupying the space in the very beginning of his book.

The task committed was not as simple as envisaged. To begin with it required a snapshot of the growth trajectory of our discipline as also an understanding of the issues involved in regulation of the periphery zone of a planned city. This led to revival of my own learning.

Geography has ever been evolving since it got its first nomenclature in Greek through Eratosthene's book *Geographica* in 3rd century B.C. Finding its early moorings in earth configuration, exploration and cartography, it acquired the title of Chorography or Chorology during the Middle Ages. Since the beginning of the 19th century, it has been institutionalised as an ever expanding and diversifying discipline with a distinct identity.

Geography has been subject to a series of definitions, such as study of the variable character of the earth surface, or that of man-land relationships or that of spatial organisation and so on. Focus on spatial specificity, interaction and diffusion has been the hallmark of the discipline. At the same time, it was put under the lens of a variety of perspectives, including positivistic, radical, behavioural and humanistic, among others. A number of regularly upgraded methodologies of fieldwork, cartography, quantitative analysis, remote sensing and geographical information systems was put in service to refine the research tools of this discipline.

If all this is distilled, one finds that the persistent focus of geography has been on spaces, places and environment, all in a holistic sense and in interrelationship with each other. Now cyberspace is emerging as a new area of interest, with a belief that technology can never do away with the relevance of spaces and places. It simply gives them a new form.

While the study of the present or contemporary has been fairly exhaustive in Geography, and that of the past has been a regular interest in Historical Geography, a visualization of future of geographic scenarios is yet to take shape. The underlying belief is that since geography has to deal with a variety and complexity of phenomena and processes, it would be hazardous for it to enter in the realm of prediction. No longer tenable is this line of thinking. In the context of the rapid transformation of landscapes taking place all over, and the need of managing them effectively being urgent, a growing realisation is that the 'future of geography' hinges on 'geography of future'. The availability of sophisticated research technological tools has made it possible to work this out. The expectation is that Geography may visualise future scenarios of different parts of world and suggest optimal use of land, identify best locations, and draw an ecologically viable road map for meeting the challenge. The interlinkage between the global and the local, and its implications for future spaces and places, has become a critical point of enquiry in Geography.

In that light, this book by Dr. Sharma is one of the few species of a new genre. It focuses on the 'Periphery Zone of the Planned City of Chandigarh in a futuristic perspective. At the centre of the whole exercise is the testing of the Periphery Control Act, which was legislated to retain the overwhelmingly rural character of the tract up to 16 kilometers from the project site of the city. To arrive at an authentic assessment and to project the scenario as it would emerge, data by villages and towns was marshalled for a time period of half a century, the existing literature and government documents were scrutinised carefully, and ground realities were captured through extensive fieldwork. Tremendous was the task involved in overall terms.

A salient finding is that under the prevailing populist political culture and indifferent bureaucracy, the Periphery Control Act was grossly violated not only by the people at large but equally by the government itself. In the process, the intended rural character of the Periphery Zone could not be conserved and it is going to be completely urbanised in not too distant a future. The periphery is now an extension of the core, a case of the core swallowing its periphery. This confirms the vulnerability of any Periphery *vis-a-vis* the dynamism of the Core.

Dr. Sharma's contribution is highly commendable and valuable. Free from any generalities based on impressions, it processes all available information through rigour of quantitative analysis, looks at population growth and land-use transformation as two basic components of a geographical change, and arrives at dependable projections on the count of both. It offers much for policy-makers to heed, for town planners to redefine their strategies, and research students to emulate.

A book is expected to represent a distinct perspective, demonstrate a convincing methodology and convey a fresh message. The book scores high on all this. I need not go further and leave the book for you to read.

DR. GOPAL KRISHAN
Professor Emeritus
Panjab University,
and Principal Advisor (PDC)
State Institute of Public Administration, Punjab
Chandigarh

Preface

A book is a journey for its author. Any journey undertaken prompts one to narrate its story. The same holds good for the present one.

Most fascinating to me, among different branches of geography, has been the Futuristic Geography. It explores evolutionary process of the present and past of places and spaces into future. This probably is linked with my natural tendency to go through horoscopes published in a magazine or newspaper. More often these are couched in good English and promise an optimistic future to arrive.

This said, my interest in the present study is rooted in a realization that while geographers have often dealt with the existing scenario of any area or region and have also been at times, interested in their past, the exercise in working out their future has been a rare effort.

Which area should be taken up for projecting its future? A natural choice went in favour of city of my abode, Chandigarh. Not only is it a completely planned city but also its periphery up to 16 kms. was expected to retain its predominantly rural landscape through a legislative measure. This defined an additional point of enquiry. To what extent the government has been successful in ensuring the implementation of the Act legislated? If not, why not and who were responsible for its violation? Above all, in futuristic perspective, what is in store for the periphery was also prognosticated?

Guided by these considerations, I decided to attempt a futuristic scenario of the Periphery Zone of Chandigarh. Which are the most critical modules to scrutinize for the purpose? The realization was that the people and the land qualify on this score. Therefore, the entire structure of analysis was raised on these two pillars.

The construction of the future calls for not only a situational analysis of the present but also a digging into the past. How far one should go back in an exercise of the present kind? This could be placed at 'one generation'. Hence, all the necessary data since 1971 were collected for every village and town in the periphery zone. The task was colossal but electronics were there to help.

Outcome of the whole effort is presented in the book. The finding was most revealing. It turned out to be a case of the 'core swallowing the periphery'. In the process, the legislative provisions got violated. This was a doing not only of the people at large but more so of the government itself.

The spirit, substance and style of the book owe a lot to the guidance and support of a number of individuals and institutions. I am deeply indebted to Professor (Emeritus) Gopal Krishan for the research training that he imparted; for generating in me the confidence to strike out on my own; for his valuable inputs to this book; for being there whenever I needed him; and most of all, for tolerating my tantrums.

At the Centre for Research in Rural and Industrial Development (CRRID), this challenging endeavor was possible largely because of the indispensable support that Dr. Rashpal Malhotra, Executive Vice Chairman, CRRID, rendered. I am grateful to him for his confidence in my ability to perform to my best, his constant encouragement in the course of the study, and also for granting me access to the infrastructure at the Centre. Beholden am I also to Professor Sucha Singh Gill, Director General, CRRID for strengthening and sustaining my belief in the value of research.

To Professor Surya Kant, Department of Geography, Panjab University, I owe a deep gratitude for his constant advice and help as also for allowing me an access to the department's infrastructure in his capacity as the Chairman.

Thanks are due also to all other members of the faculty at the department for sharing their ideas on the theme.

The help rendered by Dr. Simrit Kahlon, faculty at the D.A.V. College, Chandigarh, was very special. She is a factor in the quality that this work could acquire. Abiding will be my gratitude to her.

The book would have remained incomplete but for the logistic support given by my friends and well wishers. I wish to thank Mr. Madhav Shyam and his team at the Census of India and Mr. Pankaj Bawa, Assistant Town Planner, for allowing me access to data as well as explaining its nuances; Raman and Sombir for so painstakingly preparing the base map; Mr. Gopal Johri, Dr. Shaik Iftikhar Ahmed, and Dr. Manisha Bhatia for endless rounds of tea and peptalk; and Dr. Rajni Lamba for care in going through the manuscript. Most touching was the concern of Dr. Komila Parthi, who has ever been a source of sound advice and moral support. All this kept the flagging spirit high.

I am grateful to my family for the support that they provided. It was their patience, understanding and deep affection which made the task easy. Thanks to them for keeping the faith alive. I am grateful especially to my wife, Anjula Sharma, who took care of our children, Anshuman and Aakash, and stood in for me during the time I spent away from them.

Tomorrow back to the arenas of my both work and family. life !

PAWAN KUMAR SHARMA

1

Introduction

The global explosion of population that characterized much of the twentieth century was accompanied by another significant transformation: the urban implosion on an unprecedented scale. While about one-tenth of the world's population was inhabiting the urban centres in the beginning of the century, the proportion increased to one-fourth by 1950, one-third by 1975 and virtually half by 2000. The world is expected to become an urban majority for the first time in human history on 16 August, 2008, according to recent projections by the United Nations. In the beginning of the twentieth century, only 16 cities in the world—a larger majority in advanced industrial countries—had a population of a million plus. Today about 500 cities qualify this benchmark. More than two-thirds of these are located in the developing countries. The developing world is also likely to become progressively more urban than rural in 2017 (United Nations, 2005).

Natural increase (difference between birth and death rate), rural-urban migration, and reclassification of settlements are the three basic determinants of urban growth. Since the rate of natural increase is generally lower in urban than in rural areas, the primary reasons for rapid pace of urbanization are rural-urban migration, geographic expansion of urban areas through seizure of nearby land, and upgradation of villages to the status of urban settlements (Cohen, 2005, p. 69). The speed and scale of increase in the urban population, because of any of the reasons cited above, tend to create enormous pressure on the immediate vicinity of the existing towns posing a major challenge for their sustainable development. In most of the larger cities, the population is increasingly moving towards unplanned settlements on the periphery where land is cheaper (Brockerhoff, 2000, p. 2). The management of this magnitude of urban growth has emerged as one of the most critical challenges of the 21st century. The future transition and emerging scenario *vis-à-vis* urbanization is to be visualized and prepared for.

Geographers in the past have predicted various kinds of future landscapes—physical as well as cultural. They are fairly equipped in doing this since one of their orientations is to understand how societies are located and tend to get relocated, how man-land relationships get transformed over time and the kinds of landscapes that will emerge under varying circumstances. It is rightly admitted that, with their grounding in quantitative methods, geographers are competent in concerning themselves with the future of human settlements (Johnston, 1985, p. 6). An overriding concern of the next several decades will be to decide the kind of spatial organisation that is desirable to man for his future in various parts of the world.

The nature and magnitude of urban problems differ between evolved and planned cities. Chandigarh is one of the planned cities. It was raised to serve as the capital of the Indian Punjab. The city was to have a finite population of half-a-million on a well defined site. To check urban sprawl in the Peripheral area of the city of Chandigarh, an Act technically known as the 'Punjab New Capital Periphery Control Act, 1952' was enacted to ensure the sustenance of the primarily rural character of the area surrounding Chandigarh. The Act ensured that any haphazard urban sprawl was to be pre-empted. Initially, it brought within its purview, a Periphery Zone up to a distance of eight kilometres from the boundary of the original site of the Chandigarh Capital Project. This was extended to 16 kilometres in 1962 (Map 1.1). The Act envisaged a control over the spread of the city beyond its physical limits onto its peripheral areas.

A long time has passed. The future perceived for the Periphery Zone at that time has become a past at present. When the capital city of Chandigarh was planned, it could not have been visualised that its political status would undergo a radical change. As a consequence of the reorganisation of the former Punjab in 1966 into Punjab, Haryana and Himachal Pradesh, the Union .Territory of Chandigarh was carved out. The Periphery Zone was fragmented into three sub-zones under Punjab, Haryana and the Chandigarh Union Territory. The enforcement of the Periphery Control Act became the responsibility of the respective states/union territory.

Things began to get beyond control. Punjab planned the urban estate at Mohali, called Sahibzada Ajit Singh Nagar (S.A.S.), in 1967 and Haryana followed with another planned urban estate, Panchkula in 1970. By 2001, S.A.S. Nagar (Mohali) had a population of 123 thousand and Panchkula of 141 thousand. Subsequently, the Periphery Zone started getting dotted with additional urban settlements, gradually changing its predominantly rural character. Though the pressure on housing in Chandigarh was now being shared by the satellite towns, these in turn also made heavy demands on the educational, health and other services available in the city. Added to this was the phenomenon of large scale speculation in land and unauthorized constructions in the surroundings of the city.

The resulting pattern of development around the city, as well as buoyancy of socio-economic conditions within the city, makes it imperative for the academic world to attempt to envision the future of Chandigarh. This cannot be done without considering the evolving situation in its periphery. A lot of current research is focussed on the city itself. What is needed, all the more, is a detailed study of the changing landscape of the Chandigarh peripheral zone technically known as the Periphery Zone so as to construct its landscape likely to emerge in the future. A detailed review of the available literature will put the issues in an objective perspective.

MAP 1.1

India : Location of Chandigarh Periphery Zone : 2006

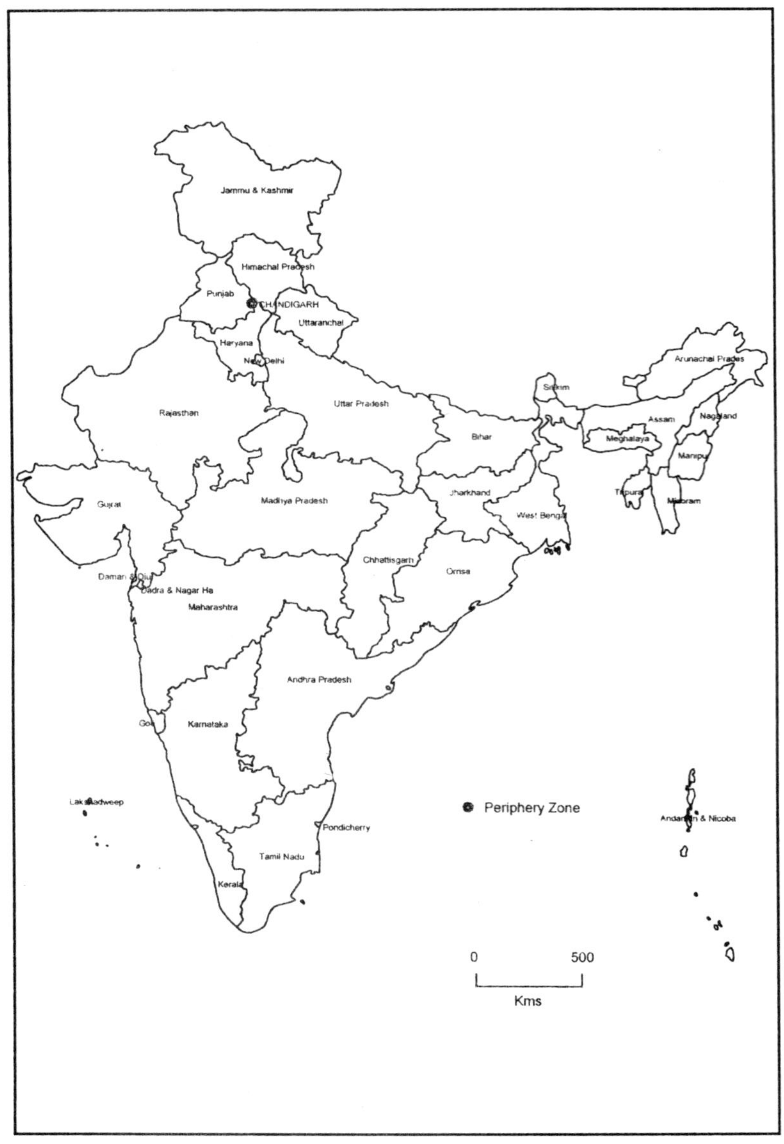

STUDIES ON THE SUBJECT

The contemporary research on the 'future' is put under varying titles in different contexts. In France, it is Futuribles; in the United Kingdom, Future Research; in the United States of America, Futurism, and in Russia, it is popularly called Prognostics. In India, the study of this subject is gaining credence under the broad heading of Futuristic Studies.

Though the future had been studied in one form or the other for quite some time, it was applied for the first time in a systematic manner by the group known as 'Club of Rome' in the sixties. 'Limits to Growth' is their most renowned work. It delves into the issue of interplay between demand and supply of resources over time.

In a wider global context, Gould (1971) describes the situation that the doubling of population in the next thirty years would place so much pressure on existing resources that geographers and other scientists will have to re-evaluate the potential productivity of some parts of the earth. The seas of the world will be seen as a source of mineral and food resources. Certain species of marine life are already domesticated and cultivated. Such a trend will continue in the future. In another context, Smith (1983), while studying 'Communication in the Year 2000', found that the new information technologies were bound to progress. Cities will not disappear, together with their traffic jams, just because of the arrival of the word-processor (as some have predicted), but then the psychological acceptance of fixed locations for work and residence, vacation and entertainment, may well evaporate. He further added that future linkages would not necessarily be based upon shared location or physical proximity. All this would result in the formation of different kind of landscapes.

Iyengar (1972), India's leading Futurist, is mostly concerned with strategies of application of science and technology. He is of the view that the less developed or developing nations can move into the future leaving the advanced nations behind without adhering to any of the conventions and formalities of phased progress. Beyond these statements by eminent scholars at the global level, a note may be taken of the observations made by Indian scholars on the emerging urban scene.

Mehta (1962) remarked that the senseless destruction of landscape in our cities is a tragedy of the high-handedness of people with little application of long range consequences. By the year 2000, a five-fold increase in the urban population in as many decades would pose an unmatched challenge. He further noted that the relationship between cities and the surrounding rural areas would remain obscure. He observed that the future development of towns and cities would form an integral part of a well thought out regional development initiative.

Bijlani (1977) suggested that the city of the future should be designed in a flexible manner so that it can adapt itself to the ever-changing requirements of technology. All new cities at present were meant to accommodate motor traffic. In the case of depletion of petroleum resources, it is difficult to say whether the future belongs to an automobile or to some other form of locomotion yet to be invented.

There are some other such micro-level studies which have been conducted by town planners as well as geographers. Here are the ones focusing on Chandigarh.

Evenson (1966) visualized a better future for the city if the role of restrictive planning was reduced. She opined that if Chandigarh were ever to become a true city, it would be only when its people have given it a history and when it becomes free of planners to acquire a destiny of its own. Randhawa (1967), while commending the tempo at which development work was going on in Chandigarh, observed that the city had a bright future. It was reflected in the prices of residential and commercial building sites sold. He emphasized that if freedom from political vicissitudes is assured, the city would definitely grow and prosper.

Bichsel (1986) describes the changes that have taken place in the villages on the periphery of Chandigarh as a consequence of the influx and settlements of migrants. Within a short period of their arrival, migrants have brought significant changes in the social and economic life of these villages. This trend is likely to reduce the chances of slum formation.

Kalia (1987) believed that 'Chandigarh would not develop according to a fixed master plan conceived some thirty-five years ago'. Thousands of people from neighbouring towns and villages commute daily to the city for one reason or another. As far as future is concerned, he observed that any plan for Chandigarh that fails to develop social and economic opportunities in its surrounding areas will not succeed.

Krishan (1994), in his report prepared for the Chandigarh Administration, projected the population of the Chandigarh as 1.26 million by 2020. He adds a note of caution that in case rehabilitation schemes are not undertaken in the near future, the proportion of slum population will rise from one-tenth to over one-fifth of the total population in 2020.

Vimal (1994), in her critical evaluation of the plan parameters of Chandigarh, observed that the immediate periphery of the city was undergoing rapid transformation. This development was contrary to what the planners had wanted to pre-empt.

Ruch (2002) while commenting on the unbuilt open spaces in Chandigarh concluded that the construction of the city was still in process. He felt that the master plan prepared half a century ago had not been updated which resulted in construction of unauthorized settlements and fast growing traffic. His solution for the future development of the city lay in the revision of the master plan, following a regional approach, which also includes Panchkula and S.A.S. Nagar (Mohali), and seeks international support for it.

Strangely enough, there is hardly any comprehensive study of the Periphery of Chandigarh. Some sporadic research or conference papers are, of course, available. These are referred to here in detail.

One of the earlier studies beyond Chandigarh was that by Krishan and Aggarwal (1970) who delimited the umland of Chandigarh. The study concluded that though Chandigarh was superimposed on its region, it created an umland around itself. The study demonstrates that any city, planned or evolved, cannot remain in isolation from its surroundings.

According to the Interstate Chandigarh Region (ISCR) Working Group Committee Report (1982), there is a need to delimit the Chandigarh Urban Complex, which is to be planned in a phased manner so that the immediate urban development takes place in and around the places where it is required. This Committee projected the population of the city at one million by the year 2001 against the planned population of only half-a-million. The projected population of the city region is estimated to be about 2.5 million by 2001, with a break up of 66 per cent urban and 34 per cent rural.

The Department of Town and Country Planning, Government of Punjab in its report on the Inter-State Chandigarh Sub Region Punjab—2021, had underlined the need to formulate a plan to control and regulate development in the periphery in the context of changed scenario. Several alternatives were reviewed for the purpose. These included physical expansion of the city, building of linear townships, development of ring towns around Chandigarh, and raising of a new town. A twin-town by the name of the New Chandigarh, was recommended. It was argued that the concept of a twin city, as represented in the success of Hyderabad-Secundarbad, Mumbai-New Mumbai and Delhi-Gurgaon-Noida, would prove helpful in an orderly development of the Periphery Zone. It was also proposed that the rural and urban settlements of the future should be promoted in accordance with the envisaged future hierarchy of settlements.

While pointing out the issues concerning the Chandigarh Periphery Zone, Batra (2002) opined that the development taking place in the area was without any relationship or integration with the mother city and the unplanned industrial growth herein has resulted in the degradation of the city environs. Such a pattern of development was not sufficient to meet the future requirements of population. To meet this situation, it is essential to delineate Chandigarh City region on scientific lines considering various physical, demographic, socio-economic and administrative parameters. Based on identifications of problems and potential of the city, the drafting of a 'Perspective Plan for 20 Years' was recommended. The idea of setting up of a Regional Planning and Development Authority or Board on the same pattern as that of the National Capital Region Planning Board was put forth.

Another viewpoint expressed did not favour regional planning (Verma and Nimbokar, 2002), especially in the case of

Chandigarh where the jurisdictional boundaries cut across three different administrative units. It was pointed out that land being a state subject, regional plan proposals of inter-state nature were likely to have no future in India. In the case of Chandigarh, the neighbouring states of Punjab and Haryana had different motivations for developing the peripheral areas around the city. A commonality between the two states, however, existed in terms of their exploitation of the city infrastructure. Under the prevailing culture of market forces, only better transport linkages with the mother city could meet the demands of a well-developed periphery. Chandigarh would acquire greater dynamism and pressure on its service base would intensify. A well-developed periphery could help it in sharing the burden on its infrastructure, including housing.

In the wake of massive onslaught on the periphery by the government as well as private agencies, things have not worked out as visualized (Krishan, 2002). Due to the escalating prices of land in Chandigarh, its periphery is being encroached upon for construction and speculation with impunity. Emergence of the planned towns of S.A.S. Nagar (Mohali) in Punjab and Panchkula in Haryana have given a further boost to the process. Extensive haphazard, and unauthorized urban growth is taking place. The remedy lies in working out a web-kind of development along the major roads radiating out of Chandigarh. A free flowing transport system to and from the city is a necessary condition for the success of such a system.

Chandigarh and its periphery have experienced a lot of changes in terms of the intent and content, as pointed out by Gupta (2002). The process of development as envisaged and designed by planners and administrators has diverged. The settlements in the proximity of Chandigarh have assumed the form of unplanned territory. The arbitrariness adopted by the government while permitting change of land use has caused this damage. It is essential that potential areas for future urbanization, in terms of areas to be preserved and conserved, areas fit for agriculture and afforestation, and the areas where large size institutions should be identified and developed accordingly. Regularization of the unauthorized constructions should be minimised and special courts be set up for speedier disposal of cases pertaining to the legalities involved herein.

Bhogal (2002) found the unwillingness on the part of government to take decisions related to demolition and prosecution as one of the main reasons for the emergence of unauthorized colonies scattered in the Periphery Zone. Given the present status of demand and supply of residential houses the illegal process of raising residential colonies is going to be further accentuated. He recommends the development of the ring towns of Kharar, Morinda, Derra Bassi, Banur, Kurali and Lalru. Simultaneously, a provision should be made for highways and the entire transportation network for speedy connectivity of the entire zone.

Khurana (2002) suggests that the departures from the original concept should be dealt with before the problem gets out of hand. He adds that when the first deviation in the form of the Army Cantonment took place, the Master Plan should have been modified at that very time and necessary efforts should have been made to accommodate the new towns to regulate foreseeable urban growth. The government should now invoke the freeze in land use of the Periphery Zone till the time the master plan, specifying phases of development, is not ready.

Dutt and Pomeroy (2003), while taking stock of the urban problems of the cities in South Asia observed that the modernism of Le Corbusier's design looks out of place in the Indian cultural setting. The experience of the city of Chandigarh reflects the impropriety of hiring western designers to plan cities for non-western cultures. Due to the heavy demand on space by a variety of land uses, the planners in Chandigarh are in the process of relaxing the regulations on vertical development of the residential quarters in order to accommodate a higher density of population. This will destroy the original concept of the city. The city is poised to grow faster and this is to be seen as a threat to its environs. Despite all the shortcomings, the city was assessed as more liveable than most other cities of India, by them.

Sandhu (2002) believes that the private colonizers, with their nexus with decision-makers in the government, were primarily responsible for land grabbing in the periphery of Chandigarh. They could exploit the situation by purchasing land from the villagers at low prices. Since, in most cases, large land owners are in a position to sell a part of their holding, the owners of small pieces of land are at a loss. He recommends a reform in the system which could curb this practice, especially by fixing the responsibility of the officials involved.

Sharma (2006) observed that the periphery of Chandigarh was dotted with unauthorized residential colonies and these were increasing at a fast pace. Such colonies have come up at places having low land prices. There are no roads in such type of localities and wherever roads are existing these are substandard. No facilities for proper disposal of solid waste, no sewerage system, untreated drinking water supply, and growth of wild weeds have created unhygienic conditions in these colonies. On the other hand, the authorized colonies have a better integrated planning process. The cumbersome and time consuming procedures to get a colony approved have forced colonisers to raise such structures. A strict enforcement to check the growth of unauthorized colonies and a good bye to their regularization would only ensure liveable conditions in the periphery.

Thus, the Periphery Zone of Chandigarh is emerging as a critical area. It is experiencing rapid and sporadic growth, which is neither planned nor has a conceptual linkage with Chandigarh. Such developments are likely to have detrimental effects. Nonetheless, it is essential to obtain a futuristic view of the disposition which this zone is likely to acquire.

CHANDIGARH PERIPHERY ZONE

Chandigarh Periphery Zone, the area selected for the present study, is an instituted region. It had a population of 1.04 million in 2001. It covers 458 villages and 12 urban centres (Map 1.2). It is nearly circular in shape with minor irregularities caused partly by the shape of the boundaries of villages on the margin and partly by the shape of the city (as the distances were taken from the outer boundary of the city project site and not from the centre). It is spread over an area of 1,362 km^2.

The region was conceived in 1952 when the Punjab New Capital (Periphery) Control Act was enacted. The Act forbade the sale of reserved land up to a periphery of 8 kilometres around the city, for any purpose other than agriculture. The Act was amended in 1962 and the boundary of the Periphery Zone was extended up to 16 kilometres. The Act was meant to regulate the physical growth of Chandigarh and ensure a green belt of rural territory around it.

The Periphery Zone has been provided with a dense network of roads so as to connect Chandigarh with all its parts. These roads have played a vital role in changing the personality of the region. A liberal provision of a variety of other infrastructure, in addition, was instrumental in bringing about significant changes in the surroundings of Chandigarh.

The formidable land prices in the City Beautiful of Chandigarh and the escalating land prices in its two satellite towns of S.A.S. Nagar (Mohali) and Panchkula have intensified pressure on the land of the Periphery Zone. A tendency toward urban sprawl even in a prohibited zone is conspicuous. Such a scenario offers itself as an exciting space to examine and give projections in terms of its future size of population, distributional pattern of urban-rural settlements, and land-use transformation. All this forms the scope of the present study.

A brief note on the special character of the present study will be in order here. The theme of Futuristic Geography stands virtually by-passed in Indian Geography. A perusal of the contents of four volumes of the Survey of Research in Geography, sponsored by the Indian Council of Social Science Research, revealed that of the total of 6,429 studies reviewed only three dealt with the theme on futuristic trends. The concern of these studies was more on the future trends in demand and supply of the natural resources like water, coal and electricity. Of the 180 articles in the Population Geography, published during the 1979-2003, none focused on the theme of the future. Almost the same was found true in the case of articles published in the Annals of the National Association of Geographers, India. Of the 312 articles published during the 1981-2002, only one focussed on this theme. In that light the present study can claim to be one of the few so far.

displaced homeless refugees. For the last category in fact, it embodied a new hope of promise, peace and prosperity.

Pandit Nehru, perhaps, best articulated this sentiment when he described the site 'free from the existing encumbrances of old towns and old traditions . . . the first large expression of our creative genius flowering on our newly earned freedom . . . symbolic of freedom of India—unfettered by tradition—an expression of the nation's faith in the future' (Kalia, 1987, p. 21).

The new city was to serve not only as a model of city planning both within the country and the Third World, but also as a model of the spirit of independent India, a proclamation of its march to the future. It was required to be pristine, flawless and incorruptible as well as slightly removed from all that existed before. It perhaps was within such a milieu in mind that the planners worked on a controlled periphery around the new capital which was to serve as much as a green envelope, as a buffer separating the new capital from the indigenous urban expression all around.

PERIPHERY CONTROL ACT : AN EVOLUTIONARY PERSPECTIVE

To translate this concept into reality, an enactment in the form of the Punjab New Capital (Periphery) Control Act, 1952 was enacted which received the assent of the President on 12th January 1953 and was first published in the Government of Punjab Gazette (Extraordinary) of 16 January 1952. The Act initially notified under section 3(1) brought within its purview, a periphery zone up to a radius of five miles or eight kilometres around Chandigarh, Le Corbusier conceptualized and crystallized the debates held on the floor of Punjab Vidhan Sabha, while passing the bill for Act 52 in the form of the following pronouncements:

> "We must take care that any temptation does not kill the goal which was foreseen at the moment of the foundation of the city . . . Industry must be outside the protected peripheral zone. . . . The function of the city and periphery

must not be interchanged; otherwise confusion and anarchy is sure to follow".

The statement of objectives and reasons for enactment of the laws under the Punjab New Capital (Periphery) Control Act, 1952 were as follows: "The Punjab Government are constructing a New Capital named "Chandigarh". The Master Plan providing for the future extension of the Capital will extend over a much greater area than the area acquired so far for the construction of the first phase of the Capital. To ensure healthy and planned development of the new city it is necessary to prevent growth of slums and ramshackle construction on the land lying on the periphery of the new city. To achieve this objective it is necessary to have legal authority to regulate the use of the said land for purposes other than the purposes for which it is used at present".

Thus, the Act envisaged a control over the spread of the city beyond the stipulated boundary under 16 different sections. The rationale of the said Act was to protect the surrounding rural community from getting urbanised, to prevent the growth of slum like inhabitations, to freeze the land use in the demarcated boundary, and to stop conversion of agricultural land into uses other than agriculture or subservient to agriculture (agriculture here includes horticulture, dairy farming, poultry farming and the planting and upkeep of orchards). The overall emphasis was on giving a green cover to the city, in addition to meeting its requirements of daily perishable commodities from the surroundings and leaving little scope for future speculation in land.

Section 3 of the Act empowered the state government to declare any part of the area or the entire area to which the provisions of the Act apply, as a controlled area. Section 3(1) reads as follows: "The State Government may by notification in the official Gazette declare the whole or any part of the area to which this Act extends to be a controlled area for the purposes of this Act".

Section 5 of the Act further empowered the state government to impose certain restrictions in the area falling in the controlled area. It laid down that "except as provided hereinafter, no person shall erect or re-erect any building or make or extend any excavation, or layout any means of access to a road, in the controlled area, save in accordance with the plans and restrictions and with the previous permission of the Director in writing".

Section 10 of the Act authorized the government to acquire land or to impose restrictions upon the use and development of the land falling in the controlled area under any law operative in the state. Section 11(1) prohibits the use of land within the controlled area for any purpose other than that for which it was being used on the date of issuance "no land within controlled area shall, except with the permission of the State Government [and on payment of such conversion charges as may be prescribed by the State Government from time to time] be used for purposes other than those for which it was used on the date of notification under sub-section (1) of Section 3 and no such land shall be used for the purposes of a charcoal-kiln, pottery firing kiln, lime-kiln, brick-field or brick-kiln or for quarrying stone, *bajari* or *kankar*, or manufacturing *surkhi*, or stone crushing, or for other similar extraction or ancillary operation except under and in accordance with the conditions of a license to be obtained from the Director on payment of such fees and on such conditions as may be prescribed or as may be specified in the order". Section 12 provides for the penalties to be imposed for the offences committed under the Act by the violation.

Keeping in view the present as well as future requirements for the proper growth of the city a few exemptions were made under Section 15. Construction of buildings within the *lal dora* boundaries as defined in the revenue record of the villages, digging of wells or other excavations made for use in the agricultural operations, construction of the unmettalled road for providing access to the land used exclusively for agricultural purposes, and erection or re-erection of a place of worship, tomb, or cenotaph or a wall enclosing a grave-yard, place of worship, cenotaph or *samadhi* on land which existed as such on the date of notification of controlled area were allowed. The powers to make rules for effectively carrying out the provisions of the Act vested with the state government under Section 16.

The limit of the Periphery Zone was extended in 1962 from five miles to eight miles that is 16 kilometres. It was argued that the land confined to the boundaries up to five miles was coming under pressure due to the setting up of a cantonment, the Hindustan Machine Tools Factory and an Air Force Station. To tackle the problem, the limit of the Periphery Zone was doubled within the first decade of its enactment. The delineation of the zone up to five miles seemed to have been guided by the Greater London Plan where in 1944 a limit up to such an extent had been proposed. Enhancing the peripheral limits by two times in 1962 was a long-term precautionary step.

In November 1966, upon the trifurcation of the state of Punjab, the state of Punjab and Haryana were asked either to adopt or to extend the 1952 Act into their respective territories. Under section 88 of the Punjab-Reorganization Act, 1966, the Act, however, continued to remain in force even after November 1, 1966 whether or not its adoption was notified by the state of Punjab (Gupta, 2001, p. 34).

The first transgression into what was envisaged as an impregnable green wall around Chandigarh's countryside, preserved and guarded so cleverly by the Punjab Periphery Control Act, 1952 took place in 1966. A host of exemptions were given to those who had land in the periphery and wanted to take part in activities subservient to agriculture. M.S. Randhawa (1967), the first Chief Commissioner after formation of the Union Territory of Chandigarh in 1966, mentioned that "Consequent modifications in the policy have been made and greater freedom has been given to farmers to build farm houses, tube wells, cattle sheds and poultry sheds."

Further, agro-based uses such as construction of farm houses, cattle sheds, farm houses, small-sized poultry farms, tube wells of standard size and design were permitted in the belt beyond 5 miles subject to the condition that these would be located 300 feet away from the national or state highway and 100 feet from a link or approach road. Construction of houses for residential purposes within the extended *abadi* (settlement) part of the village but not within the communication zone (belt reserved for road or rail transport) was allowed. All construction was prohibited within the five miles belt.

The area notified under the provisions of the Punjab New Capital (Periphery) Control Act in the year 1952 fell entirely in the state of Punjab. However, with the reorganization of the state in 1966, while the Periphery Zone remained the same 16 kilometer belt around the city, a single geographical unit was divided and brought under the control of three different governments. Of the 1,362 square kilometer total periphery area, Punjab's share was the largest, 1021 km^2 (72 per cent), followed by that of Haryana, 297 km^2 (24 per cent), and Union Territory of Chandigarh, 44 km^2 (4 per cent). This development was going to have far-reaching effect on the future of Chandigarh, as also of its periphery.

CONTROLLED AREA : INSTITUTIONAL ONSLAUGHTS

Government itself took no time in interfering with the byelaws laid under the Act for regulating the change of land use in the Periphery Zone to its own advantage. The encroachment on the rural land in the periphery had begun as early as in 1953. The proposal pertained to laying out a cantonment at Chandimandir, a site that spread over Manimajra, Saketri, Bhainsa Tibbi, Bilaspur, Surajpur, Dhara Karori and Chandimandir villages to the northeast of Chandigarh. The site covered an area of 775 hectares and was located within the Periphery Zone. Corbusier reacted to this in a letter: "I feel it to be my most urgent duty to interfere in this as it constitutes one of the most dangerous threats that could destroy the best in Chandigarh". He viewed the proposal as a violation of the city byelaws. However, the concerned official authorities viewed their decision as justified and irrevocable in the larger context of the defence needs of the country in the changed circumstances along the northern belt (Vimal, 1994, p. 58).

This was a critical decision. It provided freedom for further changes to be introduced by the government in the original proposal and eventually changing the rural character of the periphery. Le Corbusier died in a swimming accident in 1965. His demise gave rise to apprehensions about not only the sustainability of the planned character of Chandigarh but also the preservation of the desired disposition of its Periphery Zone. The later developments gave credence to such fears.

On the reorganization of Punjab on 1 November, 1966 Chandigarh was carved out as a Union Territory and its Periphery Zone got segmented into three parts, falling in Punjab, Haryana and the Union Territory itself. Anticipating changes being imposed on the Periphery Zone in terms of the assertive overtures of the respective states/union territory, the Government of India constituted a Coordination Committee, as early as on 7 November, 1966 to ensure continuity in policy toward the Periphery Zone. The Committee consisted of the Chief Commissioner, Chandigarh; Directors of the Town and Country Planning Offices of Punjab and Haryana; Chief Architect and Assistant Estate Officer from the Union Territory; and the sub-divisional officer of Kharar tehsil (Punjab). The exercise proved futile as the Committee did not have any statutory powers (Kalia, 1987, p. 138).

In 1967, the Punjab Government launched a scheme for the economic development of villages at select focal points, to provide promotional infrastructure for industry. Mohali, a village on the fringe of Chandigarh, was one of the sites. Subsequently, a decision was taken to develop Mohali into an industrial town. The real motive behind this move was to demonstrate its natural continuity to Chandigarh and thereby strengthen Punjab's case for transfer of Chandigarh to Punjab. The nomenclature of Mohali was changed to Sahibzada Ajit Singh Nagar (S.A.S. Nagar) in mid-1970s and the town has, by the turn of the century, grown into a large industrial centre. It covers an area of 5800 acres.

The Haryana Government, not to be outdone, started the work on establishing a new town Panchkula with the same intent in 1971. The new town bordered Chandigarh on the southeast and was meant to function as a big service centre. The strategy of the Haryana Government was to ensure that it did not lose ground on its equal claim on Chandigarh. Since Chandigarh had acquired a new politico-administrative status and became a joint capital of Punjab and Haryana, apart from being the headquarters of the Union Territory, it assumed a great demographic dynamism. It recorded the highest growth rate among cities of the country during 1961-71, associated with its functional upsurge as an administrative, educational, health and business centre.

Both Punjab and Haryana wanted to cash in on their proximity to Chandigarh and evolved a series of novel ways to bypass and exploit the bye-laws laid in the Periphery Act. Most notably, a number of towns were carved out by merging a group of existing villages. The emergence of S.A.S. Nagar (Mohali), Panchkula and the Cantonment area did not conform to the original Plan of Chandigarh. Once, they were set up, they were there to stay, flourish and expand. They made a significant and lasting impact on Chandigarh and its periphery.

The conspicuous effects of the townships of S.A.S. Nagar (Mohali), Panchkula and Chandimandir cantonment on Chandigarh have been the consequent squeezing of the city's green belt, infraction of the agricultural zone around it, and imposition of an industrial landscape in its vicinity. The location of industries in the adjoining towns of S.A.S. Nagar (Mohali) and Panchkula, especially the former, have also taken their toll on the environment. A positive impact was that these townships took the pressure off Chandigarh by deflecting a sizeable population, oriented towards Chandigarh, to settle there.

This, however, was just the beginning. The Periphery Zone, with the passage of time, was declared as a controlled area, where all land use changes were permitted subject to prior approval of the state government. The decisions and action taken by the concerned states exposed the fragility of the Periphery Act making the Act loose its essence. The controlled area gradually became uncontrollable, courtesy the intentions of the stakeholders involved, including private sector builders, professionals and technical institutions, individual speculators, and of course, the governments as well.

FORMATION OF COORDINATION COMMITTEE AND ITS RECOMMENDATIONS

As noted above, Punjab and Haryana governments instead of protecting the green belt established satellite towns adjacent to Chandigarh bringing thousand of acres of agricultural land under the urban carpet. With the setting up of two big townships, Mohali and Panchkula, it became increasingly necessary to coordinate their growth *vis-à-vis* each other for a balanced development of the region as a whole. The Government of India took special cognizance of the associated deforestation process and instructed the Coordination Committee to guide and channelize the growth of Chandigarh and resolve the urban problems coming up in its neighbourhood. The defined objectives of this Committee were to:

(i) study the development plans of the Union Territory of Chandigarh besides those of Mohali and Panchkula townships and suggest measures for a coordinated development of the region;
(ii) assess the impact of development programmes already implemented and those being implemented in the two townships on the development of the region as a whole and suggest remedial measures to be taken up by the state governments as well as the union territory; and
(iii) prepare an outline regional plan for Chandigarh and the urban areas falling within its zone of influence

The Committee constituted vide notification K16014/3/72-UD II, dated 26 July 1975, New Delhi was to be chaired by the Secretary, Ministry of Works and Housing, Government of India with the Quarter-Master General, Army Headquarters, Ministry of Defence, Chief Commissioner, Chandigarh, Chief Secretaries, Government of Punjab and Haryana, and the Secretary, Department of Environment as members. It was to work in close coordination with the three concerned governments. The Committee held periodic meetings and took important decisions having a bearing on the city and its surroundings.

In its meeting held on 22nd May 1979, the Coordination Committee recommended the conducting of a detailed planning exercise for the development of Chandigarh and its surroundings. In pursuance of this, the Committee, in its meeting held in 1981 appointed two working groups, one for the preparation of the Regional Plan for Chandigarh Inter-State

Region and the other for the framing of requisite legislation for its effective enforcement and implementation. Following this, the Town and Country Planning Organization, New Delhi prepared the Inter State Chandigarh Region (ISCR) Plan in April 1981 in consultation with the three concerned governments. It was argued that the influence of the city was intensive in its defined Peripheral Zone but the area beyond it was also experiencing the impact of the city. The immediate and actual zone of influence of Chandigarh had an approximate radius of 35 kilometers and it was delineated as the Inter State Chandigarh Region (TCPO, Punjab, 2000).The plan was approved on 23rd October 1984 for implementation and enforcement. However, the Draft Plan could not be translated into an actuality and remained a paper document in the absence of any legal support. The concerned states did not take any notice of the document, as it was merely advisory in nature.

In the 8th meeting of the Coordination Committee held at Chandigarh on 23 October 1984, the Chairman, Secretary, Ministry of Works and Housing stated that due importance should be given to urban development as per the Approach Paper of the Seventh Five Year. He stressed that proper development of infrastructure, such as roads, communications, and telecommunication links were basic to any form of regional development planning. He highlighted the significance of the National Capital Region (NCR) model. It could serve as a model for all the areas where inter-state regional development and planning coordination were required. A need of preparing three separate sub-regional plans by the three governments, keeping in view the overall framework of the objectives, was mooted. The sub-regional plan could include elements which were critical to future urban scene and major rural settlements. The idea of raising funds on the same lines as that of the National Capital Region Planning Board was also put forth. The Chairman observed that whatever uncertainty there may be in respect of the political status of Chandigarh, the overall development of the city and its neighbourhood region as a whole should be central to all plans. The recommendations were practical but could not be pursued in the absence of statutory powers to the Committee.

PUNJAB SEGMENT OF PERIPHERY ZONE

S.A.S. Nagar (Mohali): The Government of Punjab took up the planning and development of SAS Nagar project in the immediate vicinity of Chandigarh in 1967-68. The avowed objective was to provide an orderly growth and development in the Periphery Zone. It was argued that the city over time had become a regional centre for providing education and health facilities, and offered a variety of employment opportunities thereby attracted a large flow of migrants. A fear was expressed that the rural belt around the city would become most vulnerable, leading to haphazard growth. The precise statement ran as follows: "On account of the shortage of industrial and residential plots in Chandigarh, S.A.S. (Mohali) Nagar was conceived, in 1967, to contain the overspill of Chandigarh, to prevent haphazard growth and prevent speculation in land within its periphery". However, a contradiction was involved. On the one hand, it was said that the city and its surroundings were coming under heavy pressure while on the other hand the Chandigarh Administration was liberalizing conditions involved in the construction of houses as there were "no takers for the experiment even after 16 years of establishment". It seems that a complete stock of the situation was not taken while elaborating the need of a new town in the vicinity of Chandigarh.

Right from its inception, the city of S.A.S. Nagar (Mohali) was conceived as an integral part of Chandigarh, ultimately to become Phase III of Chandigarh. The development of the township was undertaken as a continuation of the existing grid road pattern of Chandigarh. Originally the new township was conceived as only an industrial estate but with its growing popularity and proximity to the state capital, the government started developing it into an urban estate. An area measuring approximately 5800 acres was acquired initially for the establishment of the town.

Free Enterprise Zone: The second major infringement of the periphery, also perpetrated by the administration, came about when a huge area measuring 4792 hectares comprising 23 villages, was declared as a Free Enterprise Zone (FEZ) in the

Derra Bassi-Mubarakpur belt vide Notification No. 3/4/87-3IBI/311 dated 9 January 1990 (Map 2.1). Industries could be set up in this zone, without taking any permission for conversion of the land use, subject to certain restrictions.

The roots of this decision could be traced to 1979 when the Department of Industries, Punjab announced incentives for attracting industries to this sub-mountainous tract. It was designated as a Free Enterprise Zone and formed a part of the Punjab segment of the Periphery Zone. The underlying intention seems to be to circumvent the provisions of the Periphery Control Act. By 1986, as many as 404 industrial units had come up and their number continued rising at a rapid pace. In addition, several residential colonies had also emerged, the number being 126 in 2005. A lot many informal activities have also sprung up in this Zone. On the top of this, several industries continued finding a location outside the Periphery Zone. All this gave a spurt to the process of haphazard urbanization in the environs of Chandigarh (Krishan, 2002, p. 209).

Anandgarh Project: In the meantime, the Punjab government made a proposal to set up another planned city by the name of Anandgarh, to the West of Chandigarh. It was to be developed on land falling almost entirely in the Periphery Zone. In a meeting held on 30th August 1994, chaired by Advisor to the Administrator of the Union Territory of Chandigarh, a view was taken of existing developments and future proposals for the development of the Chandigarh region. The Punjab Government aired their intention of creating a new town on the North-western side of the City. It was stated that "in view of the magnetic effect of an urban node, such as Chandigarh, there was a live danger of haphazard and unplanned development by unscrupulous elements, in the immediate vicinity of the town. It was precisely to pre-empt and prevent such developments, that the Punjab Government was considering a proposal for establishing a planned township adjacent to Chandigarh". The city was to be self-sufficient in all respects and was meant to share the load on the existing infrastructure in Chandigarh.

In pursuance of this decision, the Punjab Government constituted a sub-committee to look into the issue of giving a

MAP 2.1

Chandigarh Periphery Zone
(Villages Falling under Free Enterprise Zone : 2006)

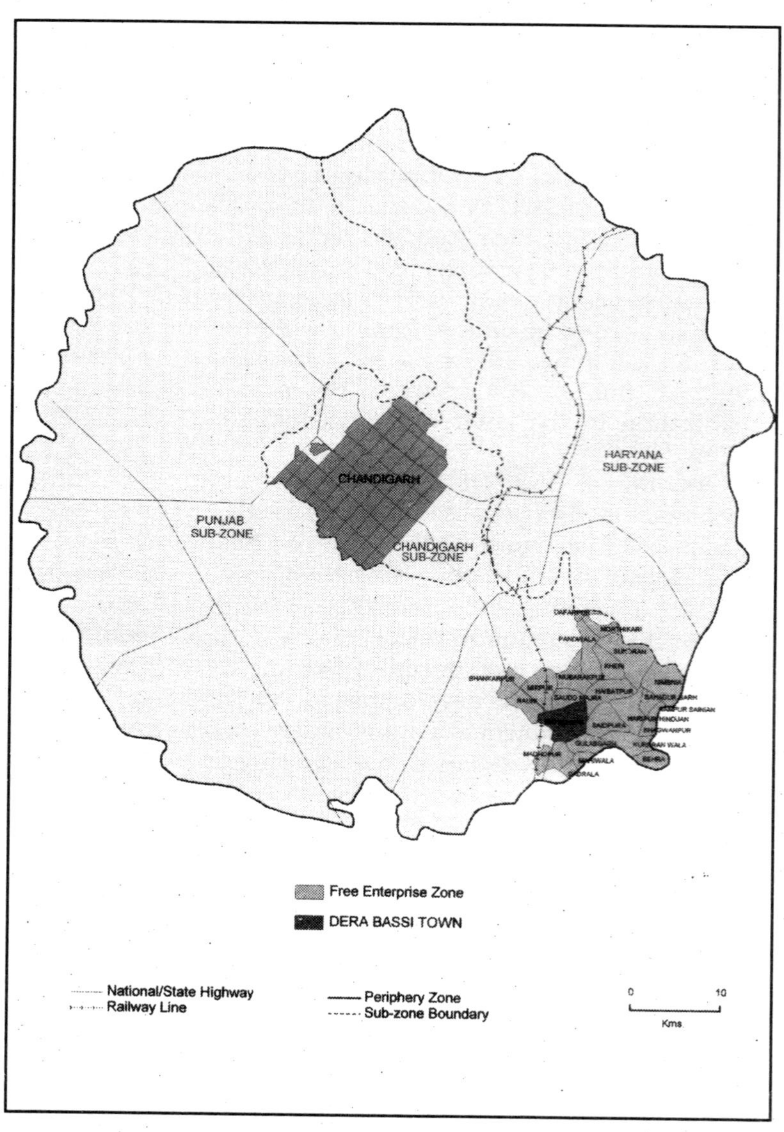

practical shape to the proposal. The sub-committee met on 23rd December 1994 and 25th January 1994 and decided to establish a new town on the North-western side of Chandigarh that is between Patiali-Ki-Rao and Siswan River. An area of 7170 acres in 15 villages was notified to be acquired by the state government. Subsequently, it was decided to acquire a larger chunk of land measuring 10,500 acres in 29 villages. On March 28, 2001, the Punjab and Haryana High Court quashed the various notifications issued by the Punjab government to acquire the land to develop the new town in response to a number of Public Interest Litigations by affected villagers (Khurana, 2002, p. 222). The proposal was shelved. The general impression was that this probably saved Chandigarh from possible further ecological degradation in its vicinity.

Also the periodic extension of the municipal limits of towns, such as Derra Bassi, Banur and Kharar, served to merge the adjoining rural areas, proliferated by illegal residential and industrial development, and steady development of urban centres, gradually removing them from the precincts of the Periphery Control Act.

There has been a general notion that an illegal and unauthorized structure becomes both legal and authorized if the status of the area is changed from rural to urban. This strategy was frequently resorted to by the government in defeating its own provisions of the Periphery Controlled Act. Such a process of upgrading select villages as towns fuelled the tendency towards land speculation in the areas adjoining Chandigarh, S.A.S. Nagar (Mohali) and Panchkula, in particular. Speculators and landowners became all the more daring in carrying out all types of violations in the hope that these would be regularized sooner or latter. Such unplanned development in the Periphery Zone was linked to and often perpetuated by the nexus of the political, bureaucratic and corporate sectors. Politicians who were to be the guardians of the Act turned out to be its violators. In fact, the "periphery has become a classic case of '*heraphery*' (scam) and has emerged as the greatest exercise in land speculation, unplanned, haphazard, illegal and sub-standard urbanization" (Gupta, 2002, p. 218). The underlying spirit of the Periphery Act was trampled by those who were supposed to safeguard it.

Punjab Urban Planning and Development Authority (PUDA) invited requests from residents in this regard for regularization of their unauthorized structures, and ordered an aerial survey of the area. However, within days of the proposal having been made public, the Punjab and Haryana High Court stayed the implementation of this decision on a protest lodged by the law abiding residents to the decision. The state government was also directed that "no construction shall be carried out or will continue in the area covered by the notices".

Upgradation of Villages to Urban Status

In November itself, another notification was issued by the Punjab Government to declare the cluster of Karoran, Nada and Kansal villages as Notified Area Committee (NAC), thereby giving them an urban status. This move too was stayed by the High Court. It became increasingly apparent that the states of Punjab and Haryana had evolved a novel method to bypass and violate the Periphery Act by transforming rural areas into urban ones by declaring them as Notified Area Committees.

A decision to create Zirakpur Nagar Panchayat, by covering Zirakpur, Lohgarh, Himmatgarh, Bishangarh, Bishanpura, Baltana and Dhakauli as its villages was taken up in 2000. This led to the regularization of another batch of illegal structures, which mushroomed in blatant breach of the Act.

More recently in 2001 Mullanpur-Garibdas, Karoran, Bhabat, and Bhankarpur villages have been raised to the urban status, under similar considerations.

Regularization of Unauthorized Constructions

Despite the provision of all controls laid down under the Periphery Control Act many illegal structures appeared in the Punjab segment of the Periphery Zone. It was an administrative failure. Conceding the governments incapacity to monitor things, the Punjab government, at a meeting on 24-8-1998, took the following populist decision to overcome the situation:

- The existing construction in the periphery area would not be demolished and parameters for regularization of these structures would be worked out by a committee headed by the Chief Secretary.

- Further construction in the periphery would be permitted only in accordance with the policy guidelines and development plans to be approved by the government.
- Till the policy guidelines and development were prepared, no further construction would be permitted.

Thus, in a so called one time amnesty, the State Government regularized all those structures that had come into existence up to and including December 7, 1998. This followed the pressure exerted by land colonizers, property dealers, landowners' lobby and many others who had ventured into illegal construction in the restricted areas. While granting this reprieve, no distinction was made with regard to the nature of the violation (whether residential, commercial or institutional) nor their location (whether in the forest areas or in the communications zone). Thus, thousands of unauthorized and illegal structures, most of which were sub-standard, became legal overnight, irrespective of the seriousness or nature of the violation.

The above measure proved totally counter-productive. A large number of structures continued to come up in the Periphery Zone in violation of the provisions of the Act with a hope that at some future date those too would be authorized. They were not wrong in their anticipation. In November 2001, the Punjab government took a decision to regularize the construction in the Periphery Zone that had come up between 8th December 1998 and 3rd November 2001.

Overtime the renewed efforts to regularize the unauthorized constructions in the Periphery Zone of the Punjab segment continued unabated. The Periphery Policy Report by the Department of Housing and Urban Development, Government of Punjab, vide notification dated 20th January 2006, proposed the granting of a reprieve to 1500 such cases since 8th December 1998. For the third time in the last decade, one-time regularization of such unauthorized constructions, adopting specific criteria with imposition of reasonable land-use conversion charges, was recommended. This was to come into effect on 1st November, 2005 as the cut-off date for the purpose.

Unauthorized construction abounds along most of the major roads radiating from Chandigarh, especially the roads like the Chandigarh-Zirakpur-Derra Bassi, Chandigarh-Zirakpur-Banur, Chandigarh-Kharar and Chandigarh-Zirakpur-Panchkula. Easy accessibility from Chandigarh and considerably lower land prices than those of Chandigarh have attracted many people to such places. The basic reason for such a phenomenon is that demand for residential plots in Chandigarh has soared (Bhogal, 2002, p. 200). A number of residential colonies, both authorized as well as unauthorized have come up along these belts. These have been built both by individuals as well as the corporate sector. It seems that the failure of the Anandgarh Plan seemed to have prompted the government to urbanize the periphery 'by any means', both through the formal and informal features of housing and colonies (Khurana, 2002, p. 222).

Unauthorized constructions on a large scale have taken place also in villages like Baltana, Naya Gaon, Dhakoli, and Kansal which are in the proximity of Chandigarh. There was hardly any agricultural land left in Baltana village in Punjab before its merger with the Zirakpur Nagar Panchayat. By now the Act had been grossly violated. The constructions outside the *lal dora* (boundary of the village settlement) were often without power and drinking water connections, making for slum-like conditions in these areas.

Paradoxically, land prices of an acre of land in Punjab villages, such as, Naya Gaon, Nada, and Kansal adjacent to Chandigarh is six times higher (Rs. 2.9 crores per acre *versus* Rs. 50 lakh per acre) than those of other villages viz. Khuda Alisher, and Mauli Jagran in Chandigarh. Regular demolition drives in Chandigarh prevented land prices from escalating and Punjab on the other hand gave the hope of unauthorized constructions getting regularized sooner or later leading to a big demand. The Chandigarh experience in contrast to that of Punjab has shown how effective the enforcement of law under the Act can help in containing the process of land speculation, leading to unauthorized constructions.

The number of authorized colonies in the Punjab segment of the Periphery Zone was 25 as compared to 216 unauthorized ones (Sharma, 2006, p. 85). Private builders in Nadda village continued rising constructions till Patiala Ki Rao, besides raising the plinth level of plots so high that it was above the flow of rainwater. These villages housed big residential societies in violation of the Act to the extent the unauthorized colonies were emerging at a faster pace than the authorized ones.

Administrative Apathy

The calculations of the land colonizers are pragmatic and simple. They ignore the cumbersome procedures of raising an authorized colony under the premise that the government would regularize these unauthorized ones eventually, especially on the eve of elections. They have already done so thrice in the past seven years. Or at the most, the unauthorized colonies will gradually be merged into a nearby town. This way they will automatically end up acquiring legal authorization.

The extent and scale of the unauthorized construction can be gauged from the fact that 6,883 cases of unauthorized construction were identified in the Punjab segment of the Periphery Zone during the 1990s. All of them had been issued show-cause notices. Only 1,045 cases were dealt with under the relevant legal provisions while 5,888 cases are still awaiting processing. While, demolition orders were issued in 594 cases they were carried out actually only in 160 cases (Gupta, 2001, p. 36).

Changed Perspective

The periodic regularizations of unauthorized structures forced the Punjab and Haryana High Court to direct the Punjab Government to constitute a committee to look into the matter. In response, an empowered committee was constituted in 2003 to facilitate the Punjab Government in laying out a comprehensive policy to streamline development within the Periphery Zone and suggest a plan for its future development.

The committee submitted a policy document in January 2006. The document took note of the wide disparity between the level of civic and urban infrastructure in the city of Chandigarh and its surrounding towns and villages. The committee was of the view that "it would be unrealistic for any state government not to take advantage of this opportunity and leverage its proximity to Chandigarh to its best economic interest". This was enough to provide stimulus to what was already happening. It was against this backdrop that the committee formulated the policy framework for the Chandigarh periphery controlled area.

The committee allowed construction in areas beyond the existing *'lal lakir'* in the villages. The area falling between the *'lal lakir'* and the *phirni* was allowed to be used for meeting individual residential and minor commercial needs of the existing and future population of the village. In other words, the *abadi* area was allowed to be extended but no formal colonization or industry was permitted into it.

In addition, the committee liberalized the guidelines in respect of farm houses. The provisions for construction of the farm house were liberalized. Earlier the farm house could be constructed in an area beyond 5 miles from the outer boundary of Chandigarh. It was also mandatory that a farm house could be raised on agricultural land at least 5 acres in area. The new guidelines allowed construction of farm houses within 5 miles from the boundary of Chandigarh and these could be raised in agriculture land less than 5 acres in area.

The New Economic Policy was not without its effect on the Periphery Zone. Promotion of private sector in education, health, recreation and housing made the most visible impacts. Several institutions like engineering colleges, management institutes, housing colonies, golf courses, country clubs and amusement parks, sprang up in the Periphery Zone, in response to the proximity of the fully planned city beautiful, i.e. Chandigarh. The availability of relatively cheap land, developed infrastructure, willingness on the part of non-resident Indians to invest and above all, the presence of thousands of students and other clients in Chandigarh, in particular, gave a spur to this process.

Private development could be undertaken on the payment of external development charges as per the policy framed by PUDA. The imposition of the conversion charge was meant to be spent on augmentation of physical and social infrastructure such as roads, educational institutions, and health centres, in the Periphery Zone. These charges were not to be levied on public utilities, such as government schools, dispensaries, veterinary centres, post offices, and police stations.

Proposed Development Plan

The committee in fact had highlighted the need for identifying areas for urbanization within the Periphery Zone, something contradictory to its very spirit of delineation. A recommendation for the preparation of a master plan for the existing towns in the Periphery Zone was also made. In addition, a freeze on the boundaries of the existing towns was suggested.

The Periphery Policy Report by the Department of Housing and Urban Development, Government of Punjab, vide notification dated 20 January 2006, was issued to check unregulated growth in this part of the zone. Suitable pockets of land, for housing, in particular, for development by the private sector, government, and semi-autonomous bodies were identified. A careful analysis of the Policy reveals that it has been formulated to give benefits to the big investors who after paying heavy conversion charges, were free to do things their way. Normally the colonizers went for large pieces of cheap land at places which are not even accessible through main road and are without the proper facility of water supply and proper drainage facilities. Under the agreement the Punjab Urban Development Authority (PUDA) is expected to provide reasonable infrastructural services at these sites. This may prove expensive for PUDA. In other words, the new planned housing development by the private sector will not be only sporadic in location but also entail heavy cost for the public sector.

Greater Mohali Plan

Mohali has recently (in 2006) been carved out as a separate district and already the Government of Punjab is considering undertaking the Greater Mohali Plan. The purpose of this decision is to develop Mohali as an investment destination and to check haphazard development in its surroundings. The proposed Greater Mohali will spread over 1,000 square kilometers, covering not only S.A.S. Nagar (Mohali) town but a large number of villages around it. The execution of plan would once again eat away a major chunk of the rural land in the Periphery Zone. This will lead to urbanization of virtually the entire Punjab segment of the Periphery Zone, giving a burial to the Periphery Control Act in this case.

In order to regulate future development around S.A.S. Nagar (Mohali), 16,642 hectares of area falling in the periphery has been declared as planning area under the Punjab Regional and Town Planning and Development Act, 1995, for which the master plan is under preparation. In the process S.A.S. Nagar (Mohali) would be extended to 106 sectors with a large chunk of the Periphery Zone being transferred to urban use.

HARYANA SEGMENT OF CONTROLLED AREA

Haryana did not want to be left behind in making a capital out of its share of the Periphery Zone. In reaction to the Punjab Government's decision to establish the new town, Mohali bordering Chandigarh, Haryana went in for the creation of Panchkula on these very lines. The advantage of Chandigarh's proximity was the underlying incentive. Also the claim of Haryana on Chandigarh was not to be weakened, by default.

The reasons put forward for setting up Panchkula as a new, fully planned town, had a different tone. It was highlighted that agriculture in the Panchkula region was stagnating, population pressure was intensifying, and out-migration from villages was picking up. The rural land, thus made available, is not likely to withstand encroachment of urban sprawl and would be prone to haphazard and ill-planed growth. Hence a strategy to cater to the anticipated urban development was to be worked out (Panchkula Project Report).

There was a precedent to seek appropriate guidelines. The development plans for the habitation ring towns around Delhi, like Faridabad, Bahadurgarh, Gurgaon and Sonepat were already in place. These towns were meant to derive benefits emanating from proximity to Delhi. The major problem faced by most of these towns was lack of requisite quantity and quality of water. Thus, the site to be selected for Panchkula was to be free from this constraint.

In a meeting held at Pinjore in 1970 and subsequent approval of that in 1971, it was proclaimed that "Keeping in view the overall development proposals for the whole region, the Haryana Government has decided to establish a New Town for 125,000 of population near the Panchkula trinjunction". The site finds a location, south of the Chandimandir Cantonment. The new town was to cater not only to its own needs but those of the entire region, covering the cantonment, and villages along the Chandigarh-Kalka road.

The site proposed for the Panchkula town marked its boundary with the cantonment to the north, the Ghaggar river in the east, Chandigarh to the west, and Punjab to south. The site had several merits. It has a scenic drop of the Shivalik hills, enjoys an amiable climate throughout the year, and water from the Ghaggar river is closeby. The building materials are in plenty, including sand and *bajri* in Ghaggar river bed, cement factory at Surajpur and brick kilns in large numbers which had come up to meet the construction demands of Chandigarh. Of course, the most critical, though unrecorded, consideration was the factor of contiguity with Chandigarh.

It was ensured that while benefiting from the contiguity with Chandigarh, Panchkula should not face any undue competition from nearby towns. Panchkula Project Report took into account the typology of existing towns in respect of their population, dominant function, and distance from Panchkula. Table 2.1 depicts the details.

It was highlighted that within a range of 60 km. from Panchkula, there were only two cities of Chandigarh and Ambala, which had a population of over 100,000. The nearby suburban centres such as Surajpur, Pinjore, Manimajra, and the Cantonment were expected to depend upon the new town for their needs. By virtue of its location on the Delhi-Shimla National Highway, the new town was to act as a distribution centre for the region North of Delhi (Panchkula Project Report).

TABLE 2.1

Typology of Existing Towns and Distance from Proposed Site of Panchkula Town

Sl. No.	*Name of town*	*Total population in 1971*	*Distance from the selected site*	*Typology of the town*
1.	Manimajra	14,197	2	Service and industry
2.	Chandigarh	218,807	5	Capital city
3.	Kharar	10,582	21	Industrial town
4.	Derra Bassi	6,415	21	
5.	Kalka	17,615	22	Transport town
6.	Banur	5,458	24	
7.	Sirhind	18,031	37	Trading and service town
8.	Rajpura	29,953	40	Rehabilitation town
9.	Kurali	9,774	41	Trading town
10.	Rupar	16,458	45	District headquarters and cantonment
11.	Naraingarh	6,885	48	Tehsil headquarter
12.	Ambala city	83,649	49	District headqurter and cantonment
13.	Ambala Cantt.	102,519	56	Cantonment
14.	Patiala	155,905	67	District headquarter
15.	Simla	55,326	110	Hill station and capital of Himachal Pradesh
16.	Ludhiana	401176	115	Industrial city
17.	Yamunanagar	72,630	115	Industrial city
	Jagadhri	35096	115	

Source : Panchkula Project Report.

For providing an economic base to the proposed city, the importance of both services and industry was emphasized. The city was to be the hub for workers engaged in commerce, housing, transportation and industry. The proposed site is very close to the exit point of Himachal Pradesh and it was envisaged as a collection-*cum*-preservation and distribution centre for the hill products. Hindustan Machine Tools factory and the Tractor Plant at Pinjore had come up in proximity to the site and these were interpreted as an opportunity for a town like Panchkula to satisfy their housing and other service needs. In addition, the proposed town was to house small and medium sized industries. The industrial growth of the new site was to get a further boost after the introduction of the Chandigarh-Ludhiana railway line.

The future perceived for the proposed town in early 1970s has now been relegated to the past. The rationale offered for the new town worked on somewhat different lines. The city has acquired the status of a satellite town of Chandigarh, accommodating largely, the overspill from the main city. It has assumed the character of a haven for those who could not or did not want to house themselves at Chandigarh. Of course, the quality of life in the new town was high and its industrial growth has been picking up regularly. The major industries located here include pharmaceuticals and machine tools.

Gradually, the Government of Haryana planned the extension of Panchkula, in phases. The first one was to come up in the form of Mansa Devi complex, a high class residential locality sandwiched between Chandigarh and Panchkula. A further expansion of the town came up in 2000 towards the east of the existing site. The Haryana Government in its official communication stated that "no space is left out within the site to meet the future demand of public for urbanization. In order to cope with the ever increasing demand of the public for planned and developed urban estate, the government has taken a decision for extension of Panchkula township by developing the urban area situated across the Ghaggar river". Thereby, the government earmarked land beyond river Ghaggar for future urbanization, encroaching on the rural land. A land measuring approximately 3,000 acres was to be acquired. This was called the Panchkula Extension.

Panchkula Extension is located along the Ghaggar river on the other side. It has undulating topography requiring leveling to a developable level. Almost one-third of the land acquired for the purpose was to be used for residential purposes, organized into seven sectors, namely 23 (partial), 24, 25, 26, 27, 28 and 31. The planning for the two sectors 29 and 30 could not be undertaken as these came under the restricted Terminal Ballistics Research Laboratory (TBRL) belt.

The unstated but actual consideration underlying the setting up of the Panchkula Extension is not difficult to understand. The huge profits made by the Government of Haryana, through its Haryana Urban Development Authority, by the sale of residential, commercial and industrial plots in Panchkula enticed the government to go in for this extension. The government filled its coffers but at the cost of further loss of the rural character of the Periphery Zone.

Pinjore and Kalka Towns

The process of encroaching on rural land is not restricted to Panchkula. Two other towns, namely, Pinjore and Kalka located in the Haryana segment of the Periphery Zone, are also spreading over rural lands around through periodic acquisitions. Government of Haryana on the lines of Government of Punjab, found it to be a convenient route to bypass the rules laid under the Periphery Control Act by extending the territorial jurisdiction of these towns..

Unauthorized Developments

The Haryana segment of the Periphery Zone was similarly prey to unauthorized construction, as in Punjab. As many as 8243 unauthorized constructions have taken place in the sub-zone during the 1972-2006 period (HUDA, 2006). Most of these illegal constructions are found on the rural land located in the vicinity of the existing towns, especially Panchkula and Kalka, and around Ramgarh village, a service centre. Many of these violations were due to the construction of small residential units outside the *lal dora* limits of these villages. As many as 540 cases related to illegal constructions were identified in Mansa Devi Complex and the Panchkula Extension.

Almost 10 per cent of these violations were carried out on government land reserved for forests in the Bir Ghaggar area. No less than 236 illegal structures were raised within the restricted belt of the TBRL. Land along the National Highway is in high demand especially for the use of roadside *dhabas* and vehicle repair shops. As many as 339 illegal structures were identified as having been built within 30 meters of the distance from the National Highway.

Ironically, hardly 269 structures have been demolished by the Enforcement Department under the provisions of the Periphery Control Act. And only 61 FIRs have been lodged under Section 12 of the Act. On legal lines, permission for carrying out the change in land use was granted in 38 individual cases during 1971-2006. These included six during the 1970s, six during the 1980s and thirty-one during the 1990s. With the adoption of a liberal policy, the path to land-use conversion has become easier.

The details of the permitted land use conversions present an interesting picture. Almost one-fourth of these were for setting up of petrol pumps. The ever-increasing traffic on the National Highway has picked up during the 1990s and to meet the demand for petrol and diesel the necessary permission was given in respect of landuse conversion. Another purpose for which the change in the land use was granted was pertaining to the setting up of poultry farms and farm houses. Some industrial units, related to agro-food, chemical and earthen materials, were also permitted due change of land use.

CHANDIGARH SEGMENT OF CONTROLLED AREA

The Chandigarh segment of the Periphery Zone covered an area of 44.4. km^2. The situation in Chandigarh was slightly better. This was under bureaucratic and not political control. Populist measures to circumvent provisions of the Periphery Control Act were decidedly less in play.

The Periphery Control Act framed to retain the essential character of Chandigarh by preventing the emergence of unplanned localities ran into rough weather within a short span of time. Since no provision in the city plan has been made for accommodating the workers in the informal sector, they resorted to raising of huts or residential units on unauthorized locations. In fact, the fully planned city of Chandigarh had also started its life with first slum localities, providing shelter to thousands of construction workers. The site of the City Centre, Sector 17 as of today was the venue of one of the slums in the city during the 1950's.

In 1958, the existing slums were relocated on the city's periphery in different cardinal directions, Sector 25, and Sector 26. These were intended as transit colonies but they soon acquired a permanent character. A process of rehabilitation had started but then the population in the unauthorized colonies was also increasing fast (Dubey, 1999, p. 117). In 2006, the city has 26 slum localities and 19 rehabilitated slum colonies. No less than 33,260 households with a population of about 118,000 are residing in unauthorized colonies.

The process of rehabilitation of slum-dwellers to nearby villages began in 1974. A number of villages, namely Karsan, Dadu Majra, Dhanas, Maloya, Mauli Jagran, Khudda Lahora and Palsora were targeted for rehabilitating the slums which had emerged in different parts of the city. What is important here is that the process of converting agricultural lands into residential ones was led by the city government itself. Three different agencies, Estate Office, Chandigarh Housing Board and Chandigarh Municipal Corporation have been responsible for undertaking such exercises of rehabilitation.

In the 1970s, eight rehabilitation schemes were undertaken; the same number was taken up in the 1980's, two during 1990's and one during 2001-06. In all, 35,796 sites have been allotted under various schemes of rehabilitation during 1974-2006. The nature of services provided to these sites differed. In 37 per cent of the cases sites and services or plinth sites were provided, in almost 25 per cent of the cases bare sites were given, in 26 per cent cases houses were provided to the economically weaker section of the society, and in the remaining 12 per cent cases, it was in the nature of tenements (Estate Office, 2006). In the process, the Chandigarh Administration regularized thousands of unauthorized structures which were in violation of the basic design of the city since its birth. The problems faced within the city have been only pushed outwards towards the villages located on its periphery. As a corollary, the city lost a part of its green girdle.

According to the estimate of the Estate Office of the Union Territory, 472 acres of unacquired land is currently under periphery violations. The majority of the violations are in Mauli Jagran (150 acre), Daria (75 acres), Burail (50 acres) and Palsora (40 acres). Unlike in Punjab and Haryana, in the case of

Chandigarh, the government has been able to check the emergence of brick kilns and marriage palaces on its rural land. It has, however, not been successful in checking the use of farm houses for renting these out for arranging marriage functions.

Besides about 3000 unauthorized structures have been identified in the villages of the Union Territory (Sharma, 2005, p. 65). Majority of these unauthorized structures were in Kishangarh, Hallo Majra and Mani Majra. In an effort to regulate the haphazard developments in its periphery, the Chandigarh administration has raised an Information Technology Park in Kishangarh village, a Botanical Garden near Sarangpur village, an Industrial Area near Raipur, and a Kalagram (House of Artisans) near Sector 26. As such, the Chandigarh segment of the Periphery Zone also stands witness to its violation at the hands of both the government itself and the private stakeholders.

CONCLUSION

That the Periphery Zone has been pillaged and ravaged hardly comes as a revelation after half-a-century of its inception. The manner, in which it happened, however, bears some understanding. Envisaged by planners as a belt that would remain more or less static in terms of land use and demographic change, it got transformed over a period of time, almost beyond recognition. This process of transformation had its seed perhaps in the plan for the city itself which did not cater to the residential needs of the informal sector like construction workers, general services providers and rickshaw pullers and as their low levels of affordability could not effectively enable them to procure houses within the city and force them to settle in slums on the periphery. Secondly, the plan also failed to foresee and even take into account the political realities, especially the one that emerged after 1966. Whereas the city itself was largely maintained as sacrosanct, the privilege could not be extended to its periphery, especially once it came under three different administrative governmental controls. Finally, the impact of Chandigarh as a growth centre that would encourage dynamism in its surroundings was also misjudged. The impressive transformation of the Periphery

Zone that has taken place owes its sustenance largely to the fact of its proximity to Chandigarh.

Politicians, planners and people have all contributed alike to defiling the Periphery Zone. Whereas the role of the first and the last is more visible within the Punjab segment of the periphery, planning bodies are somewhat more active within the Haryana and Chandigarh segments. Periphery violation in the Haryana and Chandigarh segments is better structured and organized than in the Punjab segment. The latter's response was characteristic of knee jerk reactions and efforts at public appeasement.

What is required probably is an empowered body the authority of which transcends state boundaries and which plans for the Periphery Zone as a region rather than as a series of patches of land. Only if all efforts could be geared towards optimizing the development strategies for the periphery it is expected that the Periphery Zone will continue to grow and transform with or without institutional and governmental support. The new emphasis should shift the focus from conservation to development and lay emphasis on a few potential areas rather than the entire periphery. It should aim at preserving the character of the periphery rather than allowing haphazard and unauthorized growth occurring in an isolated and sly manner. The content and intent of the Act requires a reform, keeping in view the existing ground realities and those to emerge in recent and distant future.

3

Rural Population Growth Dynamics

The Capital Periphery Control Act, legislated in 1952 and further strengthened in 1962 by way of extending the limits of the Periphery Zone, was meant to ensure sustainability of the rural landscape around Chandigarh. In addition, the *abadi* (settlement) part of the villages was not expected to expand beyond their *lal dora* (settlement boundary), thereby regulating population growth therein. To what extent could this objective be achieved? What has been the pattern of growth of rural population in the Periphery Zone? How do different sub-zones differ from each other on this count? What is the effect of the location, especially with regard to distance from Chandigarh, site conditions and population size of villages on their growth behaviour? The present chapter is devoted to seeking answers to these questions.

The time frame under consideration is 1971-2001. Evidently, the analysis begins with the first census conducted after the reorganization of Punjab in 1966 and the consequent trifurcation of the Chandigarh Periphery Zone. The year 2001 marks the point in time for which the latest census data at village level is available. The Periphery Zone had 497 villages in 1971; 328 of these fell in Punjab, 143 in Haryana and 26 in the Union Territory of Chandigarh. In 2001, the number of villages decreased to 458; 306 in Punjab, 129 in Haryana and 23 in the Union Territory of Chandigarh. Among the 39 villages which lost their entity, 20 were merged into existing towns, 5 were upgraded to urban status and the remaining 14 remained without population due to acquisition of land.

RURAL POPULATION GROWTH : AN OVERVIEW

The rural population in the Chandigarh Periphery Zone increased from 236,875 to 572,590 during 1971-2001; a doubling in thirty years, a dynamics normally associated with urban populations. The compound annual growth rate of the rural segment of the periphery was worked out as 2.9 per cent. Despite this impressive increase, the proportion of the rural population in the total population decreased during this period, with the urban growth rate being higher than the rural. Urban population recorded a compound annual growth rate of 8.6 per cent, almost three times that of the rural growth rate (2.9 per cent). Simultaneously, the number of towns in the periphery also increased from 4 in 1971 to 12 in 2001. In 1971, no less than 86 per cent of the total population in the Periphery Zone was rural by residence; by 2001, this percentage had come down to 55 per cent. Thus, even though the Periphery Zone remains a rural majority, it has shown a marked shift towards the urban at least so far as the population composition is concerned.

The three sub-zones differed in their population size and growth rate of rural population. The Chandigarh Sub-zone accounting for one-sixth of population, recorded a compound annual growth rate of 6.2 per cent and grew the fastest, followed by Haryana (sharing about one-fourth of the population) at 3.3 per cent and Punjab (partaking two-thirds of the population) at 2.2 per cent (Table 3.1 and Figure 3.1). Underlying this differential population growth rate is the factor of varying incidence of net-migration, being relatively of

TABLE 3.1

Periphery Zone : Sub-zonewise Villages and Share in Rural Population, 2001

Sub-zone/Zone	*Number of villages*	*Population and per cent share*	*Average population size of village*
Punjab Sub-zone	306 (66.8)	326611 (57.0)	1067
Haryana Sub-zone	129 (28.2)	153859 (26.9)	1193
Chandigarh Sub-zone	23 (5.0)	92120 (16.1)	4005
Periphery Zone	458 (100.0)	572590 (100.0)	1250

Note : Figures in parenthesis represent percentage share.

Source : Primary Census Abstract of Chandigarh, Punjab and Haryana, Census of India, Office of the Registrar General, New Delhi, 2001.

FIG. 3.1

Percentage of Villages and Population in Punjab, Haryana and Chandigarh Sub-zones : 2001

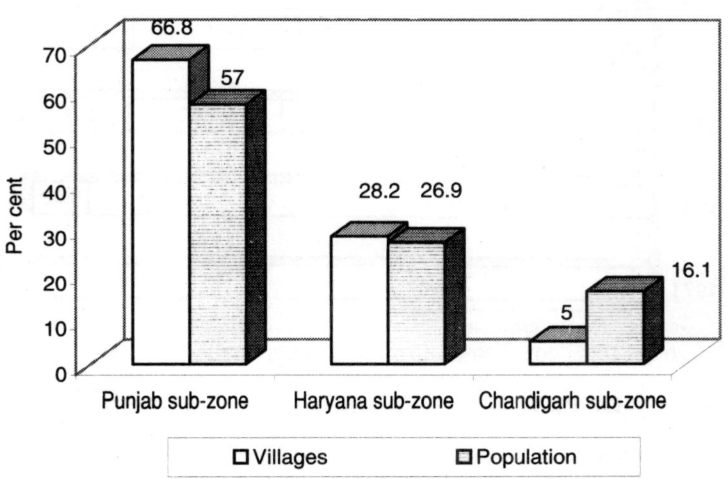

Source : *Primary Census Abstract of Chandigarh, Punjab and Haryana,* Census of India, Office of the Registrar General, New Delhi, 2001.

TABLE 3.2

Periphery Zone: Per cent Share in Rural Population of Sub-zones, 1971-2001

Sub-zone/Zone	*1971*	*2001*	*Change in per cent points*
Punjab Sub-zone	70.0	57.0	- 13.0
Haryana Sub-zone	24.0	26.9	+ 2.9
Chandigarh Sub-zone	6.0	16.1	+ 10.1
Periphery Zone	100.0	100.0	

Source : Village and Town Directory, Village and Town-wise Primary Census Abstract, District Census Handbooks of Chandigarh, Rupnagar, Patiala, Ambala Districts, 1971, Directorate of Census Operations of Chandigarh, Punjab, and Haryana and Primary Census Abstract of Chandigarh, Punjab and Haryana, Census of India, Office of the Registrar General, New Delhi, 2001.

FIG. 3.2

Share of Rural Population at Sub-Zone Level, 1971-2001

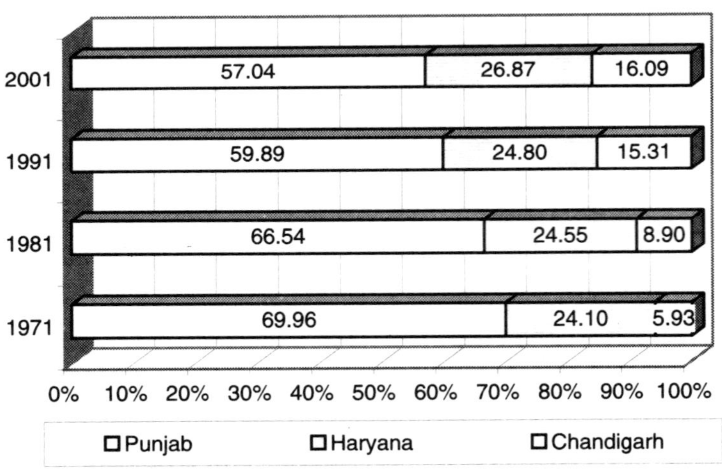

Source : Village and Town Directory, Village and Town-wise Primary Census Abstract, District Census Handbooks of Chandigarh, Rupnagar, Patiala, Ambala Districts, 1971, Directorate of Census Operations of Chandigarh, Punjab, and Haryana and Primary Census Abstract of Chandigarh, Punjab and Haryana, Census of India, Office of the Registrar General, New Delhi, 2001.

highest order in Chandigarh Sub-zone and the lowest in Punjab Sub-zone. In the case of the Punjab Sub-zone, the merger of several villages in the existing towns or upgradation of some to the urban status explains partly the relatively lower growth rate of the rural population.

This is reflected in the decrease in Punjab Sub-zone's share in rural population from 70 per cent in 1971 to 57 per cent in 2001 (Table 3.2 and Figure 3.2). By comparison, Haryana and Chandigarh Sub-zones marked an increase in their share. Meanwhile, within the Punjab Sub-zone, the share of the rural population in total population declined from 88 to 55 per cent; the corresponding decline in Haryana Sub-zone was 76 to 43 per cent. In the Chandigarh Sub-zone, by contrast, the rural population saw a notable rise in its share from 6 to 19 per cent.

UPWARD MOBILITY IN POPULATION SIZE OF VILLAGES

Another noticeable feature of population dynamics within the Periphery Zone was the rapid movement of villages from lower size class categories to higher ones. In 1971, only 40 per cent of the villages had a population size of over 500 persons, the corresponding figure was 70 per cent in 2001 (Table 3.3 and Figure 3.3). There was not a single village having a population of 5,000 persons in 1971; by 2001, there were 16 such villages. Two villages, Hallo Majra and Kujheri in the Chandigarh Union Territory recorded a population of more than 10,000 each in 2001. Obviously most villages within the Periphery Zone have seen considerable additions to their population numbers, by the twin processes of natural increase and net in-migration. The range in population size of the villages has also widened from 3 (Nizampur) to 4265 (Surajpur) in 1971 to 6 (Hasanpur) to 13,552 (Hallo Majra) in 2001. The largest village in 2001 was more than three times that in 1971.

The critical breaks in population size of villages were identified at 1000 and 2000 in 1971 and at 1000, 2000 and 4000 in 2001.

TABLE 3.3
Periphery Zone: Distribution of Inhabited Villages by Size Category, 1971 and 2001

Population range	*1971*	*2001*
Less than 200	100 (22.8)	49 (10.7)
200-499	165 (37.6)	94 (20.5)
500-999	115 (26.2)	138 (30.2)
1000-1999	52 (11.8)	106 (23.1)
2000-4999	7 (1.6)	55 (12.0)
5000-9999	0 (0.0)	14 (3.1)
10000 and more	0 (0.0)	2 (0.4)
Total	439 (100.0)	458 (100.0)

Note : Figures in parenthesis represent percentage share.

Source : *Village and Town Directory, Village and Town-wise Primary Census Abstract, District Census Handbooks of Chandigarh, Rupnagar, Patiala, Ambala Districts, 1971,* Directorate of Census Operations of Chandigarh, Punjab, and Haryana and *Primary Census Abstract of Chandigarh, Punjab and Haryana,* Census of India, Office of the Registrar General, New Delhi, 2001.

FIG. 3.3
Distribution of Villages by Population Size, 1971 and 2001

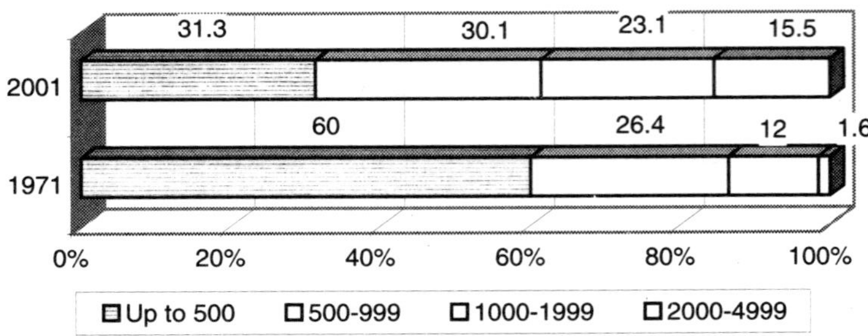

Source : *Village and Town Directory, Village and Town-wise Primary Census Abstract, District Census Handbooks of Chandigarh, Rupnagar, Patiala, Ambala Districts, 1971,* Directorate of Census Operations of Chandigarh, Punjab, and Haryana and *Primary Census Abstract of Chandigarh, Punjab and Haryana,* Census of India, Office of the Registrar General, New Delhi, 2001.

POPULATION SIZE : A NON-FACTOR IN POPULATION GROWTH

A cause-and-effect relationship is expected between population size and growth rate of a village. Bigger villages tend to accumulate more of the central functions, thereby attracting migrants, and recording faster growth rate than the rate of their natural increase. This process increases their population size.

Contrary to expectations, smaller the size of the village higher was its compound annual growth rate during the period 1971-2001 in the Periphery Zone. There was a consistent decline in the growth rate with increase in the size of the village; 3.6 per cent in villages with a population of less than 200; 3.3 per

TABLE 3.4

Periphery Zone: Decadal Compound Annual Growth Rate of Rural Population by Size Category of Villages, 1971-2001

Population range	*1971-1981*	*1981-1991*	*1991-2001*	*1971-2001*
Less than 200	5.0	8.3	7.7	3.6
200-499	3.2	2.6	3.1	3.3
500-999	2.7	2.6	2.8	2.9
1000-1999	2.4	3.6	2.4	2.6
2000-4999	1.4	3.1	3.5	1.9
5000-9999	0.0	0.2	2.7	0.0
10000 and more	0.0	0.0	-6.3	0.0
Total	2.7	3.1	2.8	2.9

Note : For calculating the compound annual growth rate, the initial year has been considered as the base.

Source : *Village and Town Directory, Village and Town-wise Primary Census Abstract, District Census Handbooks of Chandigarh, Rupnagar, Patiala, Ambala Districts, 1971*, Directorate of Census Operations of Chandigarh, Punjab, and Haryana and *Primary Census Abstract of Chandigarh, Punjab and Haryana*, Census of India, Office of the Registrar General, New Delhi, 2001.

cent in those with a population of 200 to 500 each, and so on till a growth rate of only 1.9 per cent is observed in the case of villages with a population of more than 2000 (Table 3.4 and Figure 3.4). The population growth rate of villages in the Periphery Zone was determined by the volume of net in-migration for employment in the neighbouring cities of Chandigarh, S.A.S. Nagar (Mohali) and Panchkula.

FIG. 3.4

Decadal Compound Annual Growth Rate of Population according to Size Category of Villages, 1971-2001

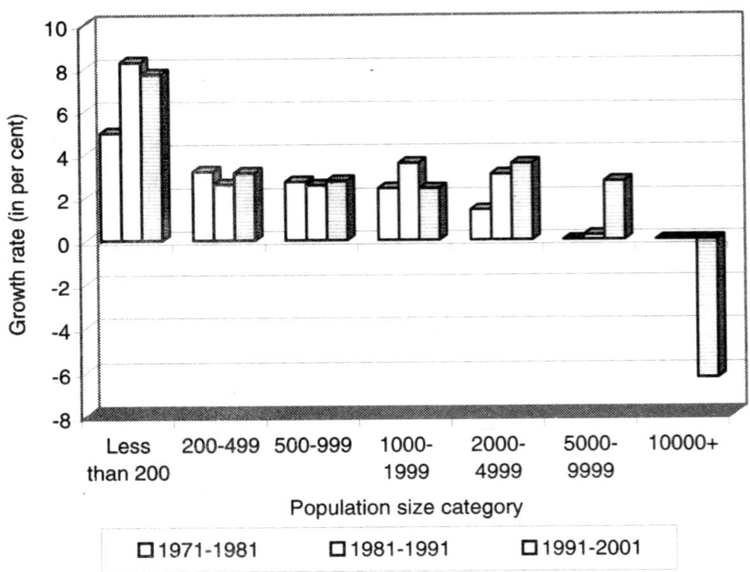

Source : *Village and Town Directory, Village and Town-wise Primary Census Abstract, District Census Handbooks of Chandigarh, Rupnagar, Patiala, Ambala Districts, 1971,* Directorate of Census Operations of Chandigarh, Punjab, and Haryana and *Primary Census Abstract of Chandigarh, Punjab and Haryana,* Census of India, Office of the Registrar General, New Delhi, 2001.

The growth behaviour of the villages by population size category, however, was not consistent over the decades. The rate at 3.1 per cent during 1981-91 was the highest in comparison with 2.7 per cent each during 1971-81 and 2.8 per cent in 1991-2001. Villages in the size category of less than 200 persons recorded the highest growth rate during all the three decades. A consistent rise in the population growth rate of villages with a population of 2000 and above over time was also observed. During 1971-2001, only one village, Palsaura in Chandigarh Sub-zone was noted for a population decrease from 10270 in 1991 to 5351 in 2001. This was associated with relocation of a slum locality from its site to the land acquired in neighbouring villages.

When data were examined sub-zonewise, a negative relationship between the population size and growth rate was consistently maintained in the case of Chandigarh Sub-zone. The same was true for Punjab and Haryana Sub-zones, by and large, but it was not that regular as in the case of the Chandigarh Sub-zone (Table 3.5 and Figure 3.5).

TABLE 3.5

Periphery Zone: Compound Annual Growth Rate of Rural Population by Population Size Category of Villages, 1971-2001

Population range	*Punjab Sub-zone*	*Haryana Sub-zone*	*Chandigarh Sub-zone*	*Periphery Zone*
Less than 200	4.0	3.0	8.9	3.6
200-499	2.6	4.6	6.9	3.3
500-999	1.9	3.1	6.6	2.9
1000-1999	2.0	2.8	5.4	2.6
2000-4999	1.6	2.3	0	1.9
5000-9999	0	0	0	0
10000 and more	0	0	0	0
Total	2.2	3.3	6.2	2.9

Note : Common villages in the years 1971 and 2001 were considered for calculating the compound annual growth rates.

Source : *Village and Town Directory, Village and Town-wise Primary Census Abstract, District Census Handbooks of Chandigarh, Rupnagar, Patiala, Ambala Districts, 1971,* Directorate of Census Operations of Chandigarh, Punjab, and Haryana and *Primary Census Abstract of Chandigarh, Punjab and Haryana,* Census of India, Office of the Registrar General, New Delhi, 2001.

FIG. 3.5

Compound Annual Growth Rate of Rural Population by Population Size Category of Villages : 1971-2001

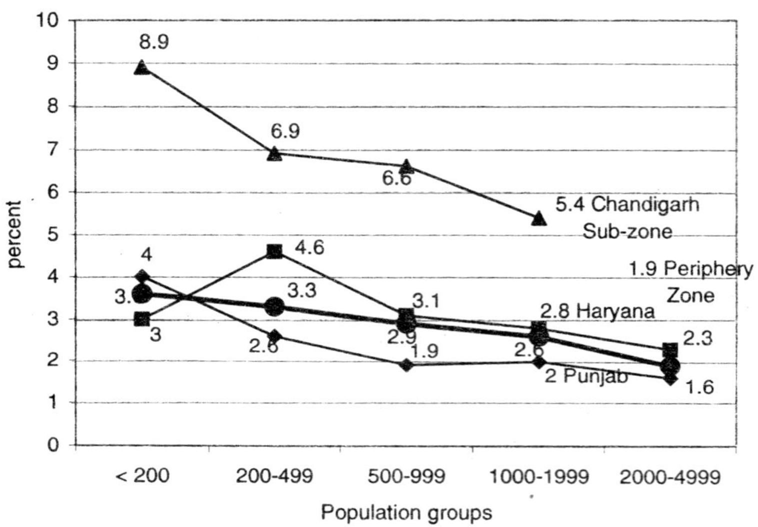

Source : *Village and Town Directory, Village and Town-wise Primary Census Abstract, District Census Handbooks of Chandigarh, Rupnagar, Patiala, Ambala Districts, 1971,* Directorate of Census Operations of Chandigarh, Punjab, and Haryana and *Primary Census Abstract of Chandigarh, Punjab and Haryana,* Census of India, Office of the Registrar General, New Delhi, 2001.

Villages close to Chandigarh, located in a sub-mountainous zone, are smaller in size and their size increases with distance. Herein lies the role of the factor of distance, which is analyzed in the following section.

DISTANCE FROM CHANDIGARH : A FACTOR IN POPULATION GROWTH

Before discussing the role of distance, it is necessary to have a look at the distributional pattern of villages by distance annules. It is learnt that 0-4 km distance annule accounted for 10.9 per cent of area, same proportion of villages and 25.8 per cent of the rural population of the Periphery Zone in 2001 (Table 3.6). By contrast, the respective figures were 40.2, 40.4 and 28.4 per cent in the 12-16 km distance annule. This is not surprising as the spatial extent of the annule is bound to grow bigger with increasing distance from Chandigarh. As noted above, the population size of villages in proximity to Chandigarh was smaller than that of others because of the sub-mountainous topography and lower productivity of agriculture in the tract wherein the city is located.

TABLE 3.6

Periphery Zone: Area and Population Parameters of Villages in Different Annules, 1971 and 2001

Distance from Chandigarh (in kilometers)	*Percentage of rural area*		*Percentage of villages*		*Percentage share of village population*	
	1971	*2001*	*1971*	*2001*	*1971*	*2001*
0-4	11.9	10.9	10.6	10.9	13.9	25.8
4-8	19.6	19.1	18.2	18.1	21.6	21.9
8-12	29.5	29.8	30.8	30.6	28.2	23.9
12-16	39.0	40.2	40.4	40.4	36.3	28.4

Source : *Village and Town Directory, Village and Town-wise Primary Census Abstract, District Census Handbooks of Chandigarh, Rupnagar, Patiala, Ambala Districts, 1971,* Directorate of Census Operations of Chandigarh, Punjab, and Haryana and *Primary Census Abstract of Chandigarh, Punjab and Haryana,* Census of India, Office of the Registrar General, New Delhi, 2001.

The marginal difference in percentage share of rural area in 1971 and 2001 in various distance annules is explained by a periodic upgradation of some rural territory to urban status.

Table 3.6 reveals that the percentage share of rural population in 0-4 km. distance annule increased from 13.9 in 1971 to 25.8 in 2001. The population share of the 4-8 kilometers distance annule experienced only a minor increase from 21.6 to 21.9 per cent. As expected, the population share successively decreased in the 8-12 and 12-16 kilometers distance annules.

The 'distance decay' phenomenon is not difficult to understand as most of the migrants, who opted to settle in villages due to lower cost of living, were keen to stay close to Chandigarh as much as possible. It is also learnt that while the Periphery Zone, as a whole, experienced a rapid growth of population during 1971-2001, the phenomenal rate of growth was marked up to a distance of 8 kilometers.

TABLE 3.7

Periphery Zone: Per Cent Share of Rural Population by Sub-zones, 1971 and 2001

Distance from Chandigarh (in kilometers)	*Punjab Sub-zone*		*Haryana Sub-zone*		*Chandigarh Sub-zone*	
	1971	*2001*	*1971*	*2001*	*1971*	*2001*
0-4	9.6	15.2	4.9	4.5	100.0	100.0
4-8	19.2	19.0	33.8	41.7	—	—
8-12	31.8	31.9	24.9	20.5	—	—
12-16	39.4	33.9	36.4	33.3	—	—

Source : *Village and Town Directory, Village and Town-wise Primary Census Abstract, District Census Handbooks of Chandigarh, Rupnagar, Patiala, Ambala Districts, 1971,* Directorate of Census Operations of Chandigarh, Punjab, and Haryana and *Primary Census Abstract of Chandigarh, Punjab and Haryana,* Census of India, Office of the Registrar General, New Delhi, 2001.

Table 3.7 presents the picture as it differs by sub-zones. The entire rural population in the Chandigarh Sub-zone was concentrated within 4 kilometers in both 1971 and 2001 from the outer boundary of the city, the extent of territorial limits of the Chandigarh Union Territory being as such. In the Punjab Sub-zone, the 0-4 km annule raised its share in population from about 10 to 15 per cent during 1971-2001; while it remained constant at nearly 5 per cent in Haryana. The Punjab villages contiguous to Chandigarh were proving stronger magnets for in-migrants than their counterparts in Haryana.

Table 3.8 synthesizes this picture which shows that the 0-4 kilometers annule accounted for one-fourth of the population on about one-tenth of the area. There was an addition of eleven per cent points in its share in total population during 1971-2001.

TABLE 3.8

Percentage Share of Area and Population according to Distance from Chandigarh

Distance from Chandigarh (in kilometers)	*Per cent share of area to total area 1971*	*Per cent share of population to total population 1971*	*Per cent share of population to total population 2001*	*Per cent point change in share of population*
0-4	11.0	13.9	25.2	+11.3
4-8	18.7	21.6	22.2	+ 0.6
8-12	30.1	28.2	23.9	- 4.3
12-16	40.2	36.3	28.7	- 7.6

Source : *Village and Town Directory, Village and Town-wise Primary Census Abstract, District Census Handbooks of Chandigarh, Rupnagar, Patiala, Ambala Districts, 1971,* Directorate of Census Operations of Chandigarh, Punjab, and Haryana and *Primary Census Abstract of Chandigarh, Punjab and Haryana,* Census of India, Office of the Registrar General, New Delhi, 2001.

The same is reflected in the compound annual population growth rate of villages located in different distance annules (Table 3.9). While the rural population in the 0-4 km. annule recorded a compound annual growth rate of as much as 5 per cent, the comparable figures for the 4-8, 8-12 and 12-16 kms annules were 3.0, 2.3 and 2.1 respectively. This is a clear case of distance decay, that is, incidence of in-migration decreasing with increasing distance from the main city.

Since all the villages in the Chandigarh Sub-zone were located within the 0-4 kilometers distance annule, the growth rate of the rural population at 6 per cent in its case was the highest among that of all sub-zones (Figure 3.6). The Haryana Sub-zone recorded a growth rate of 3.3 per cent while its different distance annules did not display a consistent pattern.

TABLE 3.9

Periphery Zone: Compound Annual Growth Rate of Villages by Distance from Chandigarh, 1971-2001

Distance up to (in kilometers)	*Punjab Sub-zone*	*Haryana Sub-zone*	*Chandigarh Sub-zone*	*Periphery Zone*
0-4	3.8 (23)	3.0 (4)	6.2 (19)	5.0 (46)
4-8	2.2 (60)	4.0 (20)	—	3.0 (80)
8-12	2.2 (99)	2.6 (37)	—	2.3 (136)
12-16	1.7 (114)	3.0 (63)	—	2.1 (177)
Total	2.2 (296)	3.3 (124)	6.2 (19)	2.9 (439)

Source : *Village and Town Directory, Village and Town-wise Primary Census Abstract, District Census Handbooks of Chandigarh, Rupnagar, Patiala, Ambala Districts, 1971,* Directorate of Census Operations of Chandigarh, Punjab, and Haryana and *Primary Census Abstract of Chandigarh, Punjab and Haryana,* Census of India, Office of the Registrar General, New Delhi, 2001.

FIG. 3.6

Compound Annual Population Growth Rate of Villages by Distance from Chandigarh : 1971-2001

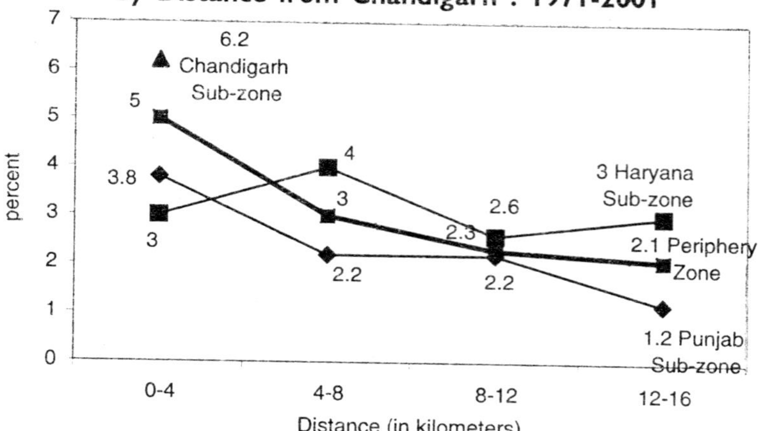

Source : *Village and Town Directory, Village and Town-wise Primary Census Abstract, District Census Handbooks of Chandigarh, Rupnagar, Patiala, Ambala Districts, 1971,* Directorate of Census Operations of Chandigarh, Punjab, and Haryana and *Primary Census Abstract of Chandigarh, Punjab and Haryana,* Census of India, Office of the Registrar General, New Delhi, 2001.

The presence of Panchkula Urban Estate in contiguity with Chandigarh disturbed the expected pattern. In the case of Punjab Sub-zone, the growth rate is high in the 0-4 kilometers distance annule, moderate in 4-8 and 8-12 kilometers distance annules and comparatively low in 12-16 kilometers distance annule. At the sub-zone level, the role of distance and land use get mixed up in influencing surface trends.

SPATIAL PATTERN OF POPULATION GROWTH

During 1971-2001, the natural rate of increase of population in the Periphery Zone was around 2 per cent, birth rate being about 30 and death rate 9. The actual growth rate was 3 per cent. To identify ultimate-in-detail patterns of rural population growth rate, the compound annual growth rate of every village was calculated and mapped. The map helped in identifying three types of areas on the basis of their population growth rate: (i) 2.5 per cent and above representing net in-migration; (ii) 1.5 to 2.5 per cent signifying a dominant role of natural increase within and out-migration balancing each other, and (iii) less than 1.5 per cent representing net out-migration. Hence, one-third of the growth of rural population could be attributed to the factor of net-migration.

Table 3.10 shows that about 40 per cent of the villages in the Periphery Zone had experienced net in-migration of varying volume. The same was true of nearly three-fifths of the villages in Haryana Sub-zone and just over one-fourth of the villages in the Punjab Sub-zone. Another around 40 per cent of the villages were noted for a balance between in-migration and out-migration and their population growth was essentially an outcome of natural increase. This category covered one-third of the villages in the Haryana Sub-zone. On the other side, one-fifth of the villages in the Periphery Zone had suffered net out-migration, and this category covered nearly one-tenth of the villages in the Haryana Sub-zone and one-fourth of those in the Punjab Sub-zone. These inter-sub-zonal differences are attributed to the locational pattern of villages *vis-a-vis* the depth of the different sub-zones. A discussion on each type follows.

In-migration Areas

In–migration was most typical of the villages located in Chandigarh Sub-zone, which recorded a compound annual growth rate of 6.2 per cent (Map 3.1). Every village was a net in-migrant case. This was an outcome of a two way process: migrants targeting Chandigarh but settling in villages in its proximity, and some Chandigarh residents shifting to these villages. While vast employment opportunities available in the city attracted in-migrants, the high cost of living in the city deflected them to the surrounding rural areas. The high cost of procuring residential accommodation in Chandigarh led many to rent a house in the neighbouring villages. Not in a position to purchase a house or own a plot in Chandigarh, many middle class or better-off persons opted to settle in a nearby village.

TABLE 3.10

Periphery Zone: Villages by Compound Annual Growth Rate of Rural Population by Sub-zones, 1971-2001

CAGR (in per cent)	*Punjab Sub-zone*	*Haryana Sub-zone*	*Chandigarh Sub-zone*	*Periphery Zone*
Less than 1.49	78 (26.4)	11 (8.9)	0 (0.0)	89 (20.3)
1.5-2.49	137 (46.2)	41 (33.1)	0 (0.0)	178 (40.5)
2.5 +	81 (27.4)	72 (58.0)	19 (100.0)	172 (39.2)
Total No. of Villages	296	124	19	439

Notes : (i) Figures in parenthesis represent percentage share.

(ii) Compound annual growth rate of less than 1.5 per cent represents out-migration and depleting natural increase of 1.5 to 2.5 per cent the dominant role of natural increase, and of above 2.5 per cent in-migration adding to natural increase.

Source : *Village and Town Directory, Village and Town-wise Primary Census Abstract, District Census Handbooks of Chandigarh, Rupnagar, Patiala, Ambala Districts, 1971,* Directorate of Census Operations of Chandigarh, Punjab, and Haryana and *Primary Census Abstract of Chandigarh, Punjab and Haryana,* Census of India, Office of the Registrar General, New Delhi, 2001.

Such villages are conveniently located within a commutable distance. Several non-farm activities, such as

MAP 3.1
Chandigarh Periphery Zone
(Net In-Migration Villages : 1971-2001)

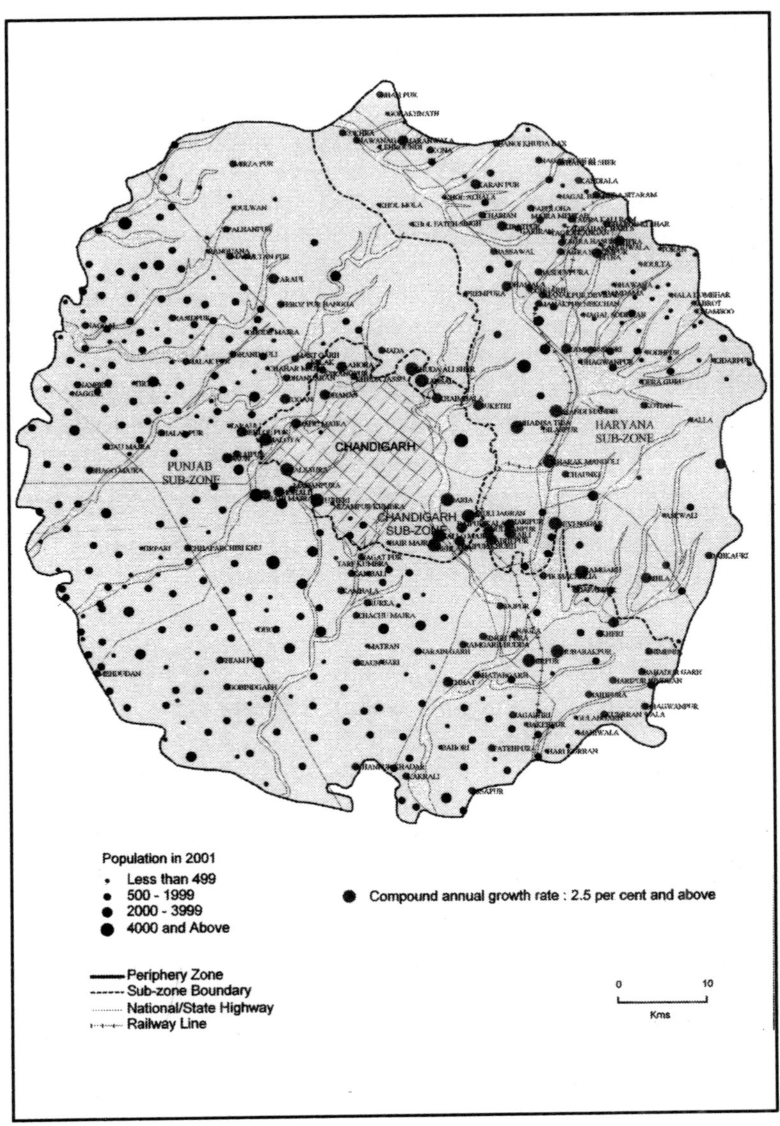

poultry farms and milk dairies, are operational in these villages. These are the activities permissible under the Periphery Control Act. Meanwhile, several households, native to these villages, have constructed low cost dwelling units especially for renting out to in-migrants in groups. This further facilitated and prompted in-migration, leading to astronomical demographic growth of these villages.

The newly planned towns, S.A.S. Nagar (Mohali) in Punjab and Panchkula in Haryana, have been raised in contiguity with Chandigarh. Both have grown to a size of a city, with a population 123,284 and 140,992, in 2001 respectively. The employment opportunities offered by these two towns, including by way of ongoing construction activity, has induced in-migration, especially of manual unskilled labour. Small and medium industry units in S.A.S. Nagar (Mohali) and Panchkula have given a further impetus to in-migration. Many of the migrants have taken residence in villages adjacent to these places, and thereby have caused rapid population growth.

PERIPHERY ZONE : LOCATIONAL DYNAMICS OF MIGRATION, 1971-2001

In-migration

Villages within Chandigarh Union Territory

- Overspill of the population of Chandigarh due to high cost of living in the city.
- Migrant labour from other parts of country settling here due to employment opportunities offered by Chandigarh.
- Availability of accommodation at low rents.

Villages contiguous to Chandigarh Union Territory

- Locational advantage of being close to Chandigarh.

- Setting up of several non-farm enterprises, such as poultry and dairy.
- Raising of residential colonies by developers.

Villages around S.A.S. Nagar (Mohali) and Panchkula

- Migration of a large number of labourers for construction work in these two cities.
- Small and medium industrial units in S.A.S. Nagar (Mohali) providing employment to skilled workers.
- Stone crushing activities on river Ghaggar near Panchkula offering employment to manual workers.

Villages adjoining Derra Bassi, Kharar, Zirakpur, Pinjore and Kalka Towns

- Emergence of residential colonies on the rural land in proximity to these towns. Labour required for construction of these colonies.
- Preference of the retired H.M.T. Pinjore employees to settle close to their previous place of work.
- Overspill of population from the fast growing congested town of Kalka.

Villages along National Highway-22 Connecting Chandigarh-Pinjore-Kalka

- Better connectivity of these villages with other major towns in the zone facilitates commuting.
- Facility of marketing local produce.
- Stone crushing activities on Pinjore-Surajpur road.

Villages adjacent to Haryana-Himachal Pradesh Border

- Employment opportunities in industries at Parwanoo and Solan, not very far away from these villages.

- Coming up of activities typical in settlements along the inter-State border.

Villages in the Belt Pinjore-Nalagarh-Baddi

- Availability of job opportunity in a large number of industrial units located in these industrial centers, coupled with inadequacy of local accommodation

Out-migration

Peripheral areas in Punjab Sub-zone

- Lowered agricultural productivity associated with undulating topography, soil erosion, and inadequate irrigation.
- Scheduled castes constituting a significant proportion of the population of these villages migrated to nearby towns.
- Progress of education in this backward area impelled outmigration for a variety of jobs.

Future Scenario

- Residential colonies on the rural land adjacent to the towns to emerge, causing redistribution of population in the periphery zone.
- New planned towns in the periphery zone to influence the growth behaviour of neighbouring villages.
- Emergence of recreational activities, marriage palaces, health and educational facilities to take place in the periphery zone due to non-availability of land or the exorbitant prices of such services in the city of Chandigarh.
- Pressure to extend the *lal dora* limits (settlements boundary) in villages to mount further as these are already overpressurised due to high natural increase and heavy in-migration.

- Upgradation of existing roads connecting rural service centers in the periphery zone likely to cause heavy in-migration to villages along these corridors.

Similar is the story emanating from smaller towns, such as Derra Bassi, Kharar, Zirakpur, and Pinjore. Several residential colonies have come up in villages adjacent to these towns. The employees retiring from the Hindustan Machine Tools factory, Pinjore preferred to settle in localities close to their previous place of work. As a result, villages around Pinjore town have experienced in-migration. Kalka town over time has got congested. There is a conspicuous overspill of population to its surrounding villages. Zirakpur town witnessed the emergence of so many residential colonies in adjoining villages that the territorial limits of the towns had to be extended recently.

In particular, villages along the National Highway-22, connecting Chandigarh-Pinjore-Kalka are growing at a fast pace. These are directly connected by road not only with Chandigarh but also other towns in the Periphery Zone. This facilitates commuting, marketing of local produce, and access to education and health services in urban places.

A spurt in the industrial activity in Solan and Sirmaur districts of Himachal Pradesh has caused sizeable in-migration to the border villages of the Haryana Sub-zone. The industrial expansion of Parwanoo town in Solan district and of Baddi and Barotiwala in Sirmaur district added several new employment opportunities of different kinds. These have been availed by the villages located in their vicinity falling in the Haryana Sub-zone as well. Kalka is the first point of contact connecting Himachal Pradesh with the rest of the country on broadgauge railway line. The town is a transactional base for transporting industrial and horticultural produce to and from Himachal Pradesh. Demand for labour is high. The inadequate accommodation facility at Kalka forces many to settle in its surrounding villages.

The process is expected to gain momentum following the announcement of the industrial package for Himachal Pradesh by the Government of India on 7th January 2003. Many entrepreneurs will prefer to set up their units in the State due to the proximity of Chandigarh. Within a short span of about three years a large number of new industrial units registered themselves at Baddi alone. Similar development would generate newer economic opportunities and stimulate in-migration. The demography of villages in Haryana Sub-zone in proximity to the Himachal Pradesh would probably acquire great dynamism during the coming years.

Out-migration Areas

One-fifth of the villages in the Periphery Zone experienced out-migration during 1971-2001. There was none of the kind in Chandigarh Sub-zone, only 9 per cent of the total in the Haryana Sub-zone, and 26.4 per cent in Punjab Sub-zone (Map 3.2). Out-migration was noted as most typical of the villages located in the inner periphery of Punjab Sub-zone. These are marked by low agricultural productivity due to undulating topography and lack of irrigation facilities. These are also relatively distantly located from Chandigarh. Efforts to improve the economy of these villages through watershed management are in process and are expected to contain out-migration.

Among out-migrants, the scheduled caste population predominates. They are generally landless and have limited stake in the village. Migration to a near by town was a gainful opportunity for them. Many of such migrants moved to villages located in the vicinity of Chandigarh. The reasons are obvious: proximity to the place of employment, and similar social milieu. Preferred locations were the villages located on the main roads, offering greater facility of commuting. The process represents a redistribution of rural population within the periphery zone.

Areas with Neutralization of and Out-migration

Two-fifths of the villages in the Periphery Zone recorded a population growth rate close to the rate of natural increase. Such villages accounted for one-third of the total in Haryana Sub-zone and nearly one-half in the Punjab Sub-zone. These do not make a cluster. Often these are located in the belts

Map 3.2
Chandigarh Periphery Zone (Net Out-Migration Villages : 1971-2001)

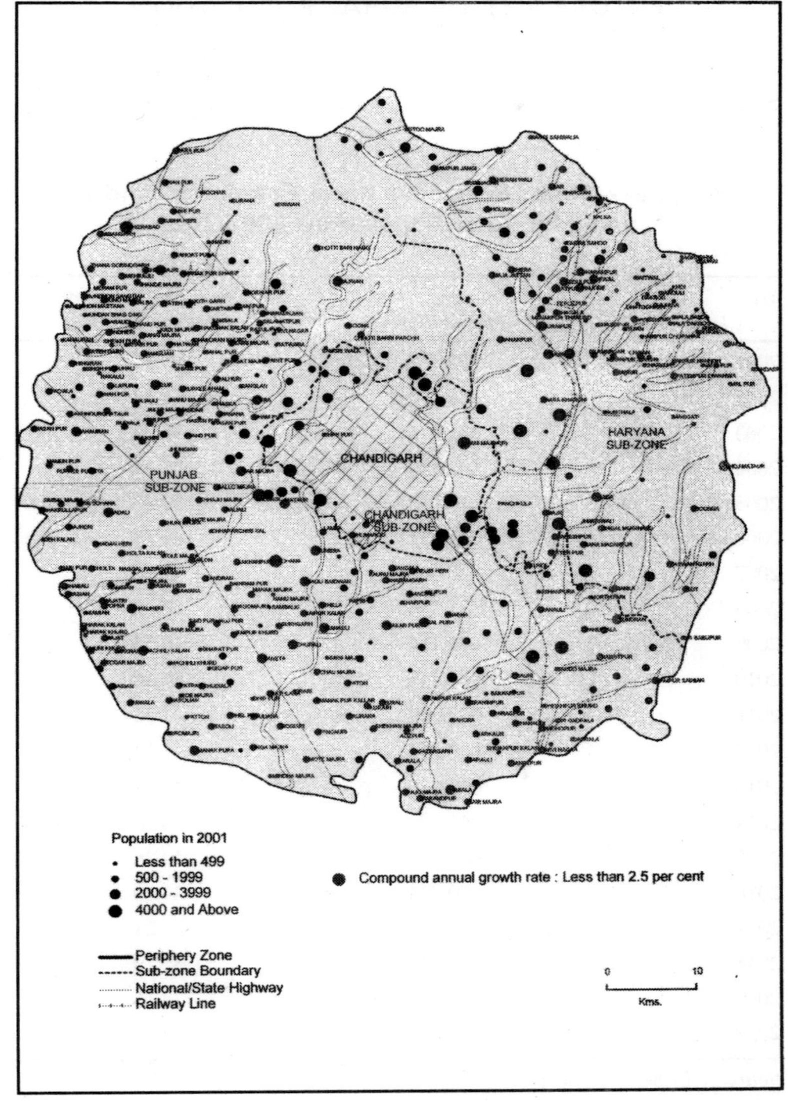

sandwiched between the areas of in-and-out-migration. A balance of positive and negative factors influencing migration is represented in their case.

FUTURE SIZE OF RURAL POPULATION

Table 3.11 shows that rural population will increase from 572,590 in 2001 to 671,174 in 2020. The share of rural

TABLE 3.11

Periphery Zone: Projected Rural Population and its Share in Total Population, 2001-2020

Year	*Projected rural population*	*Percentage share in total population*
2001	572,590 (Actual)	55.21
2002	584,496	54.12
2003	588,744	53.04
2004	602,620	51.95
2005	610,440	50.87
2006	617,272	49.78
2007	623,360	48.70
2008	633,346	47.62
2009	642,114	46.53
2010	645,248	45.44
2011	652,092	44.36
2012	658,768	43.34
2013	660,036	42.31
2014	664,608	41.28
2015	668,316	40.26
2016	670,833	39.23
2017	672,496	38.21
2018	673,139	37.19
2019	691,176	37.16
2020	671,174	35.14

Source : Projection outputs.

population would, however, decrease from 55.2 per cent in 2001 to 35.1 per cent in 2020, a decline by 20 per cent points.

The details of the projection technique to arrive at these figures are given in chapter 6. The Periphery Zone would acquire an urban majority in 2006 when more than half of the population of the Periphery Zone would be residing in urban areas. While planning the city all efforts were made to retain rural character in its surroundings. This was, however, not to be.

CONCLUSION

Contrary to what was envisaged by the planners of the city, the rural population of the Chandigarh Periphery Zone witnessed a rapid growth. During 1971-2001, the rural population grew by a compound annual growth rate of 3 per cent whereas the rate of natural increase averaged 2 per cent. A direct inference is that one-third of the rural population increase can be attributed to net in-migration.

In-migration was of higher order in villages within Chandigarh Union Territory, and those around Mohali in Punjab Sub-zone. Inflow of migrants was of larger volume also in villages located along the roads radiating out of Chandigarh, those falling in the Free Enterprise Zone of Punjab Sub-zone, and still others located in proximity of industrial complex in the Haryana Sub-zone. On the other hand, out-migration was typical of villages located at a distance from Chandigarh, especially in the Punjab Sub-zone. Considerable migration within the Periphery Zone had taken place, indicating thus a redistribution of population.

Interestingly there was a complete lack of any relationship between the population size and growth rate of villages. Small sized villages recorded the fastest increase rate of population. This is explained by the fact that most of them were located close to Chandigarh. Indeed the factors of distance from Chandigarh and matters of connectivity were most critical in determining the growth rate of individual villages.

Such a scenario is to be visualized against the drop in number of villages from 497 to 458 in the Periphery Zone. The process was associated with the merger of several villages in the existing towns and upgradation of some to the urban status. The rural population in the Periphery Zone will increase from 572,590 in 2001 to 671,174 in 2020. However, in terms of share of rural population to total population of the Periphery Zone it would decrease from 55 per cent in 2001 to 35 per cent in 2020. The Periphery Zone was thus acquiring an urban hue against what was visualized as a primarily rural girdle around Chandigarh.

Urban Population Growth Dynamics

Chandigarh is one of the 120 odd urban centres raised on planned lines since independence (Krishan, 1999, p. 1). The city was to be a manifest model of urban design and development. For this, it was necessary not only to plan the city structure within but also to protect its rural periphery from any haphazard urban growth. Initially the city was planned for a finite population size of half-a-million. The intention was not to overload its infrastructure; the periphery was also to be protected from unwarranted urban growth for the same reason. As early as in 1952, the Punjab New Capital Periphery Control Act was enacted, as mentioned before.

After a passage of about five decades the pertinent question is to what extent the Periphery Zone of Chandigarh could be protected from getting urbanized. This Chapter is geared to the task of analyzing the process of urbanization in the Periphery Zone, discerning the factors responsible for the emergence of new towns, increased rate of urban population, and additions to urban area. Implications of the scene as it emerged are also spelt out.

TOWNS AND URBAN POPULATION : 1951-2001

The efforts to retain the rural character of the Periphery Zone have not succeeded as the urban centres are continuously growing in their number and size. In 1951, that is, before the demarcation of the Periphery Zone, there were 4 towns namely, Kharar, Derra Bassi, Banur and Kalka within its limits. However, within a very short span of time considerable unplanned urban growth mushroomed within the restricted Periphery Zone. A military cantonment, the Hindustan Machine Tools factory at Pinjore, an industrial factory near Kharar, and unauthorized urban growth near the airport are some of the illustrations (Kalia, 1987, p. 139).

Of course, up to 1971 the number of towns at four remained unchanged. In 1981, there was an addition of three new towns namely, S.A.S. Nagar (Mohali) in Punjab and Panchkula and H.M.T. Pinjore in Haryana. There was an addition of one town namely, Pinjore in the 1991 census. The Census of India 2001 recorded an upsurge in the number of towns in the Periphery Zone. Five new towns, namely, Mullanpur-Garibdas, Karoran, Bhabat in Rupnager district and Zirakpur and Bhankarpur in Patiala district in Punjab were added. H.M.T. Pinjore, a new town in 1991, was de-classified and was treated as an outgrowth of Pinjore urban agglomeration in 2001. All in all, now there are 12 towns in the Periphery Zone of Chandigarh (Map 4.1).

All this was concomitant with an impressive increase in the size of the urban population in the Periphery Zone. It multiplied 17 times from 27,494 in 1951 to 4,64,451 in 2001. By comparison, urban population in the Chandigarh Union territory increased from 99,262 in 1961 to 8,08,515 in 2001, a rise by 8 times. Down the decades, a lack of uniformity is observed in urban population increase in the city and its periphery. In the Periphery Zone, the urban population grew by 1.4 times during 1951-71 and by 12 times during 1971-2001. In comparison, population of Chandigarh multiplied by 2.3 times during 1961-71 and 3.5 times during 1971-2001. Urban growth in the Periphery Zone has been phenomenal since 1971 (Table 4.1).

Map 4.1
Chandigarh Periphery Zone
(Chronological Disribution of Towns : 1951-2001)

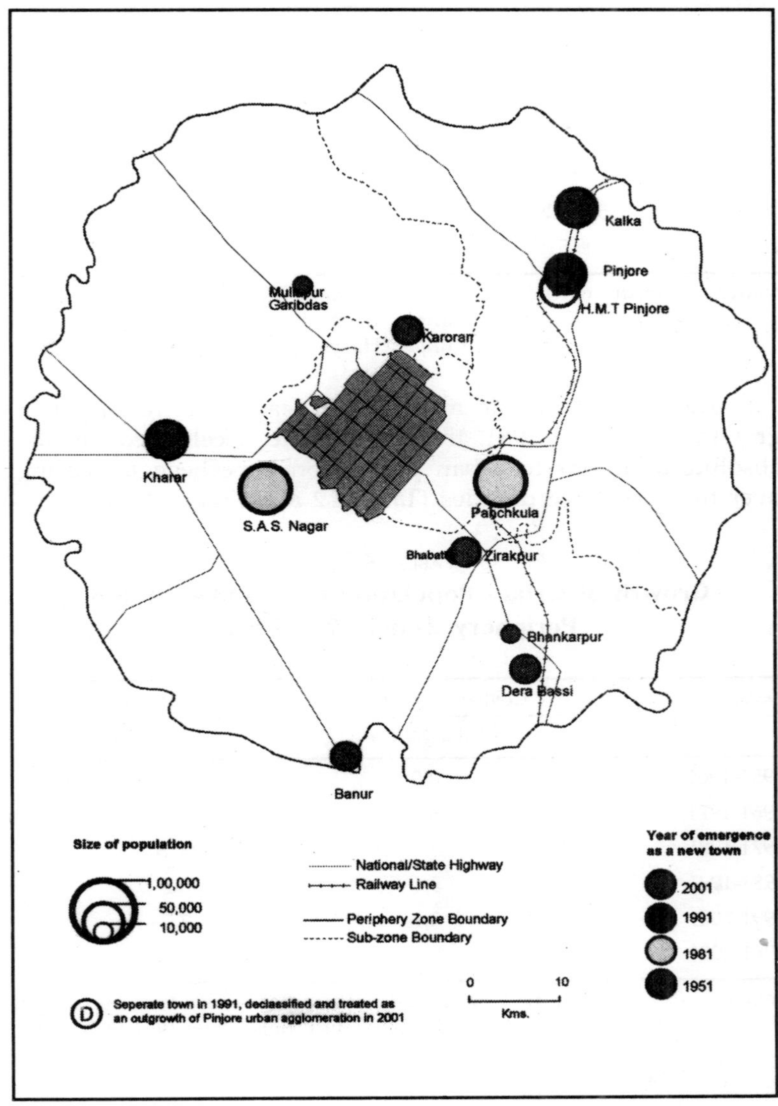

TABLE 4.1

Size of Urban Population of Chandigarh and Periphery Zone, 1961-2001

Census year	*Urban Population*		*Additions during the decade*	
	Chandigarh	*Periphery Zone*	*Chandigarh*	*Periphery Zone*
1961	99,262	34,643		
1971	232,940	39,663	133,678	5,020
1981	422,841	107,376	189,901	67,713
1991	575,829	235,367	152,988	127,991
2001	808,515	464,451	232,686	229,084

Source : Census of India, *General Population Tables and Primary Census Abstract*, different volumes from 1961 to 2001, Directorate of Census Operations, Punjab, Haryana and Chandigarh.

The 1971-81 decade marked the peak in terms of urban growth rate. Since 1981, though the rate decelerated yet the absolute additions to urban population have been increasing over the successive decades (Table 4.2 and Figure 4.1).

TABLE 4.2

Growth of Urban Population in Chandigarh and Periphery Zone, 1951-2001

Decade	*Compound annual urban growth rate (per cent)*	
	Chandigarh city	*Periphery Zone*
1951-1961	0.0	2.3
1961-1971	8.9	1.4
1971-1981	6.1	10.5
1981-1991	3.1	8.2
1991-2001	3.4	7.0
1961-2001	5.4	5.8

Source : Census of India : *General Population Tables and Primary Census Abstract, Part II-A and II-B, different volumes from 1961 to 2001 by* Directorate of Census Operations, Punjab, Haryana and Chandigarh.

FIG. 4.1
Periphery Zone: Compound Annual Growth Rate of Urban Population, 1951-2001

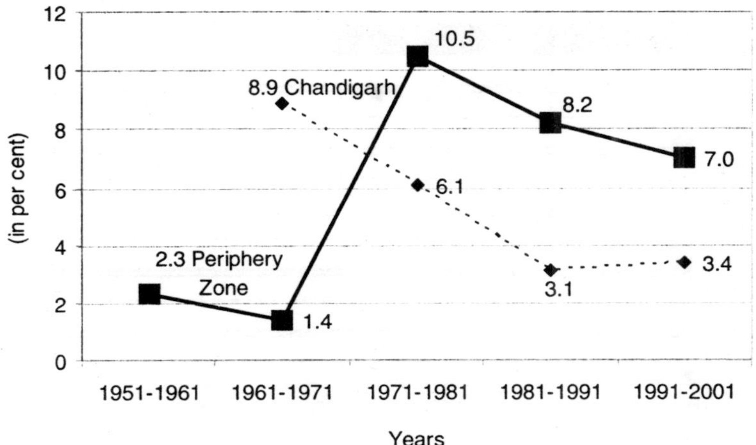

Source : Census of India : *General Population Tables and Primary Census Abstract, Part II-A and II-B, different volumes from 1961 to 2001 by* Directorate of Census Operations, Punjab, Haryana and Chandigarh.

The growth behaviour of towns since their emergence sheds an additional light on the process. Four towns existing before the delineation of the Periphery Zone, recorded a compound annual growth rate of 2.7 percent during 1951-2001. This rate was only 1.8 percent during 1951-71. By comparison the compound annual growth rate of all the existing towns in the Periphery Zone was 10.5, 8.2 and 7.0 percent respectively during the three successive decades of the 1971-2001 period.

Meanwhile the morphology of urbanization also underwent a dramatic change. While up to 1971, the entire urban population was residing in small towns of population less than 20,000 each, in 2001, 56.9 percent of urban population was concentrated in two towns of S.A.S Nagar (Mohali) and Panchkula, each with a population exceeding 100,000 (Table 4.3 and Figure 4.2). This marked the beginning of a phase wherein even cities began taking shape in the Periphery Zone.

FIG. 4.2

Periphery Zone : Share in Population of Different Size Classes of Towns, 1951-2001

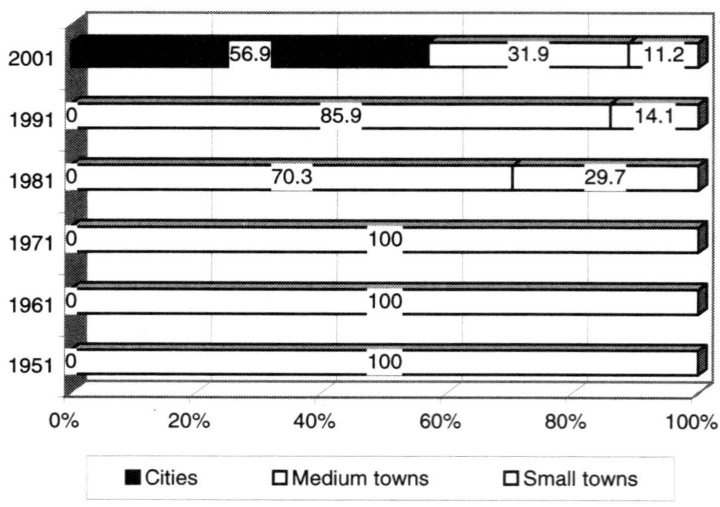

Source : Census of India : *General Population Tables and Primary Census Abstract, Part II-A and II-B, different volumes from 1961 to 2001 by* Directorate of Census Operations, Punjab, Haryana and Chandigarh.

Such developments were taking place and the envisaged rural character of the Periphery Zone was being violated mainly because the zone had been fragmented and divided among three different political entities of Punjab, Haryana and Union Territory of Chandigarh in 1966. The enforcement of the Periphery Control Act and the Controlled Area Plan became the responsibility of the respective states/union territory. However, Punjab planned the urban estate at Mohali in 1967, renamed Sahibzada Ajit Singh Nagar, and Haryana followed with another planned urban estate at Panchkula in 1970. With their emergence, the urbanization process received a great stimulus.

S.A.S. Nagar grew at the annual compound rate of 6.3 per cent and Panchkula at 20.1 per cent during 1981-91. In the

TABLE 4.3

Number of Towns and Share of Population in each Size Class in Periphery Zone: 1951-2001

Size class of town	*1951*	*1961*	*1971*	*1981*	*1991*	*2001*
100,000 and above	0 (0.0)	0 (0.0)	0 (0.0)	0 (0.0)	0 (0.0)	2 (56.9)
50,000-99,999	0 (0.0)	0 (0.0)	0 (0.0)	0 (0.0)	2 (63.2)	0 (0.0)
20,000-49,999	0 (0.0)	0 (0.0)	0 (0.0)	3 (70.3)	2 (22.7)	5 (31.9)
10,000-19,999	1 (52.2)	1 (51.1)	2 (71.6)	1 (10.5)	1 (4.2)	2 (6.6)
5,000-9999	1 (23.7)	1 (23.0)	2 (28.4)	3 (19.2)	3 (9.9)	3 (4.6)
Below 5,000	2 (24.1)	2 (25.9)	0 (0.0)	0 (0.0)	0 (0.0)	0 (0.0)
Total	4	4	4	7	8	12

Source : Census of India : *General Population Tables and Primary Census Abstract, Part II-A and II-B, different volumes from 1961 to 2001 by* Directorate of Census Operations, Punjab, Haryana and Chandigarh.

following decade of 1991-2001, Panchkula grew annually at the rate of 7.2 per cent (Table 4.4). These two towns, located adjacent to Chandigarh, rendered a feeling of its continuum. The sectors in S.A.S. have been developed in such a way as to appear extensions of Chandigarh. Panchkula also gives a practically similar feeling.

An analysis of the growth behaviour of other urban centres in the Chandigarh Periphery Zone sheds an additional light on the theme. During 1951-71, there was hardly any change in annual growth rate of Kharar and Banur towns. Kalka town was also stagnating: its population marked a decrease during 1961-71. All this was happening under the shadow effect of the city of Chandigarh. The effect persisted until the governments changed their role and stared exploiting the zone by making liberal interpretation of the rules framed to protect the rural character of the Periphery Zone.

As it emerges, the government itself has proved to be the violator of its own rules. The creation of Panchkula and S.A.S. (Mohali) towns are a violation of the Periphery Control Act. In fact, a large number of structures have come up both in the

TABLE 4.4

Periphery Zone : Compound Annual Growth Rate of Towns (in per cent), 1951-2001

Name of the town	*1951-61*	*1961-71*	*1971-81*	*1981-91*	*1991-2001*	*Growth rate since emergence as a new town*
Kharar	2.7	2.7	7.4	1.8	5.0	3.9
Kalka	2.5	-0.2	1.9	2.5	1.2	1.6
Banur	2.2	2.4	3.2	3.0	4.1	3.0
Derra Bassi	1.0	3.7	2.5	2.6	5.0	2.9
Panchkula				20.1	7.2	13.5
Pinjore				8.9	8.2	8.6
S.A.S. Nagar (Mohali)				6.3	4.6	6.9
Mullanpur-Garibdas						
Karoran						—
Bhabat						—
Zirakpur						—
Bhankarpur						—

Source : Census of India : *General Population Tables and Primary Census Abstract, Part II-A and II-B, different volumes from 1961 to 2001 by* Directorate of Census Operations, Punjab, Haryana and Chandigarh.

towns and villages in the Periphery Zone in violation of the Act. Above all, the Punjab government regularized the unauthorized structures, which had come into existence prior to 8th December, 1998.

INCREASE IN URBAN AREA

The increase in area under urban settlements was a natural corollary of the rapid process of urbanization in the Periphery Zone, as discussed above. During 1961-2001, the urban area of Chandigarh increased from 32.4 km^2 to 79.2 km^2, a rise by almost 2.5 times. During the same period urban area in the Periphery Zone shot from 10.2 km^2 to 138.9 km^2, an almost 14 times increase. The urban area of Chandigarh in 1961 was three times bigger than its Periphery Zone. The situation got reversed over time. In 2001, urban areas in the Periphery Zone became 1.7 times that of the city.

Table 4.5 provides a summary picture of the decadal increase of the urban area in the Periphery Zone, along with a

TABLE 4.5

Periphery Zone : Increase in Urban Area, 1951-2001

Year/ Decade	*Number of towns*	*Urban area (in km^2)*	*Increase in urban area during the decade (in km^2)*	*Remarks*
1951	4	10.2	—	
1951-1961	4 (1961)	10.2	0	
1961-1971	4 (1971)	10.2	0	
1971-1981	7 (1981)	41.4	31.1	This area increase was due to emergence of 3 new towns (having an aggregate area of 26.2 km^2) and territorial extension of all four existing towns by 4.92 km^2
1981-1991	8 (1991)	51.9	10.5	The area increase was primarily due to expansion of the existing towns
1991-2001	12 (2001)	138.9	87.0	Physical expansion and emergence of new towns were equally responsible for accelerating the process of urbanization
2001	12			

Source : Census of India : *General Population Tables and Primary Census Abstract, Part II-A and II-B, different volumes from 1961 to 2001 and Village and Town Directory, Village and Town-wise Primary Census Abstract, District Census Handbooks of Chandigarh, Rupnagar, Patiala, Ambala and Panchkula Districts by* Directorate of Census Operations, Punjab, Haryana and Chandigarh.

statement of the associated factors. It is observed that the urban area did not experience any change up to 1971. Subsequently, it underwent marked extension, at an accelerating pace over the successive decades. The extension of territorial jurisdiction of the existing towns in addition to, the emergence of new towns determined this process. In the ultimate analysis, changes in the urban area have been both a cause and an effect of the urbanization process taking place over the years in the Periphery Zone.

Urban settlements adjacent to Chandigarh were noted for bigger gains in their area. Punjab government increased the area of S.A.S. Nagar by almost 2 times, from 12.4 km^2 in 1981 to 25 km^2 in 2001. On similar lines, Government of Haryana increased the area of Panchkula by almost 2.5 times, from 10.4 km^2 in 1981 to 25 km^2 in 2001 even though there was no pressure of population calling for immediate physical expansion of these two towns. The two governments developed new sectors in their respective cities as a lucrative proposition through land sales. They acquired land at low price and sold it at exorbitant prices.

The emergence of new planned towns adjacent to Chandigarh was an important factor underlying the increase in urban area in the Periphery Zone. Equally critical was the factor of escalating land values and rents in Chandigarh, which gave a necessary fillip to this process. Both the towns are still physically expanding at a fast pace, by way of encroachment on the adjacent area.

In addition to the S.A.S. Nagar (Mohali) and Panchkula towns, other towns also recorded a somewhat similar experience. The area of Kharar town, which remained static at 0.7 km^2 till 1971, increased to 4.2 km^2 in 1981 and almost to 5 km^2 in 2001 (Table 4.6). Similar increase from 0.8 km^2 in 1951 to 3.1 km^2 in 1981 and 20 km^2 in 2001 was noted in the case of Derra Bassi. The area of Kalka town increased from 2.8 km^2 in 1971 to 3.4 km^2 in 1981. The towns in the Periphery Zone experienced expansion at the cost of peripheral agricultural land, which was quite often very fertile and productive. This process has resulted in the conversion of agricultural land into non-agricultural uses. At times, the towns were overburdened while extending their territorial jurisdiction.

2014	945,392	58.72
2015	991,684	59.74
2016	1,039,167	60.77
2017	1,087,504	61.79
2018	1,136,861	62.81
2019	1,168,824	63.84
2020	1,238,826	64.86

Source : Projection outputs.

Chapter 6. The Periphery Zone would become urban majority in 2006 when more than half of the population would be residing in urban areas. Its urban population will increase 2.7 fold from 464,491 in 2001 to 1,238,826 in 2020.

The rapid increase in the urban population will pose problems of its own kind. It would put further pressure on the already deficient physical infrastructure in a majority of the towns in the Periphery Zone. The process of emergence of new towns in the Periphery Zone would continue in the future as well, and the Periphery Zone is likely to take the form of an urban conglomeration. This would add another dimension to the management of the urban affairs, particularly when three governments of Punjab, Haryana and Union Territory of Chandigarh are involved. The role of local elected civic bodies in managing these towns would be crucial.

CONCLUSION

Despite the legal provisions to retain the rural character of the Periphery Zone, the process of urbanization has been rapid. The year 1966, when Chandigarh Union Territory was carved out as a separate political entity at the time of reorganization of Punjab was critical in this respect. It fragmented the designated periphery into three sub-zones under Punjab, Haryana and Chandigarh itself.

In 1981, three new towns, in addition to the four already existing emerged in the Periphery Zone as a result of which urban population increased from 27,494 in 1951 to 1,07,376 in

1981. The urban area got extended from 10.23 to 42.0 km^2 during this period. The process got accelerated further and by 2001, when the periphery had as many as 12 towns/urban agglomerations covering an aggregate area of 140 km^2 As such, the rapid pace of urbanization in the Periphery Zone could be attributed to emergence of new towns, physical expansion of the existing towns, besides the rapid increase of the urban population in the existing towns.

The growth behaviour of the urban population in the Periphery Zone has been opposite that of Chandigarh. In the initial years, Chandigarh was having a shadow effect of growth of towns in its periphery but its own growth rate was rapid. Since 1981, however, the annual urban growth rate of Periphery Zone has been more than 2.5 times that of the city. The city had started exerting its spread effect in a significant measure.

The share of urban population is expected to increase from 45 per cent in 2001 to 65 per cent in 2020, an addition of 20 per cent points. The urban population in the Periphery Zone will cross one million marks by 2016. The time is just right that the haphazard growth in the Periphery Zone should be regulated by way of preparing its perspective land use plan for the year 2020, to begin with. This requires a coordinated effort on the part of the three governments of Punjab, Haryana and Chandigarh. In absence of such steps, the undesired violations of the Periphery Control Act will continue.

5

Land Use Dynamics

Land use change is one of the most striking and visible indicators of the transformation of an area in terms of its socio-economic character. This is particularly true of the tract that lies in the immediate vicinity of an urban settlement. In the natural process, an urban area expands to encroach upon its surrounding rural hinterland and travelling outward from a city one observes a gradual change from a completely urban landscape to a urban space and then a rural hinterland. Again, in the natural order the urban spaces would continue to expand onto the rural hinterland with the speed of transformation from rural to urban depending upon the dynamism of a particular town.

In Chandigarh, however, this was not the case, for just as the city within was laid out in a planned manner, its periphery too was not to be free of control. Borrowing from the Garden City concept of Howard (1898), a view as much to isolate this planned city from its indigenous background as to provide it with a green envelope, the nature of land use within the periphery was frozen. The avowed intention was to continue primarily with a rural land use pattern around the city itself. No doubt, with the extension of the periphery from 8 to 16 kilometers, a few urban settlements also became part of this landscape, yet till around 1971 it had a dominantly rural character.

There were, of course, some exceptions to the freeze in land use. Change of land use within the *lal dora* (settlement boundary) was allowed. The contention was to allow economic activity akin to agriculture. Hence, as with time, a broadened view of agriculture emerged, activities like poultry and diary farming began to be allowed, as was the construction of farmhouses. Increased construction activity within the city necessitated the coming up of brick kilns and such associated land uses. Gradually, the landscape came to acquire a partial urban hue. An appraisal of the land use changes is crucial to understand land use dynamics in a temporal-spatial perspective for effective land management.

The present chapter seeks to analyze the nature of shift in the land use within the Periphery Zone and how far this change has been brought due to the circumstance of this land being a part of the periphery. The variations within have been examined at the sub-zone (Punjab, Haryana and Chandigarh) as well as the village level. Like the rest of the study, this section covers a period of three decades 1971-2001. Data for the purpose of the study has been sourced from records of Punjab Urban Development Authority, Mohali and Haryana Urban Development Authority, Panchkula and the Census of India publications. This secondary information has, wherever necessary, been supplemented by field observations. The situation has been observed at two levels, one the complete conversion of a rural area into an urban area through its inclusion within the municipal limits of a town or upgradation to the status of a town, two the land use changes within the rural landscape.

VILLAGE-WISE LAND USE DATA

The Census of India, in addition to its main coverage of data, also provides village-wise data on land use in the District Census Handbooks under the following categories:

Forests

This includes all lands classified as forests under any legal enactment dealing with forests or administered as forests whether state owned or private. Any cropped area within the forests and grazing lands are also counted under this category.

Net Area Sown

This represents the total area sown with crops and orchards. Area sown more than once is counted only once. Net area sown may further be divided into two sub-categories: irrigated and unirrigated.

Cultivable Wasteland

This category comprises such land, which though available for cultivation has for some reason not been brought under the plough at least for five successive years. Such lands may be lying fallow or covered with bushes or jungle, which may not have been put to any other use. Land under thatching green bamboo, bushes, which are not included under forests has been taken as cultivable waste. The village common lands and permanent pastures and grazing lands within the forests have been covered in this category.

Area not Available for Cultivation

This includes two types of lands: One, all lands occupied by settlements, roads, rails, airports, railway stations and other such features and two, absolutely barren cultivated land with associated physiography such as mountain, desert and waterways which cannot be brought under cultivation.

As a backdrop to the analysis of the land use change in the Periphery Zone, a quick look at the change in Punjab, Haryana and Chandigarh during 1971-2001 will be in order. Table 5.1 is testimony to the following facts: (i) The percentage of net area sown remained virtually the same over the period in Haryana but declined in Punjab and Chandigarh, (ii) Cultivable wasteland increased in Punjab, primarily due to the acute waterlogging conditions in part while it showed only a marginal change in Haryana and Chandigarh, (iii) The small percentage of land under forest decreased in the three political territories, and (iv) Area not available for cultivation, marked a considerable increase in all three of them, mainly due to an accelerated pace of construction activity and infrastructure development. How far this trend is represented in the Periphery Zone, which was envisaged as a controllable area in respect of land use, calls for a detailed study.

TABLE 5.1

Land Use Classification of Punjab, Haryana and Chandigarh, 1971 and 2001

(Per cent to total area)

Land Use	*Punjab*		*Haryana*		*Chandigarh*	
	1971	*2001*	*1971*	*2001*	*1971*	*2001*
Net area sown	84.4	80.8	80.1	81.0	50.3	23.1
Area not available for cultivation	8.7	12.4	10.7	11.1	32.1	68.6
Cultivable wasteland	1.3	4.6	6.6	5.6	14.7	5.3
Forest	5.6	2.2	2.6	2.3	2.9	3.0

Source : Statistical Abstracts of Punjab, Haryana and Chandigarh, 1971 and 2001.

SPATIAL PATTERNS OF LAND USE IN THE PERIPHERY ZONE, 2001

Since the land use data of the Periphery Zone is available only for its villages, the discussion here is confined to the rural segment. In 2001, the rural area of the Periphery Zone measured 1024 square kilometers, of which Punjab shared 73.4 per cent, Haryana 23.5 per cent and Chandigarh 3.1 per cent (Table 5.2 and Figure 5.1). As such, Punjab has the largest stake in sustaining or violating the spirit and substance of the Periphery Zone. Of the total rural area, 65 per cent has been recorded as net area sown, 29 per cent as area not available for cultivation, 4 per cent as cultivable wasteland, and 2 per cent as forest. Evidently, practically the entire land has been used for agriculture or non-agricultural uses and the share of the cultivable wasteland and forest is insignificant. At the sub-zone level, while there is little to distinguish between the land use

TABLE 5.2

Land Use Pattern of Rural Component of the Periphery Zone, 2001

(*Per cent to total area*)

Sub-zones/Zone	*Net area sown*	*Area not available for cultivation*	*Cultivation wasteland*	*Forest*	*Total area (in km²)*
(1)	(2)	(3)	(4)	(5)	(6)
Punjab Sub-zone	70.9 (532.78)	25.1 (188.07)	3.2 (24.18)	0.8 (6.14)	751.16 (100.0)
Haryana Sub-zone	46.1 (110.99)	41.9 (100.90)	5.4 (13.09)	6.6 (15.92)	240.90 (100.0)
Chandigarh Sub-zone	62.6 (19.91)	23.8 (7.56)	9.6 (3.05)	4.0 (1.30)	31.82 (100.0)
Periphery Zone	64.8 (663.68)	29.0 (296.53)	3.9 (40.32)	2.3 (23.36)	1023.88 (100.0)

Note : Figures in the parenthesis are for area in hectares.

Source : Calculated from the Census of India, *Provisional Village and Town Directory, Punjab, Haryana and Chandigarh, 2001.*

FIG. 5.1

Periphery Zone : Sub-zonewise Land Use Pattern, 2001

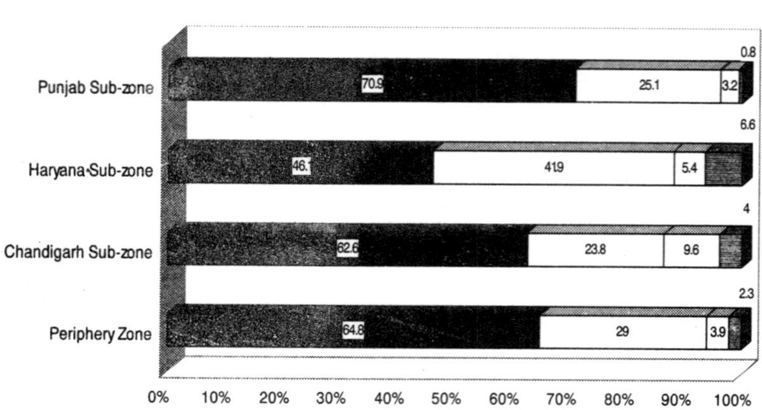

Source : Calculated from the Census of India, *Provisional Village and Town Directory, Punjab, Haryana and Chandigarh, 2001.*

pattern of the Punjab and Haryana Sub-zones of the Periphery Zone. The Chandigarh segment stands out distinctly, with over two-thirds of its rural area given over to non-agricultural uses. A detailed discussion on individual land use categories would put things in a clearer perspective.

Area Under Forests

Though Periphery Zone cannot claim any thick forests yet nearly 24 km^2 of its rural area came under the land use category of forest. The forest cover is confined to hardly 14 villages out of a total of 458, four each in Punjab and Chandigarh Sub-zones of the Periphery Zone and six in Haryana Sub-zone (Table 5.3). Most of these villages are located along different *choes* (seasonal streams) flowing through the Periphery Zone (Map 5.1). Forest land in Haryana Sub-zone is more than two times that of Punjab and Chandigarh Sub-zones put together. Bir Ghaggar village in Haryana recorded 98 per cent of its total area as forest.

Among the 14 villages, six (Gidarpur, Sahauran in Punjab and Bir Ghaggar, Kundi, Kiratpur in Haryana and Mani Majra (Rural) in Chandigarh) had no forest cover in 1971. Evidently, some afforestation was introduced here during 1971-2001.

TABLE 5.3

Percentage Share of Forest Area in Total Area in 14 Villages of the Periphery Zone, 2001

Sub-zone/Zone	*Village*	*Area under forest cover (in hectares)*	*Percentage of forest area to total area of the village*
Punjab Sub-zone	Soonk	559	66.3
	Gidarpur	38	19.0
	Madhopur	7	2.5
	Sahauran	10	1.9
Haryana Sub-zone	Bir Ghagar	162	97.6
	Nadiana	564	88.4
	Asewali	677	71.0
	Nagal Moginanad	182	54.0
	Kundi	2	3.1
	Kiratpur	5	2.1
Chandigarh Sub-zone	Raipur Kalan	36	39.6
	Hallo Majra	58	33.7
	Behlana	22	27.2
	Mani Majra (R)	14	24.6
Periphery Zone		**2336**	**2.3**

Source : Calculated from the Village and Town Directory, Punjab, Haryana and Chandigarh, 1971 and 2001.

Net Area Sown

Almost two-thirds of the area of the Periphery Zone was under crops and orchards in 2001 (Table 5.2). In about 40 per cent of the villages net area sown was more than 80 per cent of the total area. On the other hand, in nearly one-fifth of the villages, it was less than 50 per cent. The picture varied at the

MAP 5.1
Chandigarh Periphery Zone
(Villages with Some Forest Cover, 2001)

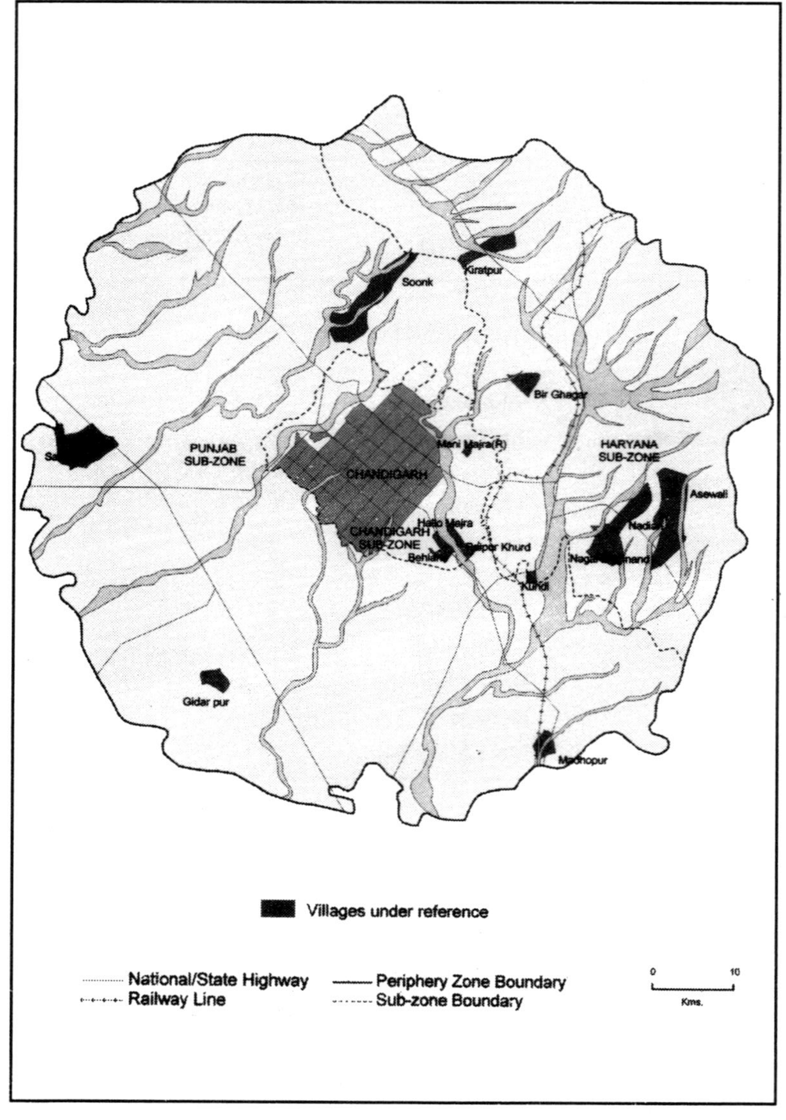

sub-zone level. In Punjab Sub-zone, 54 per cent of villages recorded more than 80 per cent of their area as net area sown as against 17 per cent in Chandigarh and 8 per cent in Haryana (Table 5.4).

TABLE 5.4

Periphery Zone: Distribution of Villages by Percentage Share of Net Area Sown in Total Area, 2001

Sub-zones/Zone	*Less than 50 per cent*	*50 to 80 per cent*	*80 per cent and above*	*All*
Punjab Sub-zone	29 (9.5)	113 (36.9)	164 (53.6)	306 (100.0)
Haryana Sub-zone	53 (41.1)	66 (51.1)	10 (7.8)	129 (100.0)
Chandigarh Sub-zone	8 (34.8)	11 (47.8)	4 (17.4)	23 (100.0)
Periphery Zone	90 (19.7)	190 (41.5)	178 (38.8)	458 (100.0)

Note : Figures in brackets denote percentages.

Source : Census of India, *Provisional Village and Town Directories, Punjab, Haryana and Chandigarh, 2001.*

Twelve villages (11 in Haryana and one in Punjab) in the Periphery Zone were without any area under crops and orchards. Most of the Haryana villages were located on the border of Panchkula city and their entire land outside the *lal dora* (settlement) limits had been acquired by the state government for raising new sectors in Panchkula township. Likewise, the one village in Punjab found its location on the outskirts of S.A.S. Nagar (Mohali) and its land had also been acquired for urban development. The same was true for villages close to S.A.S. Nagar (Mohali). More than 90 per cent of their area had gone out of the agricultural use.

On the other extreme, 50 villages in the Periphery Zone had more than 90 per cent of the total area under crops and orchards; 48 in Punjab, 2 in Haryana and none in Chandigarh. Several of these were located along the Kharar-Banur, and Kharar-Rupnagar roads and had witnessed emergence of orchards on a significant scale.

The case of villages located in the sub-mountainous zone was different. Here the proportion of net area sown was low either because of the forest cover or presence of pasture land or bushes. The underlying factor was the lack of irrigation. Efforts to tackle this problem through watershed management programme have contributed towards increase in area under cultivation in these villages.

The Periphery Zone is traversed by a number of *choes* (seasonal streams). Land along these *choes* is not that fertile, being sandy by soil. The percentage of net area sown is low in villages adjoining the *choes* (Map 5.2). Covered by sand and stones, the wide beds of these *choes* are not fit for cultivation even during the dry season. None the less, under intensifying pressure of population even this marginal land is being brought under cultivation.

Cultivable Wasteland

Nearly four per cent of the total land in the Periphery Zone was recorded as cultivable wasteland in 2001, being covered with bushes or sporadic trees (Table 5.2). Almost half the villages are without any cultivable wasteland; 58 per cent of them in Punjab Sub-zone, 33 per cent in Haryana and 22 per cent in Chandigarh (Table 5.5) On the other hand, the percentage share of cultivable wasteland was 10 per cent or more in about 15 per cent of the villages.

In Chandigarh Sub-zone, 39 per cent of the villages had at least one-tenth of their total area as cultivable wasteland. Kujheri, Kaimbwala and Mauli Jagran villages were noted for more than one-fifth of their total area as cultivable wasteland. Several of the bare sites on the outskirts were those from where slums had been cleared and rehabilitated elsewhere, particularly in villages like Khudda Lahora, Maloya, Palsora, Dadu Majra and Karsan. These evacuated sites remained reserved for some specified land use in future and no agricultural activity was allowed here.

Another factor underlying higher percentage of cultivable wasteland was speculation in land. The agricultural land in some villages had been sold at a large scale. At the same time, due to legal constraints involved in conversion of land use, it is lying vacant. Landowners are waiting for sunshine in future when they can sell their pieces of land at a much higher price in future when the situation is all in their favour.

Map 5.2

Chandigarh Periphery Zone (Villages with Less than Half of Total Area as Net Area Sown, 2001)

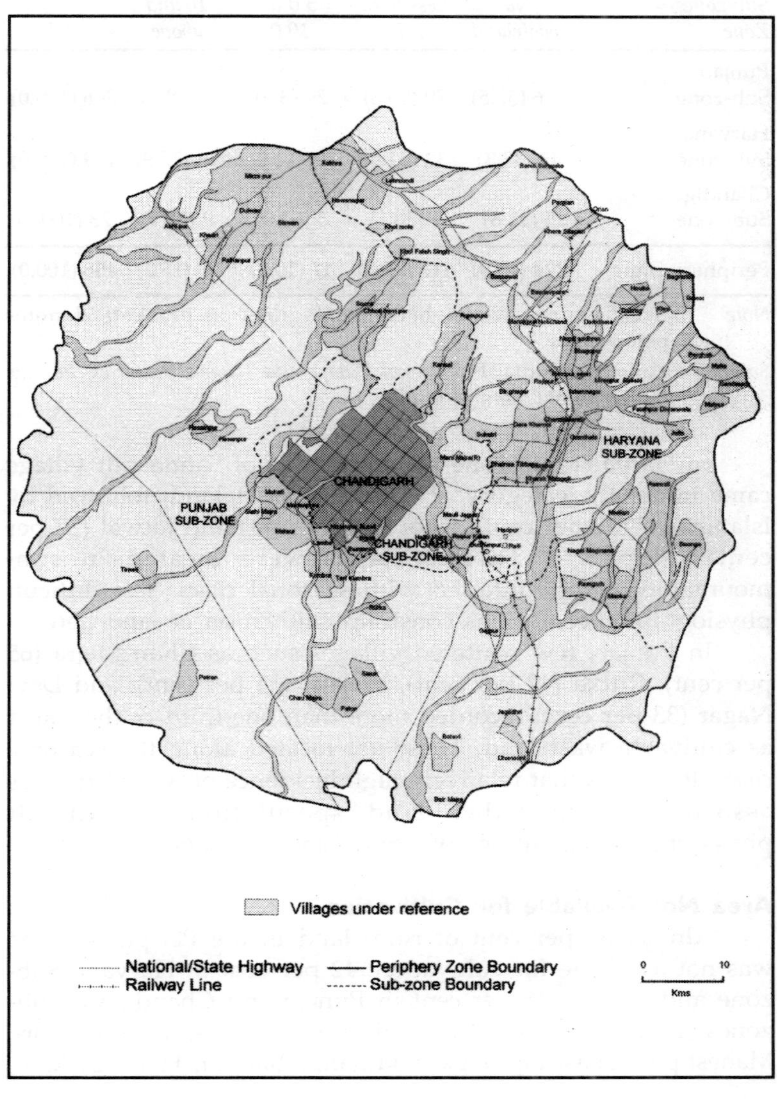

TABLE 5.5

Periphery Zone: Distribution of Villages by Percentage Share of Cultivable Wasteland in Total Area, 2001

Sub-zones/ Zone	*No wasteland*	*Less than 5*	*5.0 to 10.0*	*10 and above*	*All*
Punjab Sub-zone	176 (57.5)	79 (25.8)	26 (8.5)	25 (8.2)	306 (100.0)
Haryana Sub-zone	43 (33.3)	32 (24.8)	18 (14.0)	36 (27.9)	129 (100.0)
Chandigarh Sub-zone	5 (21.8)	6 (26.1)	3 (13.0)	9 (39.1)	23 (100.0)
Periphery Zone	224 (48.9)	117 (25.5)	47 (10.3)	70 (15.3)	458 (100.0)

Note : Area figures are in hectares. Figures in brackets denotes percentages.

Source : Census of India, *Provisional Village and Town Directories, Punjab, Haryana and Chandigarh, 2001.*

In Haryana Sub-zone the entire area of Sandaspur village came under the category of cultivable wasteland, followed by Islamnagar (52 per cent), Khoi (35 per cent) and Jatwal (37 per cent) (Map 5.3). These villages were located in sub-mountainous tract, infested with seasonal *choes*. The difficult physiographic conditions constrain cultivation of land here.

In Punjab, few scattered villages such as Chau Majra (65 per cent), Rurka (42 per cent), Majatri (33 per cent), and Devi Nagar (33 per cent) recorded more than one-third of their area as cultivable wasteland. These are located along the seasonal *choes*. It follows that relatively high incidence of wasteland was associated with either land speculation or difficult physiographic conditions of terrain and drainage.

Area Not Available for Cultivation

Almost 30 per cent of rural land in the Periphery Zone was not available for cultivation; 42 per cent in Haryana Sub-zone and around 25 per cent in Punjab and Chandigarh Sub-zones (Table 5.2). The entire land in ten villages, namely, Majri, Maheshpur, Bilaspur, Nagal Sodhian, Abhepur, Haripur, Raili,

MAP 5.3
Chandigarh Periphery Zone
(Villages with at Least Ten Per Cent of Total Area as Cultivable Wasteland, 2001)

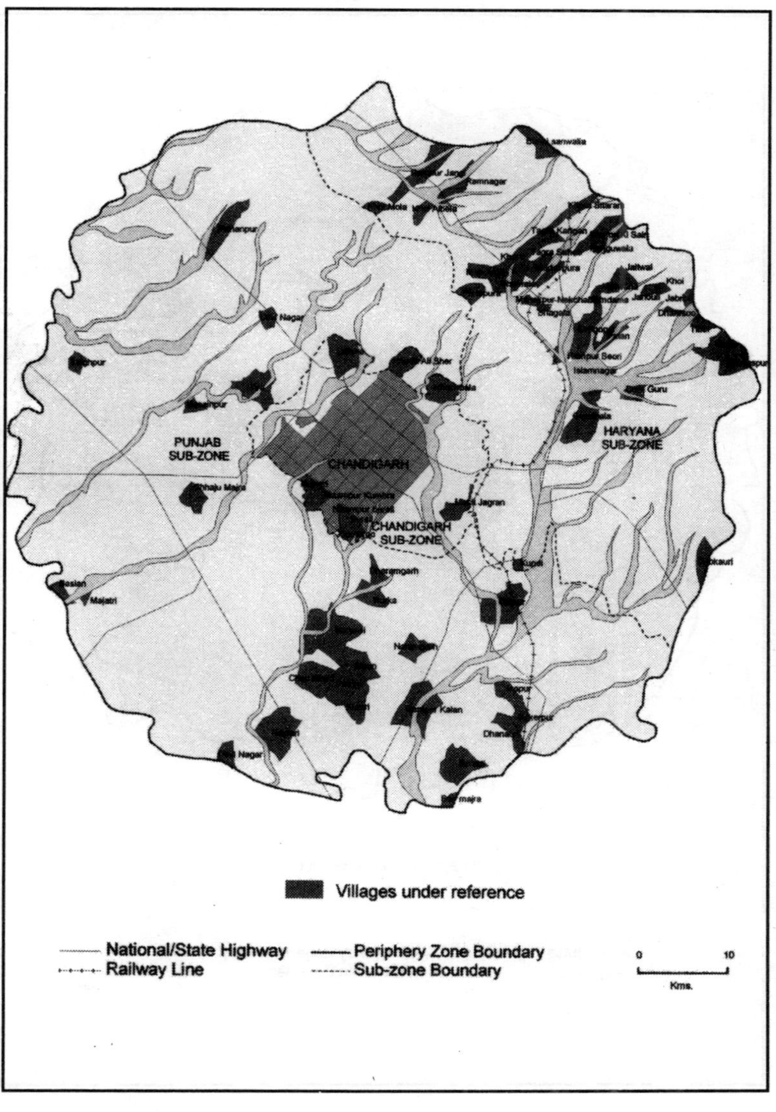

Map 5.4
Chandigarh Periphery Zone (Villages with at Least Half of Total Area as Not Available for Cultivation, 2001)

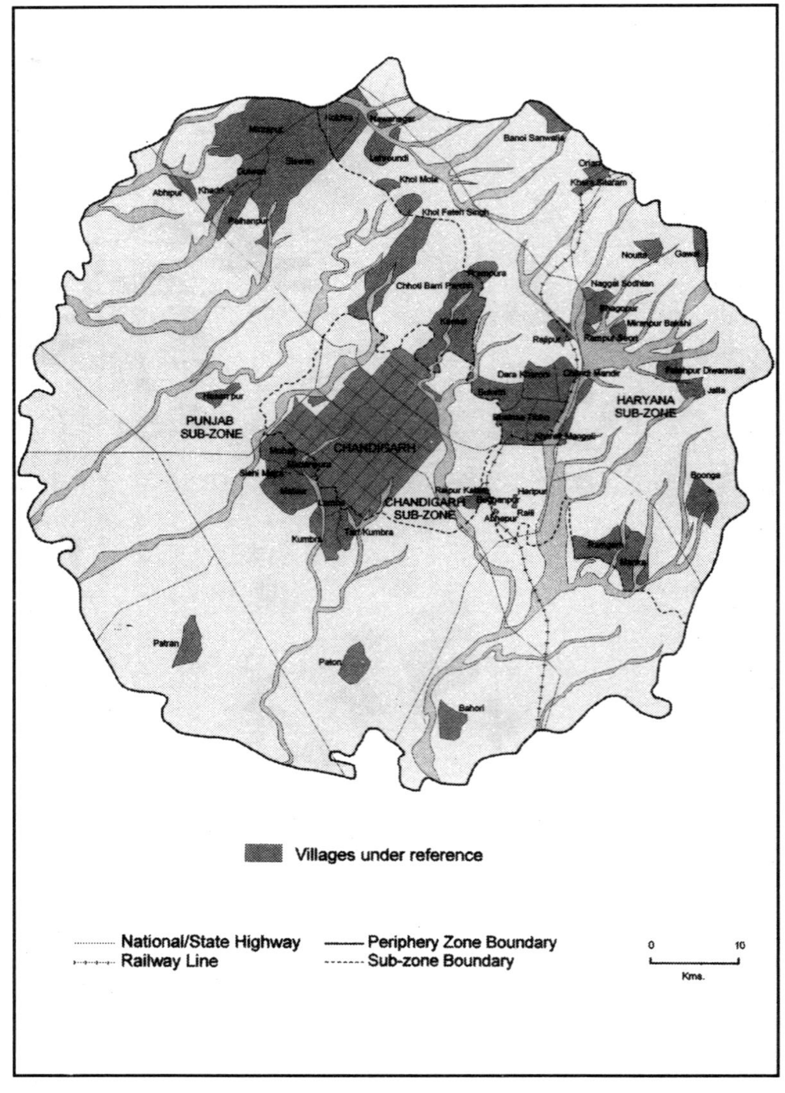

Budhanpur and Dara Kharoni in Haryana Sub-zone and Mohali in Punjab Sub-zone was not available for cultivation (Map 5.4). Almost a similar situation is observed in Lamba, Tarf Kumbra, Kumbra, Madanpur and Siahi Majra villages in Punjab Sub-zone and Kharak Mangoli and Bhainsa Tibba in Haryana Sub-zone. All these villages were located on the fringe of Panchkula and S.A.S. Nagar (Mohali) and their land had been acquired for the expansion of the two cities. In addition, there was a large scale encroachment on agricultural land by the villagers themselves, for construction of new houses or other structures for their use. All such land went out of cultivation.

In Chandigarh Sub-zone, almost two-thirds of the villages had less than one-third of the land as not available for cultivation (Table 5.6). This signifies that agricultural land within the Sub-zone did not suffer much as much as in the neighbouring villages of Punjab and Haryana. This was partly due to the pressure exerted by the community based *Pind Bachao* (save the village) Committee and partly the effectiveness of the Chandigarh Administration in implementing the Act.

TABLE 5.6

Periphery Zone : Percentage Share of Area Not Available for Cultivation in Total Area, 2001

Sub-zone/ Zone	*Up to 33.3 per cent*	*33.4 to 49.9 per cent*	*50 per cent & above*	*All*
Punjab Sub-zone	258 (84.3)	29 (9.5)	16 (6.2)	306 (100.0)
Haryana Sub-zone	59 (45.7)	36 (27.9)	34 (26.4)	129 (100.0)
Chandigarh Sub-zone	15 (65.2)	7 (30.4)	1 (4.4)	23 (100.0)
Periphery Zone	332 (72.5)	72 (15.7)	54 (11.8)	458 (100.0)

Note : Area figures are in hectares. Figures in brackets denotes percentage.

Source : Census of India, *Provisional Village and Town Directories, Punjab, Haryana and Chandigarh, 2001.*

LAND USE CHANGE : 1971-2001

If one were to compare the land use situation as it emerged in 2001 *vis-à-vis* the picture in 1971 in the Periphery Zone (Table 5.7), the two most noticeable features are the decrease in forest area by 6.1 per cent points (from 8.4 per cent in 1971 to 2.3 per cent in 2001) and an increase in the share of land not available for cultivation by 7.1 per cent points (from 21.5 per cent in 1971 to 28.6 per cent in 2001). At the sub-zone

TABLE 5.7
Land Use Change in Chandigarh Periphery Zone during 1971-2001

(Per cent in total area)

Sub-zones/Zone	*Net area sown*	*Area not available for cultivation*	*Cultivable wasteland*	*Forest*	*All*
Punjab Sub-zone					
1971	71.3	14.8	4.8	9.1	100.0
2001	70.7	25.3	3.2	0.8	100.0
Change in % points	-0.6	10.5	-1.6	-8.3	
Haryana Sub-zone					
1971	49.0	40.9	3.7	6.4	100.0
2001	47.2	40.4	5.3	7.1	100.0
Change in % points	-1.8	-0.5	1.6	0.7	
Chandigarh Sub-zone					
1971	65.9	25.6	0.9	7.6	100.0
2001	63.9	22.8	9.3	3.9	100.0
Change in % points	-2	-2.7	8.4	-3.6	
Periphery Zone					
1971	65.7	21.5	4.4	8.4	100.0
2001	65.1	28.6	3.9	2.3	100.0
Change in % points	-0.6	7.1	-0.5	-6.1	

Source : Census of India, *Village and Town Directories of Punjab, Haryana and Chandigarh, 1971 and 2001.*

level, this change was most pronounced in the Punjab segment (Figure 5.2) where the percentage of forest area recorded a decrease by 8.3 per cent points (from 9.1 per cent in 1971 to 0.8 per cent in 2001) and the land not available for cultivation increased by 10.5 per cent points (from 14.8 per cent in 1971 to 25.3 per cent in 2001).

The area not available for cultivation encroached not only on forest land but also upon cultivable wastelands and net area sown. There is also a visible conversion of unirrigated land into irrigated land, no doubt a result of the various watershed management schemes being fostered in the Zone. By comparison, the Haryana Sub-zone experienced a lower order of change in its land use as already by 1971, it had acquired a large chunk of land for new Panchkula town, which is reflected in a very high proportion of land falling under the category of area not available for cultivation. The Chandigarh Sub-zone scenario has been different where cultivable wasteland marked a big increase while land under uses of forest, net area sown and area not available for cultivation suffered a decrease. The cultivable wasteland was essentially the land acquired but not developed in the villages of the Chandigarh Sub-zone.

Forest Cover

A marked decrease in the share of forest cover has been noted above. In 1971, 50 villages in the Periphery Zone (27 in Haryana segment, 16 in Punjab and seven in Chandigarh) had some forest land. By 2001, the number of such villages had come down to 14. In fact, in the tally of these 14 villages, 6 were new additions where afforestation was a recent phenomenon. In other words, whatever forest cover existed in 42 villages under reference in 1971 it got wiped in many by 2001 (Map 5.5).

A squeezing of the forest land in the Periphery Zone is evident from Table 5.8. The number of villages with more than half of their land under forest cover declined from 11 in 1971 to 4 in 2001. The actual decrease here was from 8729 to 2105 hectares. At the same time, the number of villages with less than five per cent of the land under forests has increased from 8 to 43 during the same period. Included herein are the villages left with no forest land. In Chandigarh Sub-zone, the number of such villages had gone up from one to four.

Fig. 5.2

Periphery Zone : Land Use Change in Sub-Zones during 1971 and 2001

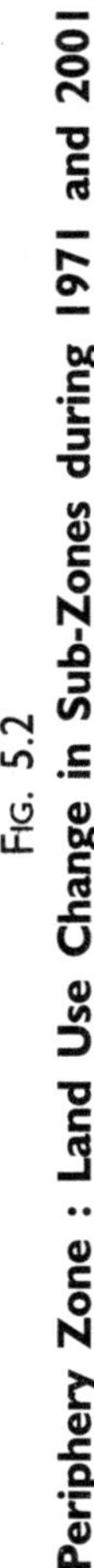

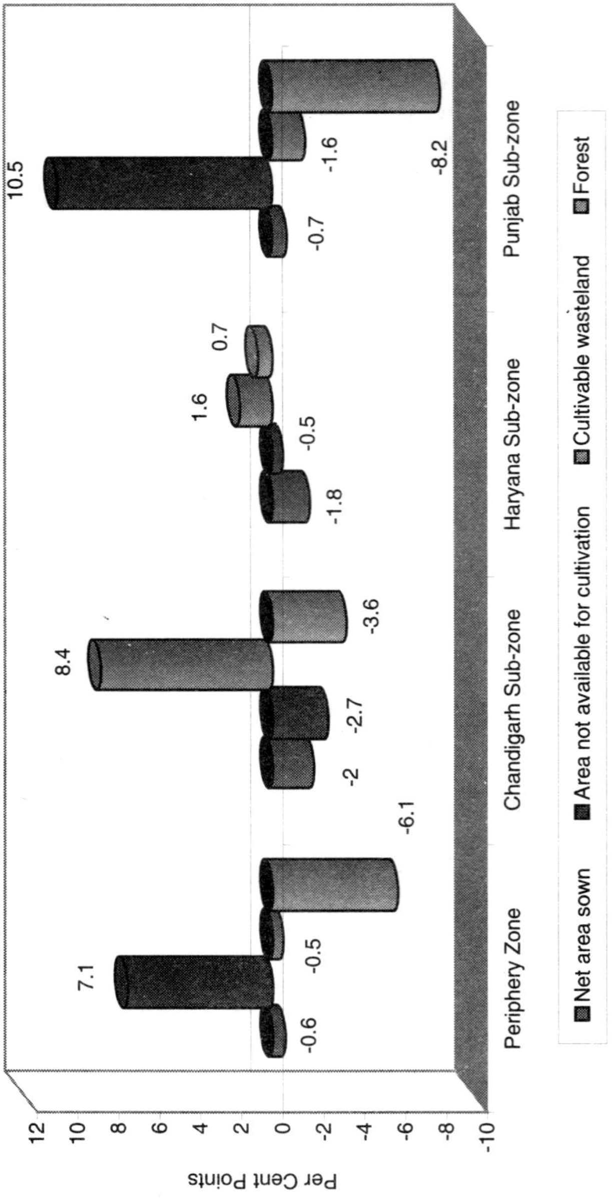

Source : Census of India, *Village and Town Directories of Punjab, Haryana and Chandigarh, 1971 and 2001.*

MAP 5.5
Chandigarh Periphery Zone (Villages Noted for Complete Erosion of Forest Cover during 1971-2001)

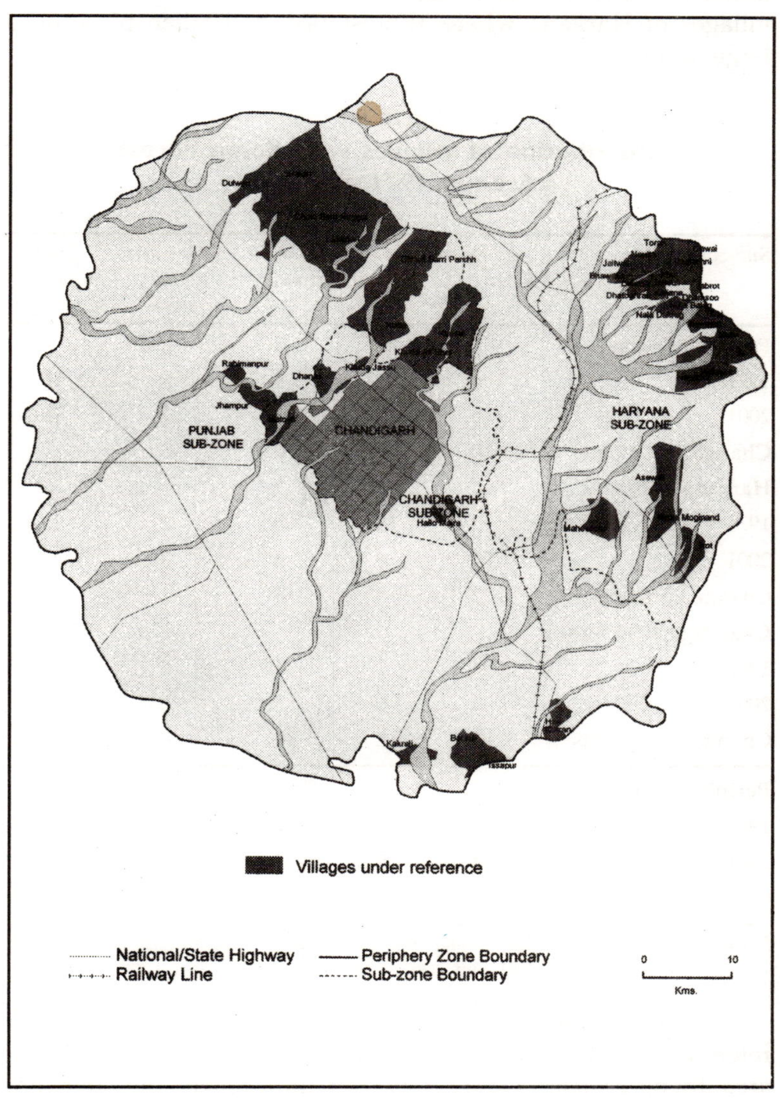

The picture varies by sub-zones. While the number of villages with more than half of the land under forest cover declined in Punjab from 9 to only one during 1971-2001, in Haryana it increased from two to three. The increase in area under forest was spectacular, from 17 to 88 per cent in Nadian villages of Haryana where afforestation had taken place on a large scale.

TABLE 5.8
Distribution of Villages with Some Forest Area in 1971 and 2001

Sub-zone/Zone	*Less than 5 per cent*	*5 to 25 per cent*	*25 to 50 per cent*	*50 per cent and above*	*Total number of villages*
Punjab Sub-zone					
1971	5	2	0	9	16
2001	15	0	0	1	16
Change in % points	+10	-2	0	-8	
Haryana Sub-zone					
1971	2	15	8	2	27
2001	24	0	0	3	27
Change in % points	+22	-15	-8	+1	
Chandigarh Sub-zone					
1971	1	2	4	0	7
2001	4	0	3	0	7
Change in % points	+3	-2	-1	0	
Periphery Zone					
1971	8	19	12	11	50
2001	43	0	3	4	50
Change in % points	+35	-19	-9	-7	

Source : Census of India, *Village and Town Directories, Punjab, Haryana and Chandigarh, 1971 and 2001.*

A quick look at the land use change in 50 villages under reference would indicate the direction of change from forest area to other uses (Table 5.9). Net area sown and area not

TABLE 5.9

Change in the Land Use Pattern of 50 Villages having Some Forest Area in 1971

(Per cent to total area)

Sub-zones/Zone	*Net area sown (%)*	*Area not available for cultivation (%)*	*Cultivable wasteland (%)*	*Forest (%)*	*Total area (in hectares)*
Punjab Sub-zone					
1971	26.3	8.4	1.5	63.9	10659
2001	46.4	46.0	2.3	5.3	10714
Change in % points	20.1	37.6	0.9	-58.6	
Haryana Sub-zone					
1971	29.9	32.9	0.5	36.7	4387
2001	34.1	26.6	6.0	33.3	4270
Change in % points	4.2	-6.4	5.5	-3.4	
Chandigarh Sub-zone					
1971	54.9	25.8	1.2	18.2	1709
2001	59.1	25.7	6.1	9.1	1275
Change in % points	4.2	-0.0	5.0	-9.1	
Periphery Zone					
1971	30.2	16.6	1.2	52.1	16755
2001	44.2	39.3	3.6	13.0	16259
Change in % points	14.0	22.7	2.4	-39.2	

Source : Census of India, *Village and Town Directories, Punjab, Haryana and Chandigarh, 1971 and 2001.*

available for cultivation (denoting land brought under new construction or acquired for the purpose) were the main beneficiaries, particularly in Punjab Sub-zone. Cultivable wasteland marked an increase in Haryana and Chandigarh Sub-zones (Figure 5.3), where large chunks of land acquired for urban development remained vacant. It follows that forest land in essence fell prey to developmental activity, completed or in process.

Fig. 5.3

Periphery Zone: Sub-zonewise Change during 1971-2001 in Land Use Pattern of 50 Villages with Some Forest Area in 1971

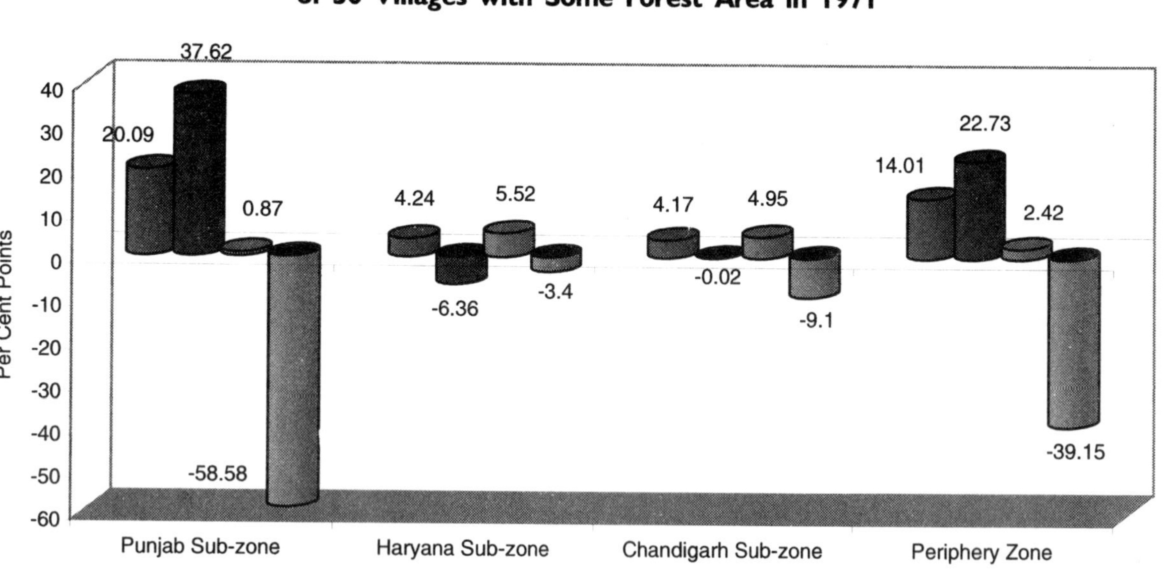

Source : Census of India, *Village and Town Directories, Punjab, Haryana and Chandigarh, 1971 and 2001.*

Net Area Sown

The proportion of net area sown to total area in the Periphery Zone remained virtually the same at two-thirds of the total during 1971-2001. In absolute terms, it marginally declined from 67214 hectares to 64367 hectares. At sub-zone level also, the change was of small order. The share of net area sown in the total area decreased by 2 per cent points in Chandigarh Sub-zone, by 1.8 per cent points in Haryana Sub-zone and by 0.7 per cent points in Punjab Sub-zone (Table 5.7).

In 1971, about 49 per cent of the villages had at least four-fifths of their total areas as net sown. This percentage had come down to 39 per cent by 2001. The decrease by 16 per cent points in Chandigarh Sub-zone was the highest, followed by 12 per cent points in Punjab Sub-zone and 3 per cent points in Haryana Sub-zone (Table 5.10).

TABLE 5.10

Distribution of Villages by Percentage Share of Net Area Sown in Total Area, 1971 and 2001

Sub-zones/Zone	*Less than 50*	*50 to 80*	*80 and above*	*All*
Punjab Sub-zone				
1971	7.8	26.7	65.5	100.0
2001	9.5	37.1	53.4	100.0
Change in % points	+1.7	+10.4	-12.1	
Haryana Sub-zone				
1971	37.1	52.4	10.5	100.0
2001	40.3	52.4	7.3	100.0
Change in % points	+3.2	0	-3.2	
Chandigarh Sub-zone				
1971	21.1	47.4	31.5	100.0
2001	31.6	52.6	15.8	100.0
Change in % points	+10.5	+5.2	-15.7	
Periphery Zone				
1971	16.6	34.9	48.5	100.0
2001	19.1	42.2	38.7	100.0
Change in % points	+2.5	+7.3	-9.8	

Note : N = 439 (296 for Punjab Sub-zone, 124 for Haryana Sub-zone, and 19 for Chandigarh Sub-zone)

Source : Census of India, *Village and Town Directories, Punjab, Haryana and Chandigarh, 1971 and 2001.*

The agricultural land in the Periphery Zone was not to be converted for other uses as per the provisions laid under the 1952 Act. This seems to have checked a drastic reduction in the net area sown in overall terms. At a more disaggregated level, it was found that in 103 villages (71 in Punjab Sub-zone, 26 in Haryana and 6 in Chandigarh Sub-zone), the net area sown suffered a decrease by at least 10 per cent points during 1971-2001. An analysis of the land use change in these villages reveals that the land not available for cultivation had increased by 18 per cent points, followed by 6 per cent points rise in the share of cultivable wasteland (Table 5.11 and Figure 5.4). The

TABLE 5.11

Change in Land Use Pattern of Villages (N=103) where Net Area Sown Decreased by at Least 10 Per Cent Points during 1971-2001

Sub-zones/Zone	*Net area sown*	*Area not available for cultivation*	*Cultivable waste-land*	*Forest*	*Total area*
Punjab Sub-zone					
1971	83.4	13.9	2.7	0.0	15901 (100.0)
2001	57.4	35.5	7.1	0.0	15418 (100.0)
Change in % points	-26.0	+21.6	+4.4	0	
Haryana Sub-zone					
1971	59.0	34.2	1.5	5.3	4739 (100.0)
2001	34.8	46.6	12.6	6.0	3070 (100.0)
Change in % points	-24.2	+12.4	+11.1	0.7	
Chandigarh Sub-zone					
1971	74.8	23.3	1.8	0.1	1432 (100.0)
2001	53.1	35.5	11.4	0.0	933 (100.0)
Change in % points	-21.7	+12.2	+9.6	-0.1	
Periphery Zone					
1971	77.6	18.9	2.4	1.1	22072 (100.0)
2001	53.6	37.3	8.2	0.9	19421 (100.0)
Change in % points	-24.0	+18.4	+5.8	-0.2	

Source : Census of India, *Village and Town Directories, Punjab, Haryana and Chandigarh, 1971 and 2001.*

FIG. 5.4

Periphery Zone: Sub-zonewise Change in Land Use Pattern of 103 Villages where Net Area Sown Decreased by at Least 10 Per Cent Points during 1971-2001

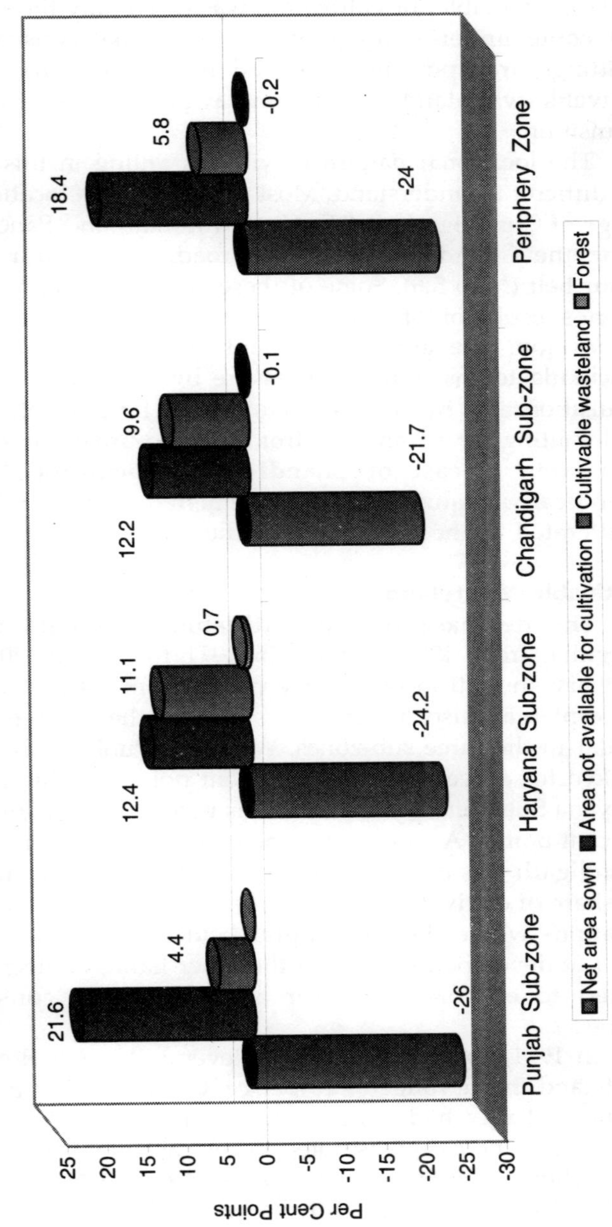

Source : Census of India, *Village and Town Directories, Punjab, Haryana and Chandigarh, 1971 and 2001.*

land not available for cultivation was essentially the one which had come under non-agricultural uses like construction of buildings, transport network and related infrastructure, and cultivable wasteland was the one awaiting development after acquisition.

The locational pattern of villages falling in this group is not difficult to understand. Most of these find a location on the fringe of Chandigarh, S.A.S. Nagar (Mohali) and Panchkula, or along the Chandigarh-Rupnagar road, and Kharar-Landran-Banur belt (Map 5.6). Some of these are located along the *choes* where speculation of land available at cheap rates is a lucrative proposition. The agricultural land around S.A.S. Nagar and Panchkula towns is under pressure by both governments for acquisition and by private sector as an investment. This is a land waiting for a transition from rural to urban, sooner rather than later. In case of Chandigarh, agricultural land was periodically acquired for resettlement of slums which had proliferated in the main body of the city.

Cultivable Wasteland

The decrease in the cultivable wasteland was just marginal: from 4500 hectares in 1971 to 3856 in 2001. As a corollary, the fall in percentage points from 4.4 per cent to 3.9 per cent was also small. The scene of the change was not similar in the three sub-zones. While the Punjab Sub-zone was marked for a decrease of 1.6 per cent points on this count; the Haryana Sub-zone, by contrast, was noted for an increase of 1.6 per cent points. A comparable increase by 8.4 per cent points in Chandigarh was of the higher order (Table 5.7). The increase in the share of cultivable wasteland was associated primarily with situations where the agricultural land has been acquired but was not developed so far. On the other hand, its decrease was linked to encroachment for agricultural or construction purposes.

In 1971, about one in every eleven villages had cultivable wasteland in the range of 10 per cent or more. The proportion of such villages had gone up to one in every seven by 2001. The biggest increase was noted in the case of Chandigarh Sub-zone followed by Haryana Sub-zone. As expected, Punjab was marked by some marginal decrease (Table 5.12).

MAP 5.6

Chandigarh Periphery Zone (Villages where Net Area Sown Decreased by at Least Ten Per Cent Points during 1971-2001)

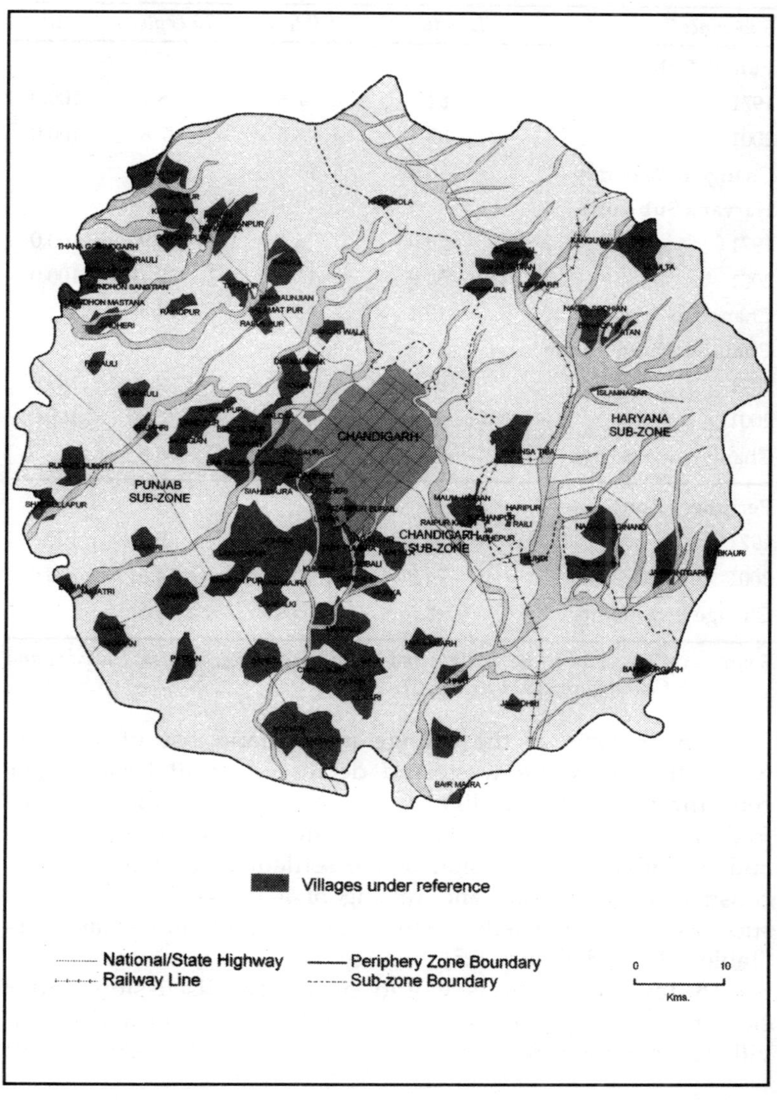

TABLE 5.12
Periphery Zone : Distribution of Villages by Percentage Share of Cultivable Wasteland to Total Area, 1971 and 2001

Sub-zones/Zone	*Less than 5*	*5.0 to 10*	*10 & above*	*All*
Punjab Sub-zone				
1971	84.1	7.8	8.1	100.0
2001	83.4	8.8	7.8	100.0
Change in % points	-0.7	+1.0	-0.3	
Haryana Sub-zone				
1971	79.0	8.1	12.9	100.0
2001	58.9	13.7	27.4	100.0
Change in % points	-20.1	+5.6	+14.5	
Chandigarh Sub-zone				
1971	100.0	0.0	0.0	100.0
2001	47.4	15.8	36.8	100.0
Change in % points	-52.6	+15.8	+36.8	
Periphery Zone				
1971	83.4	7.5	9.1	100.0
2001	74.9	10.5	14.6	100.0
Change in % points	-8.5	+3.0	+5.5	

Source : Census of India, *Village and Town Directories, Punjab, Haryana and Chandigarh, 1971 and 2001.*

An analysis of the change in the land use of villages, where the cultivable wasteland decreased by at least 10 per cent, throws additional light on the emerged situation. A two-fold shift in use of wasteland is manifest: one for agriculture and the other for extension of the settlement part of villages, constructions of roads and raising of a variety of structures, such as livestock sheds, poultry farms, and industrial units (Table 5.13 and Figure 5.5).

A few illustrations would bring the discussion under clearer focus. The cultivable wasteland in Mirzapur and Badali villages in Punjab Sub-zone decreased during 1971-2001 by 89

TABLE 5.13

Change in Land Use Pattern of Villages (N=44) where Cultivable Wasteland Decreased by at Least 10 Per Cent Points during 1971-2001

Sub-zones/Zone	*Net area sown*	*Area not available for cultivation*	*Cultivable waste-land*	*Forest*	*Total area*
Punjab Sub-zone					
1971	53.9	13.8	32.3	0.0	7554 (100.0)
2001	62.8	35.3	1.4	0.5	7324 (100.0)
Change in % points	+8.9	+21.5	-30.9	+0.5	
Haryana Sub-zone					
1971	47.7	34.5	17.8	0.0	3123 (100.0)
2001	55.1	41.2	3.7	0.0	3123 (100.0)
Change in % points	+7.4	+6.7	-14.1	0.0	
Periphery Zone					
1971	52.1	19.8	28.1	0.0	10677 (100.0)
2001	60.5	37.0	2.1	0.4	10447 (100.0)
Change in % points	+8.4	+17.2	-26.0	+0.4	

Note : There was no such village in Chandigarh Sub-zone

Source : Census of India, *Village and Town Directories, Punjab, Haryana and Chandigarh, 1971 and 2001.*

and 81 per cent points respectively. While in Mirzapur village almost all the cultivable wasteland was brought under non-agricultural activities, such as roads, business establishments and other such features; in Badali villages, the cultivable wasteland was diverted to agricultural use. In general, several villages located along the *choes* witnesses an increase in their net areas sown at the cost of cultivable wasteland (Map 5.7).

In Haryana Sub-zone, the conversion of cultivable wasteland was shared by agricultural and non-agricultural uses. While the villages located along the *choes* were noted for an extension of agriculture; those finding a location along main roads or in proximity of towns, were marked for emergence of

FIG. 5.5

Periphery Zone: Sub-zonewise Change in Land Use Pattern of Villages (N=44) where Cultivable Wasteland Decreased by at Least 10 Per Cent Points during 1971-2001

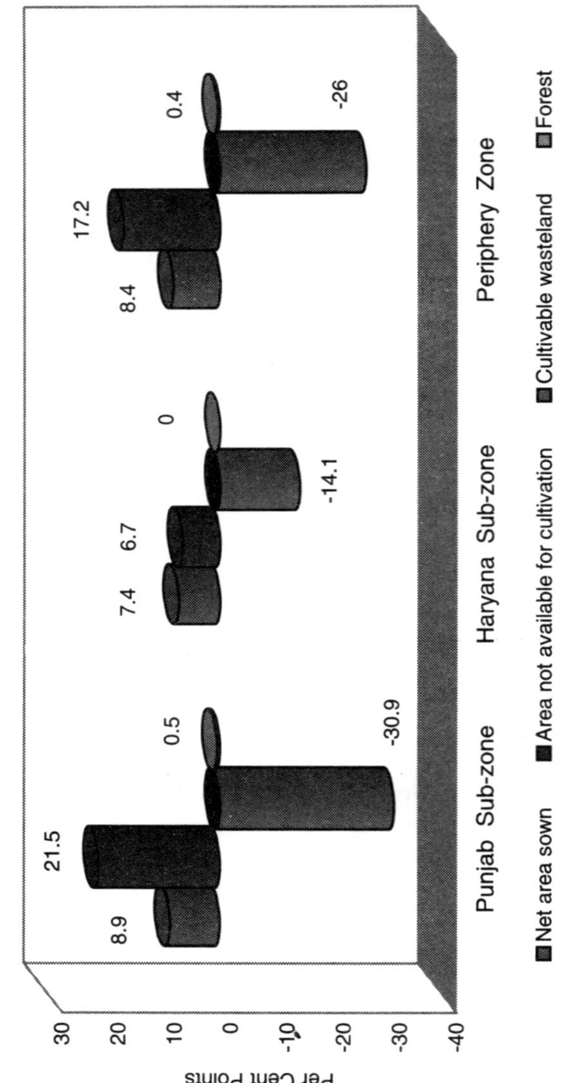

Source : Census of India, *Village and Town Directories, Punjab, Haryana and Chandigarh, 1971 and 2001.*

Map 5.7
Chandigarh Periphery Zone
(Villages where Cultivable Wasteland Decreased by at Least Five Per Cent Points during 1971-2001)

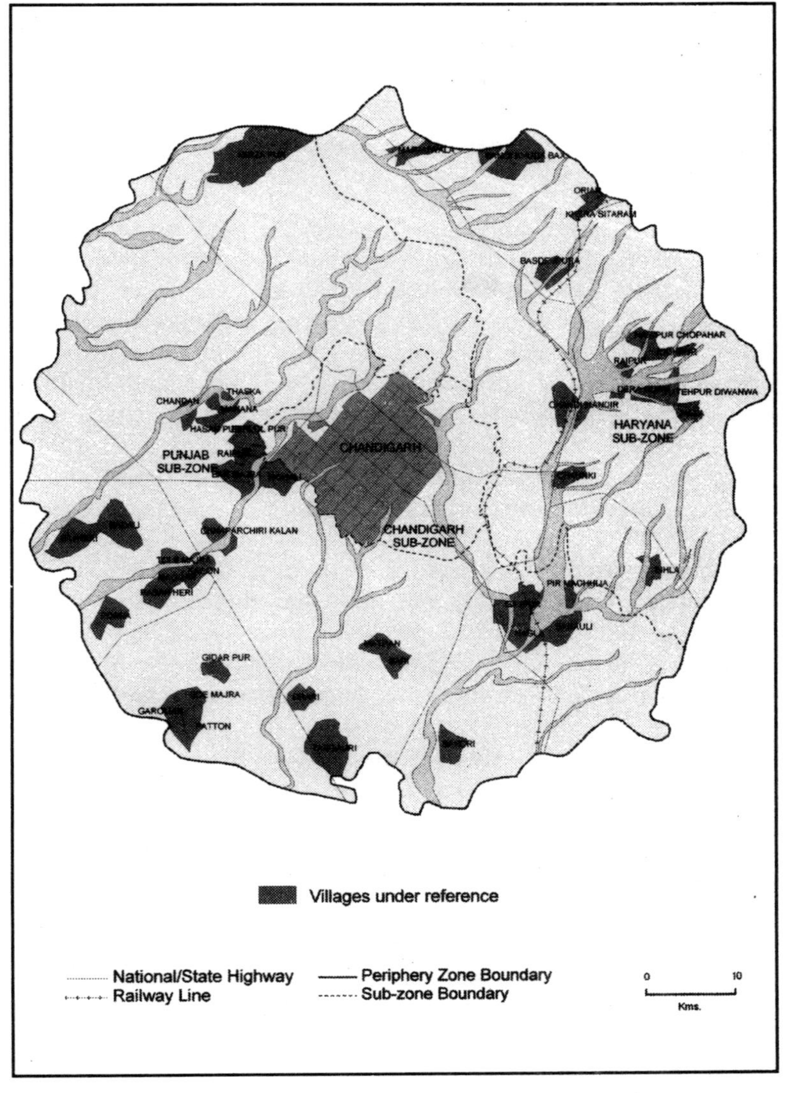

new structure or residential localities. Reclamation of land along the *choes* or on their dry beds was of high order.

In the Chandigarh Sub-zone, there was no village where the percentage of cultivable wasteland decreased by 10 per cent points and above. On the other hand, eight villages here recorded an increase in the cultivable wasteland by 10 per cent points or above. This was commensurate with the decrease in the net area sown in villages like Mauli Jagran, Kujheri, and Nizampur Burail and reduction in area under forest in Jhumaroo and Khuda Alisher villages.

Area not Available for Cultivation

The most outstanding feature of the land use change in the Periphery Zone has been a significant extension of the 'area not available for cultivation' from 21 to 29 per cent during 1971-2001. This is another way of saying that area under new housing, utility structures, such as water treatment plants and electricity stations, recreational sites, industrial and business establishments, roads and other such features has tremendously increased over the years in rural parts of the Periphery Zone. Added here is the rural land acquired but only used for development so far. The picture of course, differs by sub-zone. Punjab Sub-zone was noted for a big rise by 10 per cent points in this category of land use, Haryana Sub-zone experienced a marginal change, and Chandigarh was unique in exhibiting a decline by 3 per cent points (Table 5.7). The anomalous situation in the last case was due to the relocation of slums in the city onto earlier acquired vacant lands in the villages.

Table 5.14 shows that the number of villages having more than one-third of total area as 'not available for cultivation' increased from 19 per cent in 1971 to 27 per cent in 2001. In 1971, 8 per cent of all the villages recorded 50 per cent or above of their total area as being 'not available for cultivation'. By 2001, the share of such villages had risen to 12.1 per cent, a rise by 4.1 per cent points. Such a rise was almost similar in Punjab and Haryana Sub-zones, by 4.4 and 4.8 per cent points respectively. On the other side, Chandigarh Sub-zone marked a decrease in its 'area not available for cultivation' for cultivation by 5.2 per cent points.

TABLE 5.14

Periphery Zone : Distribution of Villages by Percentage Share of Area Not Available for Cultivation to Total Area, 1971 and 2001

Sub-zones/Zone	*0 to 33.3*	*33.4 to 49.9*	*50 & above*	*All*
Punjab Sub-zone				
1971	92.9	5.1	2.0	296 (100.0)
2001	84.1	9.5	6.4	296 (100.0)
Change in % points	-8.8	+4.4	+4.4	
Haryana Sub-zone				
1971	53.2	25.0	21.8	124 (100.0)
2001	46.8	26.6	26.6	124 (100.0)
Change in % points	-6.4	1.6	+4.8	
Chandigarh Sub-zone				
1971	79.0	10.5	10.5	19 (100.0)
2001	73.7	21.0	5.3	19 (100.0)
Change in % points	-5.3	+10.5	-5.2	
Periphery Zone				
1971	81.1	10.9	8.0	439 (100.0)
2001	73.1	14.8	12.1	439 (100.0)
Change in % points	-8.0	+3.9	+4.1	

Source : Census of India, *Village and Town Directories, Punjab, Haryana and Chandigarh, 1971 and 2001.*

For identifying the dynamics underlying the kind of change described, Table 5.15 was prepared to show the change in land use pattern of villages which had experienced an increase by at least 10 per cent points in respect of this land use category. It is learnt that at the level of the Periphery Zone as a whole, the 'area not available for cultivation' was extending at the cost of forest land, net area sown, and cultivated wasteland, in that order. At the sub-zone level, the forest land was the greatest loser in the Punjab and Chandigarh Sub-zones and net area sown in the Haryana Sub-zone (Figure 5.6).

Table 5.15

Periphery Zone : Change in Land Use Pattern of Villages (N=109) where Area Not Available for Cultivation Increased by at Least 10 Per Cent Points during 1971-2001

Sub-zones/Zone	*Net area sown*	*Area not available for cultivation*	*Cultivable waste-land*	*Forest*	*Total area*
Punjab Sub-zone					
1971	56.4	10.2	8.7	24.6	24975 (100.0)
2001	51.2	46.2	2.6	0.0	24547 (100.0)
Percentage change	-5.3	36.0	-6.1	-24.6	
Haryana Sub-zone					
1971	45.1	29.8	6.4	18.8	6309 (100.0)
2001	30.1	47.9	3.6	18.4	4693 (100.0)
Percentage change	-15.0	18.1	-2.8	-0.4	
Chandigarh Sub-zone					
1971	72.4	10.1	0.6	16.9	681 (100.0)
2001	61.3	35.2	3.5	0.0	511 (100.0)
Percentage change	-11.1	25.1	2.9	-16.9	
Periphery Zone					
1971	54.5	14.1	8.1	23.3	31965 (100.0)
2001	48.0	46.3	2.8	2.9	29751 (100.0)
Percentage change	-6.5	32.2	-5.3	-20.4	

Source : Census of India, *Village and Town Directories, Punjab, Haryana and Chandigarh, 1971 and 2001.*

In the Chandigarh Sub-zone, the land earmarked for forests was intruded upon by slum dwellers who constructed unauthorized colonies. Over time, these slum localities were cleared and slums-dwellers rehabilitated at other locations but the cleared land did not revert to forest cover. These were kept vacant for the time being for future use. In the Punjab Sub-zone, the reduction of forest land in Siswan village by 88 per cent points, Chotti Bari Naggal by 80, Chotti Bari Parchh by 72

Fig. 5.6

Periphery Zone: Sub-zonewise Change in Land Use Pattern of Villages (N=109) where Area Not Available for Cultivation Increased by at Least 10 Per Cent Points during 1971-2001

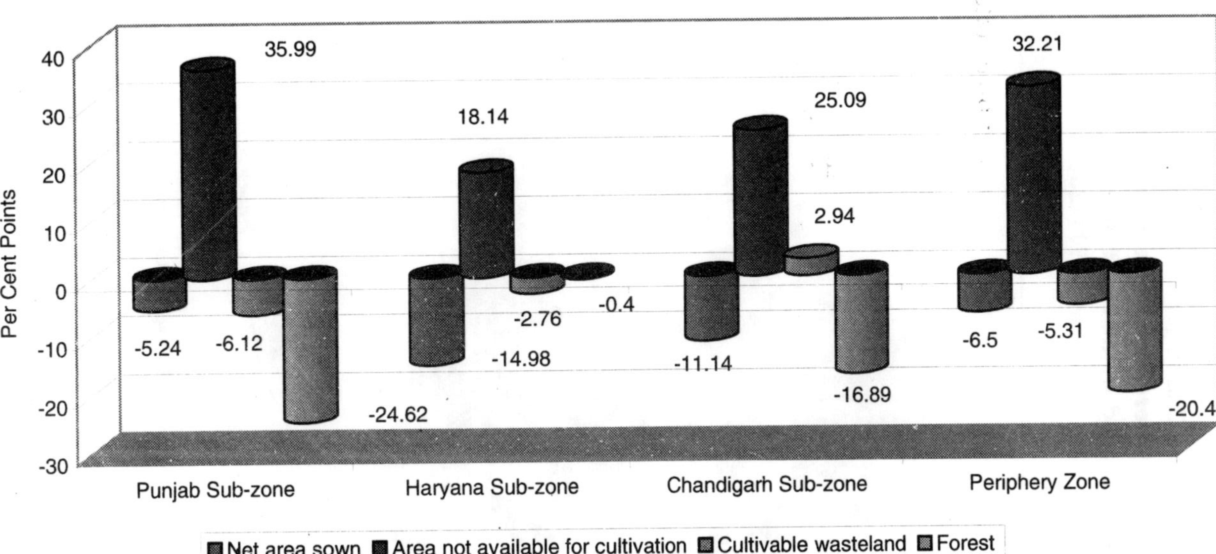

Source : Census of India, *Village and Town Directories, Punjab, Haryana and Chandigarh, 1971 and 2001.*

Map 5.8

Chandigarh Periphery Zone (Villages where Area Not Available for Cultivation Increased by at Least Ten Per Cent Points during 1971-2001)

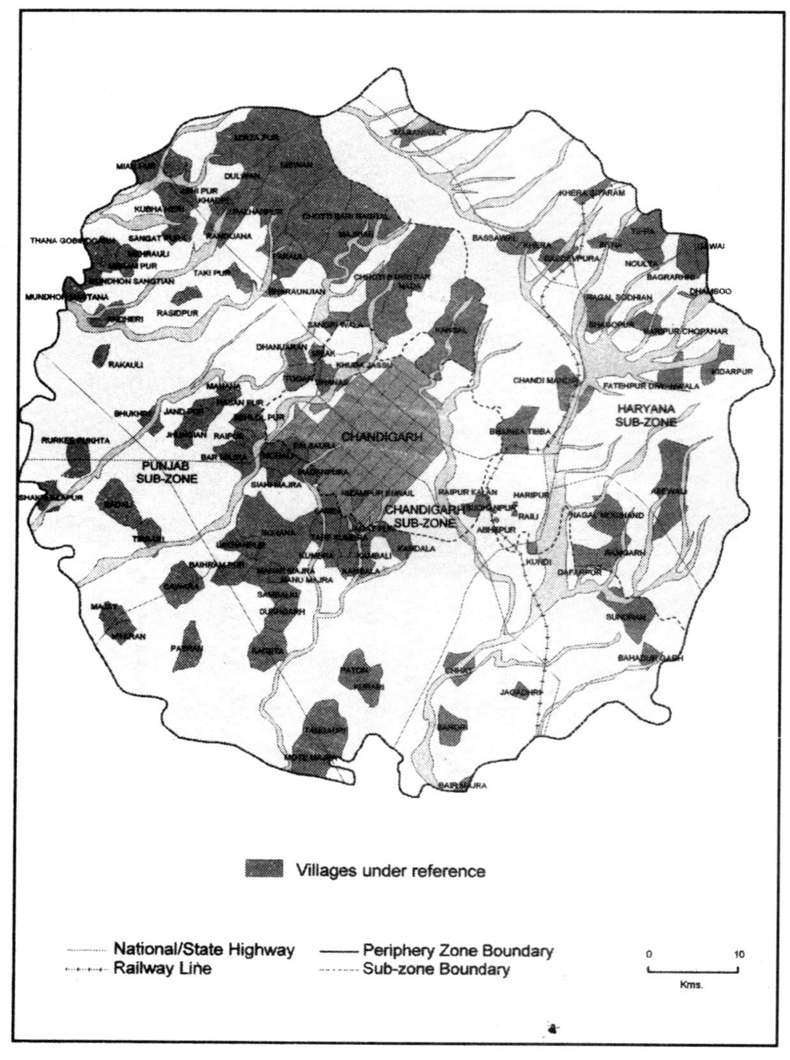

and Majri by 67 is most notable. All these villages are close to Chandigarh. In the Haryana Sub-zone, land acquisition for Panchkula on a large scale led to the gross reduction of net area sown in villages like Abhepur, Haripur, Raili, Majri and Maheshpur.

In addition, a large chunk of the agricultural land had been sold in several villages close to Chandigarh and Panchkula in response to speculation by land buyers. Similar was the experience of many villages of Punjab Sub-zone located in proximity to Chandigarh and S.A.S. Nagar (Mohali). Thus, the land use pattern of the Periphery Zone was getting significantly transformed under the impact of Chandigarh and its satellite towns of S.A.S. Nagar (Mohali) and Panchkula (Map 5.8). The rechanneling of *choes* especially by way of diversions of many into one was also not without its effect. Additional land was made available for use.

URBANIZATION AS A FACTOR OF LAND USE CHANGE

The Periphery Zone was meant to be essentially rural, by definition. Any urban place located within it was outside the purview of the Periphery Control Act. This provision became handy at the hands of the governments for it could circumvent the Act either by upgrading a village or a group of contiguous villages to urban status or by extending the territorial jurisdiction of the existing towns. This is actually what was resorted to and became a critical factor in transforming the character of the Periphery Zone and squeezing its spatial domain.

Table 5.16 shows that the urban area in the Periphery Zone increased from hardly 10 km^2 in 1971 to as much as 140 km^2 in 2001. The territorial limits of every existing town, without any exception, were extended from time to time. Derra Bassi got enlarged from 0.8 km^2 in 1971 to 20 km^2 in 2001 and Kharar from, 0.7 km^2 to 5 km^2. The spatial extension of the planned satellite towns is also noticeable: of S.A.S. Nagar (Mohali) from 12.4 in 1981 to 25 km^2 in 2001 and of Panchkula from 10.4 to 25 km^2.

TABLE 5.16

Periphery Zone : Change in Area of the Individual Towns, 1971-2001

Name of the town	*Area (in km²)*			
	1971	*1981*	*1991*	*2001*
Banur	5.8	4.5	4.5	7.0
Kalka	2.8	3.4	3.4	3.4
Derra Bassi	0.8	3.1	3.1	20.0
Kharar	0.7	4.2	4.2	5.0
S.A.S. Nagar (Mohali)		12.4	16.7	25.0
Panchkula		10.4	15.2	25.0
Pinjore		3.4	4.8	7.0
Karoran				15.0
Zirakpur				11.4
Mullanpur—Garibdas				8.5
Bhankarpur				5.9
Bhabat				5.7

Source : (i) Census of India : *Village and Town Directory, Village and Town-wise Primary Census Abstract*, different volumes from 1971 to 2001, Director of Census Operations, Punjab, Haryana and Chandigarh.

During 1991-2001, five clusters of villages or individual villages were raised to urban status (Map 5.9). This increased the urban area within the Periphery Zone by about 47 km^2. Such a process is unabated. It is likely that more of the rural pockets of the Periphery Zone will be declared as urban from time to time. Corbusiers's insistence on maintaining it as rural is under regular threat.

As expected, the emerged scene in the three sub-zones calls for a comparison. While in the case of the Haryana Sub-zone, the encroachment on rural land was associated primarily with the extension of Panchkula, in the Punjab Sub-zone, the factors of extension of S.A.S. Nagar (Mohali), upgradation of village settlement to urban status and enlargement of the territorial jurisdiction of existing towns, all played a collective

MAP 5.9
Chandigarh Periphery Zone
(Villages Merged with Towns or Upgraded to Urban Status during 1991-2001)

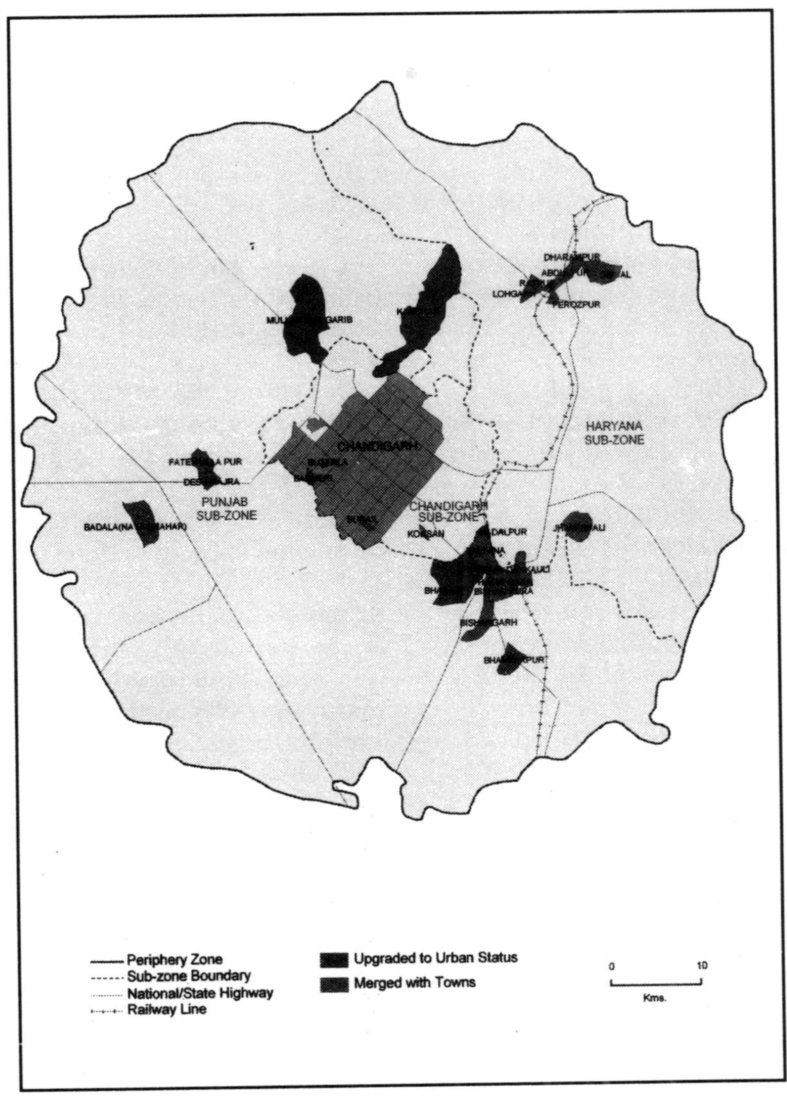

role. The usurpation of rural land for urban use was largely on planned lines in the Haryana Sub-zone but it happened to be on an ad hoc basis in the case of Punjab. In Chandigarh Sub-zone, pockets of rural land were acquired for relocation of slum localities which had proliferated in the main body of the city.

This is not to imply that Haryana Sub-zone was free from illegal conversion of agricultural land for other uses. During the past 34 years (1972 to 2006), 8,243 unauthorized structures have been detected in its controlled area. Among these, 800 had come up on government land of the Forest Department in the Bir Ghaggar area, 339 within the 30 meters of restricted distance from the national highway and 236 within the Terminal Ballistics Research Laboratory (TBRLs) restricted belt. The remaining unauthorized structures had mushroomed, either around the existing towns or along Chandigarh-Kalka-Shimla, Chandigarh-Barwala and Pinjore-Baddi-Nalagarh highways. Only 38 cases, among these were given legal sanction eventually (Table 5.17). The permission pertained to setting up of petrol pumps, farm houses, poultry farms, and agro-based industrial units. This process assumed pace during the 1990s. The outcome was both good and bad. On the one hand, the facility of petrol pumps got available on the main highways, on the other, it caused emergence of unauthorized structures.

It is difficult to gauge the nature, frequency and location of unauthorized constructions in the Punjab Sub-zone. Such violations of the Periphery Act were regularized by the government from time to time and no systematic record was kept in order. However, the detection of as many as 6883 unauthorized constructions on agricultural land which were spotted during the 1990s speak of its widespread range. Demolition orders were issued only in 594 cases but were executed actually in only 160 cases. The indifferent process of punishing the guilty encouraged others to carry out the same with impunity. The Periphery Zone stands violated.

Added to this is the effect of recent policy changes adopted by the Punjab Government for promoting residential colonies within the Periphery Zone. The government has encouraged the entry of the private sector in the acquisition of

TABLE 5.17

Haryana Sub-zone: Permission Cases of Conversion of Agricultural Land, 1972-2006

Sl. No.	*Year*	*Nature of activity*	*Location*
(1)	*(2)*	*(3)*	*(4)*
1.	1971	Petrol Pump	Chandigarh-Kalka Road
2.	1972	Petrol Pump	Ambala-Kalka Road
3.	1974	Residential building	Gorakhnath
4.	1975	Residential building	Tipra
5.	1976	Farm house	Bhainsa Tibba
6.	1979	Poultry/Farm Cattle shed	Bhainsa Tibba
7.	1986	Petrol Pump	Chandigarh-Kalka Road
8.	1990	Poultry/Farm Cattle shed	Bhainsa Tibba
9.	1990	Poultry/Farm Cattle shed	Bhainsa Tibba
10.	1990	Poultry/Farm Cattle shed	Bhainsa Tibba
11.	1990	Industry (Chemical)	Ramgarh-Barwala Road
12.	1992	Hotel	Panchkula-Barwala Road
13.	1992	Industry (earthen energies)	Billa
14.	1993	Training School (ITBP)	Bhanu
15.	1994	Industry (Agro food)	Kherawali
16.	1994	Poultry farm	Panchkula-Barwala Road
17.	1994	Poultry farm	Dabkori Road
18.	1994	Industry (Khadi Gram Udhyog)	Ramgarh
19.	1995	Industry (pesticide)	Kherawali
20.	1995	Hospital	Maheshpur
21.	1996	Nursery	Bhainsa Tibba
22.	1996	Poultry farm	Barwala Road
23.	1999	Staff quarter (police)	Moginand Madanpur
24.	2001	Religious building (Ashram)	Morni Road
25.	2002	School	Morni Road

(*Contd.*)

TABLE 5.17 (*Contd.*)

(1)	(2)	(3)	(4)
26.	2003	School (primary)	Kot
27.	2003	Petrol Pump	Billa
28.	2004	Training institute (Commando Training)	Naggal Moginand
29.	2004	Farm house	Nada
30.	2004	Farm house	Bunga
31.	2004	For acquisition (shifting of one Battalion)	Billa
32.	2004	Care taker/mali hut	Billa
33.	2004	Petrol Pump	Nalagarh Road
34.	2005	Brick Kiln	Dabkori
35.	2005	Petrol Pump	Nalagarh Road
36.	2005	Petrol Pump	Barwala Road
37.	2005	Petrol Pump	Barwala Road
38.	2006	Petrol Pump	Nalagarh Road

Source : Town Planning Department, Panchkula.

land and construction of residential units. The policy is proving highly lucrative for the private sector.

Table 5.18 is a testimony to the emergence of the Kharar, Zirakpur and Derra Bassi areas as residential hubs in the Punjab Sub-zone. All these places are close to Chandigarh and are located on main highways radiating from the city. Among the 126 residential colonies, 70 are unauthorized and 56 authorized. The authorized ones are recent additions during the last five years, when land colonizers started availing of the legal support of the state government. The most preferred site is the Kharar area which is in contiguity with Chandigarh and S.A.S. Nagar (Mohali).

It may be noted that earlier in 1990, 4792 hectares of land in 23 villages in Derra Bassi-Mubarakpur belt, located in the Punjab Sub-zone, was declared as a Free Enterprise Zone, for attracting industries (Table 5.19). Conversion of agricultural land for setting up of industrial units was made easy. A natural

TABLE 5.18

Punjab Sub-zone : Authorized and Unauthorized Residential Colonies, 2006

Area	*Authorized*	*Unauthorized*	*Total*
Kharar Area	30	58	88
Zirakpur Area	16	5	21
Derra Bassi	10	7	17
Total	56	70	126

Source : Swapnil, Sharma, 2005, *Future of the Periphery in Chandigarh.* Unpublished dissertation for B. Planning, New Delhi, School of Planning and Architecture.

TABLE 5.19

Punjab Sub-zone: Free Enterprise Zone (FEZ) Villages

Sl. No	*Name of the Village*	*Area (in hectares)*
(1)	*(2)*	*(3)*
1.	Mor Thikari	83
2.	Pandwala	263
3.	Sundran	649
4.	Mirpur (Min)	37
5.	Mubarakpur (Min)	265
6.	Haibatpur	211
7.	Dafarpur	101
8.	Kheri	126
9.	Behra	530
10.	Bhagwanpur	178
11.	Rampur Sainian	285
12.	Nimbnia	394
13.	Bahadurgarh	78
14.	Haripur Hinduan	186

(Contd.)

TABLE 5.19 (*Contd.*)

(1)	(2)	(3)
15.	Kurranwala	222
16.	Mahiwala	185
17.	Dadrala	189
18.	Gulabgarh (Min)	161
19.	Saidpura	300
20.	Madhopur (Min)	63
21.	Saudo Majra	131
22.	Rauni (Min)	27
23.	Bhankarpur (Min)	128

Source : PUDA Records.

outcome was the loss of the agricultural character of this part of the Punjab Sub-zone.

FUTURE LAND USE SCENARIO

In the context of Periphery Control Act, the land under the category of 'area not available for cultivation' assumes special significance as it represents the area brought under new constructions or acquired for future development. In the case of the Periphery Zone, the rate and magnitude of change in this land use can be deemed as indicative of overall change in the land use. The share of area not available for cultivation in total area of the Periphery Zone was 21.5 per cent in 1971 and 28.6 per cent in 2001. By using the extrapolation technique, it was worked out that in 2020, no less than 32.9 per cent or nearly one-third of the total area of the Periphery Zone would belong to this category of land use. This figure might go higher if the Greater Mohali Plan of the Punjab Government gets implemented by the year 2020. The Periphery Zone in all probability is bound to lose a large part of its agricultural land to urban use.

CONCLUSION

The Periphery Zone of Chandigarh is literally losing ground. It is being squeezed through the upgradation of villages or groups of villages into towns, extension of the territorial jurisdiction of the existing towns, emergence of authorized and unauthorized residential colonies, mushrooming of illegal constructions at strategic sites, and above all, the laying out of S.A.S. Nagar (Mohali) and Panchkula towns.

The process of urban development and increasing land use changes in response to the buoyant economy and intensifying pressure of population has quickened its pace, of late, in the Periphery Zone. However, these are not the only factors involved. Farmland owners in connivance with land colonizers and Departments of Punjab Urban Planning and Development Authority (PUDA) and Haryana Urban Development Authority (HUDA), are making land use decisions against the backdrop of a changing landscape and economic environment.

The last two decades have also witnessed increased state-level involvement in the name of countering the negative impacts of haphazard urban growth. The private sector has been invited to participate in the task of acquiring and developing land and raising residential colonies, apart from the educational health and recreational campuses. The provisions of the Periphery Control Act are being circumvented and the originally visualized green and serene landscape of the Periphery Zone has been brought under the carpet of the urban sprawl.

The emerging scenario in the three sub-zones of the Periphery Zone calls for a comparison. The Punjab Sub-zone has been the venue of a most conspicuous onslaught on the periphery. It enjoys contiguity with the Chandigarh Union Territory on three sides of north, west and south, is well connected through roads, and is relatively well-off economically speaking. Added to this is the urbanizing effect of S.A.S. Nagar (Mohali) on planned lines. The land use changes in the Haryana Sub-zone were comparatively more on planned lines as a large part of it is accounted for by the fully planned town of Panchkula. In the Chandigarh Sub-zone, acquisition of agricultural land for carrying out new sectors or for relocation of slum localities is the most noticeable feature.

Land is increasingly becoming scarce due to immense pressure on agricultural land imposed by the rapid urbanization process and demographic growth. Most of the forest area has been encroached upon and almost all fallow land stands reclaimed. The Periphery Zone of Chandigarh is now under the collective impact of the tri-cities of Chandigarh, Mohali and Panchkula.

6

Population Projections : 2020

The population of the Periphery Zone has shown a four-fold increase during the period 1971-2001; from about one-quarter to over one million. Such an eventuality was not even foreseen and much less catered for at the time of its inception. Although conceived as a rural envelope for the city, the urban component of the Periphery Zone displayed a 12-fold increase, as noted in Chapter 4. Meanwhile the rural component was also doubled in terms of population size during this same period. This called for an augmentation of the socio-economic infrastructure including transport, communication, housing, electricity, water supply, sewage, schools, hospitals and other community support services. Now the future is to be catered for. Population forecasts to that end can help project, direct and channelize the growth in a desired direction.

The present chapter seeks to present population projections for Chandigarh Periphery Zone up to the year 2020 on a yearly basis. These projections have been made not only for the aggregate population but also for its components, viz. various age groups, occupational groups, and socio-economic groups. The exercise addresses itself to the call of the Futuristic Geography of the Periphery Zone.

POPULATION PROJECTIONS

Population projections are intrinsic to all kinds of plan and policy formulations. The involvement of a plethora of agencies in the prediction of future population dynamics comes as no surprise. At the global and national level, the agencies such as the World Bank and the United National Population Division regularly work out the future estimates of population. The accuracy of these projections can be gauged by examining how close they have come in projecting the population of India in 2001.

Of the ten population projections, seven had underestimated the population for India for the year 2001 (Table 6.1). Barring the projection made by Das Gupta and Majumdar, all others come within or close to ten per cent of the census estimates for 2001. The projections made by the United

TABLE 6.1

A Comparative View of Some Population Projections for India's Population in 2001 *vis-à-vis* the Actual Count

Author/ Organization	*Year of projection*	*Population projected for 2001 (million)*	*Percentage deviation from the actual (1028 million)*
Das Gupta and Majumdar	1954	667	-35.1
United Nations	1963	922	-10.2
World Bank	1972	1109	8.0
Frejka	1972	955	-7.0
United Nations	1973	1078	5.0
Operations Research Group	1974	973	-5.3
Raghavachari	1974	935	-9.0
J.P. Ambannavar	1975	1003	-2.3
Cassen and Tim Dyson	1976	934	-9.1
United Nations	1978	1056	2.8

Source : Bhat, P.N.R., 2001. *Indian Demographic Scenario, 2025*. Delhi, Population Research Centre, Institute of Economic Growth.

Nations in 1973 and 1978 and by J.P. Ambannavar in 1975 were quite close to India's population for the year 2001. The exercise of making population projections for a longer time is likely to go wrong as the assumptions made for the future shape on indicators of fertility and mortality might not take place as visualized. The Indian experience is that the rigour of the methodology adopted is more critical. For example, the population projections for India's population made in 1973 by the United Nations are much closer to the actual in 2001 than the one by Cassen and Dyson in 1976.

Besides this, the exercise of projecting India's future populations at the country as well as the state level at the behest of the Planning Commission of India, has been a continuous exercise since 1950s. The Office of the Registrar General and Census Commissioner, India constituted Expert Review Committees from time to time to work out population projections on a regular basis. Table 6.2 summarizes the projections made by the technical groups and their accuracy level, since 1971. The actuals outnumbered the projections in most cases.

The projections made by different Technical Groups deviated by within two per cent of the emerged reality. Most were underestimates. The final population totals in 1991 were fairly close to the projected one. The projected population for the year 2001 fell short by over 14 million. This situation implies that either mortality has improved faster than the expected rate or the rate of fertility decline has been a bit slower than the one assumed.

Projecting the population at the state level is a relatively more risky affair. Estimating trends in birth rate and death rate here may not pose much of a problem. The real difficulty lies in working out the role of migration in shaping the future population growth scenario. This factor may be insignificant at the national level but assumes criticality at the state-level or below.

Population projections at the regional level cutting across state boundaries are still more difficult to manage. This is the case with the Periphery Zone which is composed of three sub-zones under different political dispensations. Each tends to follow its own developmental policies, further compounding

TABLE 6.2

Projected and Actual Population of India, 1971-2001

(*in 000*)

Year	*Projected population*	*Actual population*	*Difference*	*Per cent difference*
1971	5,59,622[(1)]	5,48,160	-11462	-2.05
1981	6,72,014[(2)]	6,83,329	11315	1.68
1991	8,37,249[(3)]	8,46,388	9139	1.09
1991	8,43,596[(4)]	8,46,388	2792	0.33
2001	10,12,386[(5)]	10,28,610	14629	1.42

Notes : (1) According to the Report of the Expert Committee on Population, Registrar General, India, July 1968.
(2) According to the Report of the Expert Committee on Population Projections, Registrar General, India, October, 1978.
(3) According to the Report of the Expert Committee on Population Projections, Registrar General, India, January, 1988.
(4) According to the Report of the Standing Committee on Population Projections, Planning Commission, India, October, 1989.
(5) According to the Population Projections for India and States, Registrar General, India, New Delhi, 1966.

Source : *Population Projections, Provisional Population Totals, Series 1, India, Paper 1 of 2001*, Census of India, Registrar General of India, New Delhi.

the issue of population projections. None of the three concerned governments of Punjab, Haryana and Chandigarh have tried to take a holistic picture of the emerging demographic scene of the zone. Each treats the territory under its jurisdiction in isolation. The present study is an attempt to correct this situation.

Assumptions

Population projections are based on a certain set of assumptions. These in turn flow from an understanding of the short-term and long-term historical trends, government policies, and other relevant information influencing the population change in any area. The foremost assumption in this case is that there will be no change in the territorial organization of the Chandigarh Periphery Zone, till the year up to which the population projections are made. Secondly, it is visualized that the prevailing trends in the fertility, mortality and migration will remain the same not only in the Periphery Zone but also in the region of which it is a part and in India. Finally, non-demographic factors, such as natural catastrophes, would not come into play. One may say that the present sets of projections would be more explorative than prescriptive.

In order to neutralize the debilitating impact of assumptions on the projected population figures, and make these more dependable, it is proposed that more than one technique be put into service and the results be compared. In the present exercise, five different techniques, with varying conceptualizations were used and the ones which gave population projections close to each other were averaged to work out more reliable projection figures.

Techniques

A variety of techniques, both mechanical as well as analytical, are used to project future populations depending upon the availability of data. Mechanical techniques deal with aggregate population while the analytical ones differentiate between the relative contributions of the three vital processes - fertility, mortality and migration in population growth. The population of the Periphery Zone has been projected through a combination of both mechanical and analytical techniques. Mechanical ones are the techniques of ratio, extrapolation, compound annual growth rate, and urban-rural growth differential. The cohort component technique is an analytical one which has been used with the help of Demoproj software (Constella Futures, Washington DC). Each technique has been critically examined in terms of its assumptions, data requirements, properties and limitations. While projecting the population by using any of the techniques all the steps followed and the calculations done have been presented with a view to making it available for simulation by any other scholar.

RATIO

The method assumes that the share of the Periphery's Zone's population in that of Punjab and Haryana put together will remain virtually the same in the short run, and any change in the degree (quantum) and direction (positive or negative) of this share will be sustained over a long period. The current behaviour of a part is seen as linked to that of the whole. The availability of necessary data and ease in understanding and convenience of computation makes it a popular technique (Krishan, 1994, p. 13).

Two sets of data are required for the purpose. The first is the total population of Periphery Zone and that of Punjab and Haryana over a number of previous years. The second is the projected population of Punjab and Haryana for the years over which population projections for the Chandigarh Periphery are to be made. The data to meet the first requirement was collected from the Primary Census Abstracts of Punjab and Haryana, Census of India, 2001. For resolving the second requirement, the projected populations of Punjab and Haryana for the respective years were taken from the Report of the Technical Group on Population Projections constituted by the National Commission on Population, Registrar General and Census Commissioner, Census of India, May 2006. The following sequential steps were taken to operationalise the technique.

Steps

Projections for 2011

(i) Calculated the percentage share of Periphery Zone's population in combined population of Punjab and Haryana in 1971, 1981, 1991 and 2001 (Table 6.3);

(ii) For projecting the population of Periphery Zone for the year 2011, calculated the difference between the population share of Periphery Zone to combined population of Punjab and Haryana in 1991 and 2001, as follows:

TABLE 6.3

Percentage Share of Periphery Zone's Population in Combined Populations of Punjab and Haryana : 1971-2001

Year	*Combined population of Punjab and Haryana*	*Population of the Periphery Zone*	*Percentage share of the Periphery Zone's population in combined population of Punjab and Haryana*
1971	23,587,868	286796	1.216
1981	29,711,533	417773	1.406
1991	36,745,617	663065	1.804
2001	45,503,563	1037041	2.279
2011	53117,000	1462842	2.754
2021	59685000	1927229	3.229
2020	58993211	1874821	3.178

Source : Census of India, *Primary Census Abstracts of Punjab and Haryana, 1971 to 2001,* and *Population Projections for India and States 2001-26,* Report of the Technical Group on Population Projections, Office of the Registrar General and Census Commissioner, India, New Delhi, May 2006.

Share of Periphery Zone's population in the combined population of Punjab and Haryana in 1991 (S_{1991}) = 1.804

Share of Periphery Zone's population in the combined population of Punjab and Haryana in 2001 (S_{2001}) = 2.279

$$\text{Difference (D)} = S_{1991} - S_{2001} = 1.804 - 2.279 = -0.475$$

This tendency, in degree and direction, was forward to project the population in 2011. The steps followed were as follows:

$$S_{2011} = [S_{2001} - D] = [2.279 - (-0.475)] = [2.279 + 0.475] = 2.754$$

In other words, the Periphery Zone would have 2.754 per cent of the combined population of Punjab and Haryana in 2011.

(iii) The combined population of Punjab and Haryana in 2011 was noted as 53,117,000.
Hence projected population of the Periphery Zone in 2011 can be worked out as
(53,117,000 × 2.754)/100 = 1,462,842

Technically this could be expressed as follows:

$$
\begin{aligned}
CPZ_{2011} &= (T_{2011} \times S_{2011})/100 \\
&= (53{,}117{,}000 \times 2.754)/100 \\
&= 1{,}462{,}842
\end{aligned}
$$

(iv) Following the same procedure, the Periphery Zone's population was projected as 1,927,229 in 2021.

$$
\begin{aligned}
CPZ_{2021} &= (T_{2021} \times S_{2021})/100 \\
&= (59{,}685{,}000 \times 3.229)/100 \\
&= 1{,}927{,}229
\end{aligned}
$$

(v) To obtain the population figures for the intervening years, the technique of interpolation was used, decade by decade. Interpolation was done by calculating the annual compound growth rate of population for each intercensal period separately. An illustration is as following:

Population in the Periphery Zone in 2001 = 1,037,041
Population in the Periphery Zone in 2011 = 1,462,842
Compound annual growth rate (in percentage) during 2001-2011 $= [(1{,}462{,}842/1{,}037{,}041)^{1/10} - 1] \times 100 = 3.49$

This growth rate was applied to obtain population estimate for each figures for projected population for successive years since 2001 to 2020. The results obtained are presented in Table 6.4.

TABLE 6.4
Projected Population of Periphery Zone by Ratio Technique : 2001-2020

Year	*Population*
2001	1,037,041 (Actual)
2002	1,073,337
2003	1,110,903
2004	1,149,784
2005	1,190,026
2006	1,231,677
2007	1,274,785
2008	1,319,401
2009	1,365,580
2010	1,413,375
2011	1,462,842
2012	1,503,734
2013	1,545,769
2014	1,588,979
2015	1,633,397
2016	1,679,057
2017	1,725,993
2018	1,774,241
2019	1,823,837
2020	1,874,821

Source : Projection outputs.

Within only two decades, the Periphery Zone's population is expected to almost double itself. This technique projects the population of Periphery Zone at 1.87 million in 2020. This is nearly two times the figure recorded by the Census of India for the year 2001.

URBAN-RURAL GROWTH DIFFERENTIAL

The Urban-Rural Growth Differential (URGD) technique

was developed by the United Nations Population Division to project and estimate urban populations. The technique used here is a variant of the URGD technique, which enjoys a high degree of respectability for projecting the population of a sub-system.

The method assumes that the growth behaviour of the sub-system, that is the Periphery Zone and that of the whole of which it forms a part, that is the states of Punjab and Haryana, are complementary to each other, "If the former records a faster growth rate through net in-migration, this is construed as happening at the cost of the rest of the system, which is seen as losing in the process of migration. An opposite picture will prevail if the sub-national area/state is making a population growth rate lower than its rate of natural increase. In essence, the method takes into account the difference in growth rates of the sub-national area/state and rest of the system, and projects population for the former". The technique invokes a greater role for migration (Krishan, 1994, p. 14).

The growth differential calls for population figures for Periphery Zone for two census periods and the projected populations of Punjab and Haryana for the years for which projections are to be made. The projections for Punjab and Haryana as a whole at five-year intervals were obtained from the Report of the Technical Group on Population Projections constituted by the National Commission on Population by the Registrar General and Census Commissioner, India, May 2006. Additionally, the decennial Census data was interpolated to get the figures at five-year intervals, which is the requirement of this method. The technique followed is detailed below.

Steps

(i) Periphery Zone's 2000 population (PZ_{2000}) = 991684

Periphery Zone's 1995 population (PZ_{1995}) = 792962

Punjab and Haryana's combined 2000 population (PH_{2000}) = 44541033

Punjab and Haryana's combined 1995 population (PH_{1995}) = 40025889

(ii) Periphery Zone's compound annual growth rate (CAGR) during 1995-2000 in unit fraction was worked out as follows:

$$\text{CAGR (PZ)} = (PZ_{2000}/PZ_{1995})^{1/5}-1$$
$$= (991684/792962)^{1/5}-1$$
$$= (1.2506072)^{1/5}-1$$
$$= 1.0457411-1$$
$$= 0.0457411$$

(iii) The CAGR of non-PZ has been worked out.

$$\text{CAGR (Non-PZ)} = [(PH_{2000}-PZ_{2000})/(PH_{1995}-PZ_{1995})]^{1/5}-1$$
$$= [(44541033-991684)/(40025889-792962)]^{1/5}-1$$
$$= (43549349/39232927)^{1/5}-1$$
$$= (1.1100204)^{1/5}-1$$
$$= 1.0210951-1$$
$$= 0.021091$$

(iv) The difference between the two growth rates (D) that is of Periphery Zone and Non-Periphery Zone was found as follows:

$$D = 0.0457411-0.0210951$$
$$= 0.0246460$$

(v) Periphery Zone's population was projected by solving two equations A and B.

$$A = (PZ_{2000}/\text{Non-}PZ_{2000}) \times e^{(5\times D)}$$
$$= (991684/43549349) \times e^{(5 \times .0246460)}$$
$$= (0.0227715) \times e^{(0.12323)}$$
$$= (0.0227715) \times 1.1311446$$
$$= 0.0257578 \text{ .... equation 1}$$

$$B = [A/(1+A)] \text{ .... equation 2}$$
$$= [0.0257578/1.0257578]$$
$$= 0.0251109$$

TABLE 6.5

Projected Population of Periphery Zone by Urban-Rural Growth Differential Technique : 2001 to 2020

Year	*Population*	
2001	1037041	(Actual)
2002	1077276	
2003	1122804	
2004	1170256	
2005	1219708	
2006	1269052	
2007	1320386	
2008	1373797	
2009	1429368	
2010	1487188	
2011	1545299	
2012	1605683	
2013	1668427	
2014	1733623	
2015	1801366	
2016	1865126	
2017	1931144	
2018	1999499	
2019	2070273	
2020	2143549	

Source : Projection outputs.

PZ_{2005} = B × PH_{2005} [Combined population of Punjab and Haryana]
= 0.0251109 × 48572871
= 1219708

(vi) Same procedure for projecting the population for the successive years of 2010, 2015 and 2020 has been adopted.

(vii) Figures for individual years were obtained through interpolation.

Table 6.5 depicts the results obtained by this technique.

The projected population in 2020 by the Urban-Rural Growth Differential technique is higher by 12.6 per cent than by the Ratio technique. The population of the Periphery Zone is projected at 2.14 million in 2020, an addition of 1.10 million to the recorded population of 1.04 million in 2001.

COMPOUND ANNUAL GROWTH RATE

This method is based on the assumption that in a given set up the population growth behaviour is likely to extend both in the direction (increase/decrease) and extent (quantum) in future also, at least in the short run. The underlying belief is that the basic determinants of population growth namely fertility, mortality and migration, do not change abruptly in their level and direction. This has been found to be true of large systems of population. The technique does not permit much confidence when applied to smaller systems of population (Krishan, 1994, p. 18).

Data requirements of this technique include population figures of the sub-national area, that is Periphery Zone in this case, for the latest and as many preceding census years. In this technique, the projections of population for the sub-national area are independent of what is happening to the larger system.

The steps followed for projecting the population of the Periphery Zone are listed below:

Steps

(i) The compound annual growth rate (CAGR) was referred to the following formula:

$$CAGR = [(p_1/p_0)^{1/t}-1] \times 100$$

(ii) It is likely that some exceptional event, such as a short term construction project may distort the population growth behaviour during a particular decade. To take care and moderate the effect of such a situation, compound annual growth rates were calculated for the preceding three decades (1971-

2001), two decades (1981-2001) and one decade (1991-2001), applied to the base population and an average of the three results obtained thereby.

CAGR of 1971-2001 = $[(p_{2001}/p_{1971})^{1/t}-1] \times 100$
= $[(1037041/286796)^{1/30}-1] \times 100$
= 4.38 per cent .... (a)

CAGR of 1981-2001 = $[(p_{2001}/p_{1981})^{1/t}-1] \times 100$
= $[(1037041/417773)^{1/20}-1] \times 100$
= 4.65 per cent .... (b)

CAGR of 1991-2001 = $[(p_{2001}/p_{1991})^{1/t}-1] \times 100$
= $[(1037041/663065)^{1/10}-1] \times 100$
= 4.57 per cent .... (c)

Hence :

(a) With CAGR of 1971-2001 as 4.38 per cent

P_{2011} = $P_{2001} \times [(100 + CAGR)/100]^{10}$
= $1037041 \times [100+4.38)/100]^{10}$
= $1037041 \times [104.38/100]^{10}$
= 1037041×1.5352282
= 1592094 .... (a)

(b) With CAGR of 1981-2001 as 4.65 per cent

P_{2011} = $1037041 \times [100+4.65)/100]^{10}$
= $1037041 \times [104.65/100]^{10}$
= 1037041×1.5754054
= 1633760 .... (b)

(c) With CAGR of 1991-2001 as 4.57 per cent

P_{2011} = $1037041 \times [100+4.57)/100]^{10}$
= $1037041 \times [104.57/100]^{10}$
= 1037041×1.5634035
= 1621313 .... (c)

The average of a, b and c (1,592,094, 1,633,760 and 1,621,313) works out to be 1,615,722.

Similar procedure was adopted for projecting the population for 2021. To project the populations for intervening years on a yearly basis, the interpolation technique was employed. Table 6.6 provides the results obtained.

TABLE 6.6

Projected Population of Periphery Zone by Compound Annual Growth Rate Technique: 2001 to 2020

Year	*Population*
2001	1037041 (Actual)
2002	1084059
2003	1133210
2004	1184588
2005	1238296
2006	1294439
2007	1353128
2008	1414477
2009	1478608
2010	1545647
2011	1615722
2012	1689454
2013	1766550
2014	1847165
2015	1931459
2016	2019599
2017	2111761
2018	2208129
2019	2308895
2020	2414259

Source : Projection outputs.

The technique seems to have an inflating tendency, probably because of the increasing base of population year by year. The projected population of the Periphery Zone for the year 2020 by this technique is 2.41 million. This figure is higher by 11.2 per cent than that obtained by the Urban-Rural Growth Differential technique.

EXTRAPOLATION

This technique is based on the same lines of reasoning as that of compound annual growth rate method. There is,

TABLE 6.7

Projected Population of Periphery Zone by Extrapolation Technique : 2001 to 2020

Year	*Population*
2001	1037041 (Actual)
2002	1069472
2003	1102918
2004	1137410
2005	1172980
2006	1209662
2007	1247492
2008	1286505
2009	1326738
2010	1368229
2011	1411018
2012	1444584
2013	1478949
2014	1514132
2015	1550152
2016	1587028
2017	1624782
2018	1663434
2019	1703006
2020	1743518

Source : Projection outputs.

however, a distinct departure in its working. Herein, the increase or decrease in population is computed in absolute numbers not in terms of rate. A rationale underlying this technique is that any numerical rise in the contribution made by a natural increase, associated with a successively bigger base over the year, will be counter-balanced by a decrease in the net in-migration.

The working of the technique can be demonstrated in the case of the Periphery Zone as follows:

Steps

$$
\begin{aligned}
P_{2011} &= (2 \times P_{2001}) - P_{1991} \\
&= (2 \times 1037041) - 663065 \\
&= 2074082 - 663065 \\
&= 1411017 \\
P_{2021} &= (2 \times P_{2011}) - P_{2001} \\
&= (2 \times 1411017) - 1037041 \\
&= 2822034 - 1037041 \\
&= 1784993
\end{aligned}
$$

Interpolation was done for computing the population on a yearly basis. Thus the projected population for 2020 is only 1.74 million. Table 6.7 represents the results obtained in detail.

The projected figures seem to be depressed due to an assumed constraint on net in-migration.

COHORT COMPONENT TECHNIQUE

With the construction of 'the component technique' of projecting populations, the art of making population forecasts has acquired the rigour of a science. The rationale of the component method rests on the undisputable fact that population growth is the function of three vital processes of fertility, mortality and migration. As each of these factors have distinct age and sex profile, it becomes essential to mathematically incorporate age-sex structures in any exercise aiming at a population projection.

The cohort component population projection technique follows each cohort of population throughout its lifetime according to its exposure to fertility, mortality, and migration.

The software package DemProj (Constella Futures, Washington, DC) is directly serviceable for the purpose.

To be more specific, each age group is seen as subject to varying chances of dying, as determined by projected mortality levels by sex and age. Once deaths are estimated, they are subtracted from the population. The surviving are taken as elderly.

Fertility rates are projected and applied to the female population, in childbearing ages by estimating the number of births every year. Each cohort of children born is also followed through time by exposing it to the mortality factor.

Finally, the component of net migration is taken into account. Net-migrants are added to or subtracted from the population at each specific age. The whole process is repeated for each year of the projection period. This ultimately yields the projected population by age and the sex, birth and death rates, population growth rate, and other summary measures of fertility, mortality, and migration for each year.

The actual working of the technique, however, requires a variety of data as an input. These may be itemized as:

(i) base-year population size (for 2001, in the present case), and its break up by sex, and age categories of 0-4, 5-9, 10-14 ——— up to the final category of 80+
(ii) total fertility rate for the base-year and as well as for the subsequent years up to 2020 on yearly basis
(iii) age-specific fertility rate for the base year
(iv) sex ratio at birth, that is the number of male births per 100 females births for the base-year as well as for the subsequent years up to 2020 on a yearly basis
(v) life expectancy at birth for males and females for the base year as well for the subsequent years up to 2020 on a yearly basis
(vi) model life table which fits into the context, and
(vii) net-migrants by sex and age for the base year and for subsequent years up to 2020 on yearly basis.

The data for this projection technique has been accessed from the Census of India and the Sample Registration System (SRS) Reports. The Census provided information on the size and structure of the population while the SRS was the source of reliable time series estimates of birth and death rates.

Steps

Population size and distribution for the base year : The starting point for making population projection using cohort component technique is to obtain population data by age and sex in the base year, that is 2001 in this case. For both males and females, the population is divided into five-year age groups from 0-4 to 75-79. The final age group covers people aged 80 and above.

It is a well-known fact that the data on age is susceptible to several infirmities, such as misreporting, underreporting, and no reporting. Any distortion in the base year data could lead to wrong estimations. Consequently, an effort should be made to detect errors in age data and make the necessary rectification to correct them. There is an equal need to smoothen the age-sex distribution of population. In this case, the data smoothened by the Technical Group on Population Projections May 2006, has been used (Table 6.8).

Age-Sex Structure: The data on the age-sex structure of the population of the Periphery Zone is not available. But then Cohort Component technique cannot proceed without such data. Hence an assumption was made that the age structure of males and females in the Periphery Zone would be the same as that of Punjab and Haryana. The following procedure was followed to generate the requisite data, to begin with that of the male population.

- All males in Punjab and Haryana were added by age groups. For example males in 0-4 years in Punjab (1292 thousand) and those in Haryana (1342 thousand) are added (2634 thousand) to get the combined population of the two states in 0-4 age group.
- The process was repeated for all the successive age groups of males.
- Male population in all age groups is added up to obtain their total population. This was 24349 thousand in this case.

TABLE 6.8

Punjab and Haryana

Smoothened Population Classified by Age and Sex, 2001

Age groups (in years)	*Punjab*		*Haryana*		*Punjab + Haryana*		*Punjab + Haryana*	
	Males (in 000)	*Females (in 000)*	*Males (in 000)*	*Females (in 000)*	*Males (in 000)*	*Females (in 000)*	*Percentage share in male population*	*Percentage share in Female population*
	1	2	3	4	1+3	2+4		
(1)	(2)	(3)	(4)	(5)	(6)	(7)	(8)	(9)
0-4	1292	1047	1342	1135	2634	2182	10.83	10.31
5-9	1413	1166	1392	1168	2805	2334	11.52	11.03
10-14	1481	1249	1399	1172	2880	2421	11.83	11.44
15-19	1397	1184	1269	1028	2666	2212	10.95	10.46
20-24	1234	1069	1088	896	2322	1965	9.54	9.29
25-29	1047	961	921	819	1968	1780	8.08	8.41
30-34	925	885	799	746	1724	1631	7.08	7.71
35-39	863	806	711	649	1574	1455	6.46	6.88
40-44	766	681	603	522	1369	1203	5.62	5.69
45-49	634	540	475	395	1109	935	4.55	4.42

50-54	489	410	350	293	839	703	3.45	3.32
55-59	364	339	258	243	622	582	2.55	2.75
60-64	312	326	225	241	537	567	2.21	2.68
65-69	286	286	209	216	495	502	2.03	2.37
70-74	259	233	186	170	445	403	1.83	1.90
75-79	145	115	88	53	233	168	0.96	0.79
80+	78	77	47	35	125	112	0.51	0.53
Total	12985	11374	11364	9781	24349	21155	100.0	100.0

Source : *Population Projections for India and States 2001-26*, Report of the Technical Group on Population Projections by the National Commission on Population, May 2006, Census of India, Office of the Registrar General and Census Commissioner, India, New Delhi.

- The share of males in the 0-4 years (2634 thousand) to the male population of both states (24349 thousand) was calculated. This worked out as 10.83 per cent.
- The same process was repeated for all the successive age groups, up to 80+ years.
- The same very procedure was adopted for generating the age-structure data of females for the states of Punjab and Haryana.

Age-Sex Structure of the Periphery Zone : The percentage share of males and females as obtained for all age groups of Punjab and Haryana together, was applied to the respective male and female populations of the Periphery Zone. For example, the share of male population in 0-4 years age group was 10.83 per cent for the year 2001 in the case of Punjab and Haryana. The same percentage was applied to the male population of the Periphery Zone, 572 thousand. This worked out to be 61 thousand. The same procedure was repeated for all other groups. On the same pattern of calculation, data were generated in respect of the number of females in different age groups. Table 6.9 presents the results obtained.

Total Fertility Rates: Information on the total fertility rate for the base year and its likely disposition in coming years is another data requirement of the Cohort Component technique. Again, this data is not available for the Periphery Zone. It had to be derived indirectly from the total fertility rates of Punjab and Haryana. National Family Health Survey 1 and 2 and Sample Registration System (SRS) are the two surveys which provide the estimates on the fertility rates for these two states. Narasimhan *et. al.* (1997) opine that since SRS estimates are not subject to displacement, they are likely to be closer to the true level of fertility than either the NFHS-1 and NFHS-2 estimates (National Family Health Survey, Punjab, 1998-99, p. 61). Hence recourse was taken to the SRS data, and the following procedure was adopted for working out the total fertility rate of the Periphery Zone, as derived from the available information for Punjab and Haryana.

TABLE 6.9

Estimated Population of Periphery Zone by Age and Sex, 2001

Age group (in years)	*Males (in 000)*	*Females (in 000)*
0-4	61	48
5-9	66	51
10-14	68	53
15-19	63	49
20-24	55	43
25-29	46	39
30-34	40	36
35-39	37	32
40-44	32	26
45-49	26	21
50-54	20	15
55-59	15	13
60-64	13	12
65-69	12	11
70-74	10	9
75-79	5	4
80+	3	2
All	572	464

Source : Calculated from Census of India, 2001, *Primary Census Abstract, Punjab and Haryana*, Registrar General of India, New Delhi.

Steps

- Multiply the female population of Punjab (11374 thousand) by the state's total fertility rate in 2001 (2.4). The resultant figure is 27297.6.
- Multiply the female population of Haryana (9781 thousand) by the state's total fertility rate in 2001 (3.2). This works out as 31299.2.

- Add up the two figures that is 27297.6 + 31299.2 = 58596.8.
- Divide the above figure by the combined female population of Punjab and Haryana (11374+9781), that is 21155.
- The result obtained is 2.77. This is the total fertility rate of Punjab and Haryana Combined together in 2001.
- This figure of 2.77 was adopted as the total fertility rate of the Periphery Zone in 2001 (Table 6.10).

TABLE 6.10

Periphery Zone : Population-Weighted Total Fertility Rates Generated up to 2001

Year	*State*	*Female population (in 000)*	*Total fertility rate*	*Female population (in 000) × total fertility rate*		*Total fertility rate*
2001	Punjab	11374	× 2.4	27297.6	58596.8/	2.77
	Haryana	+ 9781	× 3.2	+ 31299.2	21155	
	Total	21155		58596.8		

Source : Calculated from the data made available by Sample Registration System, *Statistical Report, 2000, Report No. 5 of 2003*, Registrar General and Census Commissioner, India, New Delhi and *Population Projections for India and States, 2001-26,* May 2006, Census of India, New Delhi.

- For estimating total fertility rate of the Periphery Zone for the successive years up to 2020, it was further assumed that its total fertility rate would be the same as that of Punjab and Haryana together till 2020.
- By making use of the data pertaining to the number of female populations and total fertility rates in Punjab and Haryana at five year intervals till 2020, the population weighted total fertility rates of the Periphery Zone were worked out for the years 2006, 2011, 2016 and 2020.

TABLE 6.11

Periphery Zone : Population-Weighted Total Fertility Rates Generated up to 2020

Year	*State*	*Female population (in 000)*	*Total fertility rate*	*Female population (in 000) × total fertility rate*		*Total fertility rate*
2006	Punjab	12104	× 2.1	25418.4	51208.8/	2.24
	Haryana	+ 10746	× 2.4	25709.4	22850	
	Total	22850		51208.8		
2011	Punjab	12792	× 1.9	24304.8	48843.3/	1.99
	Haryana	+ 11685	× 2.1	24538.5	24477	
	Total	24477		48843.3		
2016	Punjab	13394	× 1.8	24109.2	48022.6/	1.85
	Haryana	+ 12586	× 1.9	23913.4	25980	
	Total	25980		48022.6		
2020	Punjab	13790	× 1.8	24822	48666.6/	1.8
	Haryana	+ 13247	× 1.8	23844.6	27037	
	Total	27037		48666.6		

Source : Calculated from the data made available by Sample Registration System, *Statistical Report, 2000, Report No. 5 of 2003,* Registrar General and Census Commissioner, India, New Delhi and *Population Projections for India and States, 2001-26,* May 2006, Census of India, New Delhi.

- Table 6.11 illustrates the procedure.
- TFRs generated at an interval of five years were interpolated to get figures for the intervening years. Table 6.12 gives year-wise total fertility rate of the Periphery Zone for the years 2001-2020.

Age Specific Fertility Rate: In addition to the total fertility rates on a yearly basis, the age distribution of fertility in the base-year for Periphery Zone is an additional requirement of

TABLE 6.12

Population-Weighted Total Fertility Rates Generated for the Periphery Zone, 2001-2020

Year	*Estimated total fertility rate*
2001	2.77
2002	2.65
2003	2.53
2004	2.41
2005	2.30
2006	2.24
2007	2.19
2008	2.14
2009	2.09
2010	2.04
2011	1.99
2012	1.96
2013	1.93
2014	1.91
2015	1.88
2016	1.85
2017	1.84
2018	1.82
2019	1.81
2020	1.80

Source : Projection inputs.

the Cohort Component technique. The age specific fertility rates in the 15-49 years age group at an interval of five years, starting with 15-19 and ending with 45-49 years age group, are an essential input. Since no such data on age specific fertility rates are available for the Periphery Zone, these were also generated with an assumption that the Periphery Zone would have the same age specific fertility rate as were prevailing in Punjab and Haryana put together for the base year, that is 2001.

Table 6.13 shows the data required and generated for the Periphery Zone.

TABLE 6.13

Female Population-Weighted Age Specific Fertility Rates for Punjab, Haryana and Periphery Zone, 2001

Age group (in years)	*Age specific fertility rates (ASFRs)*		*Female population (in 000) in the age group*		*Population-weighted ASFRs for Periphery Zone*
	Punjab	*Haryana*	*Punjab*	*Haryana*	
15-19	16.5	44.9	1184	1028	29.70
20-24	203.4	275.4	1069	896	236.13
25-29	181.6	186.2	961	819	183.72
30-34	62.3	79.2	885	746	70.03
35-39	20.1	28.9	806	649	24.02
40-44	3.3	15.9	681	522	8.77
45-49	1.3	4.2	540	395	2.53

Source : Sample Registration System, *Statistical Report, 2000, Report No. 5 of 2003*, Registrar General and Census Commissioner, India, New Delhi and *Population Projections for India and States, 2001-26*, May 2006, Census of India, New Delhi.

Age specific fertility rates in each group were given population-weights *vis-a-vis* the female population in the two states. For example, in respect of the 15-19 age group in the case of Punjab, female population of 1184 thousand was multiplied by the fertility rate of 16.5 in that age in 2001. Likewise female population of 1028 thousand in Haryana was multiplied by the fertility rate of 44.9 in the same age group in 2001. The two results were added (19536+46157=65693) and the sum was divided by the combined female population of the two states, that is 2212 thousand, in this case. This figure of 29.70 population-weighted fertility rate for the age group of 15-19 years was adopted for the Periphery Zone in 2001.

The process was repeated for all successive age groups. Table 6.14 shows all the calculations for deriving the fertility

TABLE 6.14

Age-Specific Fertility Rates Generated for Periphery Zone, 2001

Year	*State*	*Female population (in 000)*	*ASFRs 2000*	*Female population (in 000) × age specific fertility rate*		*Female population weighted ASFRs for Periphery Zone*
15-19	Punjab	1184	× 16.5	19536	65693.2/	29.7
	Haryana	+ 1028	× 44.9	46157.2	2212	
	Total	2212		65693.2		
20-24	Punjab	1069	× 203.4	217434.6	464193.0/	236.23
	Haryana	+ 896	× 275.4	246758.4	1965	
	Total	1965		464193		
25-29	Punjab	961	× 181.6	174517.6	327015.4/	183.72
	Haryana	+ 819	× 186.2	152497.8	1780	
	Total	1780		327015.4		
30-34	Punjab	885	× 62.3	55135.5	114218.7/	70.03
	Haryana	+ 746	× 79.2	59083.2	1631	
	Total	1631		114218.7		
35-39	Punjab	806	× 20.5	16523	35279.1/	24.25
	Haryana	+ 649	× 28.9	18756.1	1455	
	Total	1455		35279.1		
40-44	Punjab	681	× 3.3	2247.3	10547.1/	8.77
	Haryana	+ 522	× 15.9	8299.8	1203	
	Total	1203		10547.1		
45-49	Punjab	540	× 1.3	702	2361/	2.53
	Haryana	+ 395	× 4.2	1659	935	
	Total	935		2361		

Source : Calculated from the data made available by Sample Registration System, *Statistical Report, 2000, Report No. 5 of 2003*, Registrar General and Census Commissioner, India, New Delhi and *Population Projections for India and States, 2001-26*, May 2006, Census of India, New Delhi.

rates for the rest of the groups up to 45-49 years for the Periphery Zone. The results, as obtained in the following table, were treated as the inputs for the fertility rates of all age groups for the Periphery Zone as required for making the projections.

Sex Ratio at Birth : Data on sex ratio at birth that is number of male births per every 100 female births is another requirement for making projections by the Cohort Component technique. The sex ratio at birth for the period 1998-2000, as given in the Report of the Sample Registration System, 2000 and used by the Report of the Technical Group on Population Projections while making Population Projections for India and States for 2001-2026, was put in service for the present exercise. Since the data on sex ratio at birth was not available for the Periphery Zone an assumption was made here that its sex ratio at birth would be the same as that of Punjab and Haryana put together. The population-weighted sex ratio at birth of these two states in combine was worked out to get the requisite figure for the Periphery Zone.

The procedure adopted for the purpose was the same as that for Total Fertility Rate, as illustrated below in Table 6.15.

TABLE 6.15

Sex Ratio at Birth for Punjab, Haryana and Periphery Zone, 2001

State	*Population (in 000)*	*Sex ratio at birth*	*Population x Sex ratio at birth*	*Population-weighted sex ratio at birth*	*Population-weighted sex ratio at birth for the Periphery Zone*
Punjab	24359	× 126	3069234	5712359/	125
Haryana	+ 21145	× 125	2643125	45504	
Total	45504		5712359		

Source : Calculated from the data made available by Sample Registration System, *Statistical Report, 2000, Report No. 5 of 2003*, Registrar General and Census Commissioner, India, New Delhi and *Population Projections for India and States, 2001-26*, May 2006, Census of India, New Delhi.

It was further assumed that the sex ratio at birth would remain the same that is 125 in the Periphery Zone for all the years up to 2020 as demonstrated in Table 6.16.

TABLE 6.16
Sex Ratio at Birth in Periphery Zone, 2001-20

Year	*Sex ratio at birth (number of male births per every 100 female births)*
2001	125
2005	125
2010	125
2015	125
2020	125

Source : Projection inputs.

Life Expectancy at Birth: Life expectancy at birth is the average number of years that a cohort of people would live, subject to the prevailing age-specific mortality rate. Data on this parameter, both for the males and females, is one of the requisites for making population projections.

Since no data on mortality rates of the Periphery Zone is available, these were derived from those of Punjab and Haryana put together. This was consistent with the assumption made in similar cases earlier. It was also assumed that the same mortality rates prevailing in the base year that is at 2001 would persist for all the years till 2020.

Data on the existing and likely mortality rates in future for Punjab and Haryana was taken from the Report of the Technical Group on Population Projections, Census of India, May 2006. For projecting the likely levels of expectation of life at birth (e_o), age-specific mortality rates working models developed by the United Nations were adopted. An underlying assumption of these models is that increase in the life expectancy becomes relatively slower as it reaches higher levels.

TABLE 6.17

Projected Life Expectancy and Male Population for Punjab and Haryana, 2001-21

Years	*Life expectancy at birth (in years)*		*Male population (in 000)*	
	Punjab	*Haryana*	*Punjab*	*Haryana*
2001	67.7	66.4	12985	11364
2006	68.7	67.9	13956	12568
2011	69.7	68.9	14886	13754
2016	70.7	69.9	15718	14892
2021	71.5	70.9	16432	15944

Source : *Population Projections for India and States, 2001-26,* Report of the Technical Group on Population Projections by the National Commission on Population, May 2006, Census of India, Registrar General and Census Commissioner, India, New Delhi.

Table 6.17 represents the existing and projected life expectancy at birth for the male population for Punjab and Haryana from 2001 to 2021 on a five-year interval. This was used to derive the population-weighted life expectancy at birth for the males in the Periphery Zone.

The Table 6.18 demonstrates the working of the data.

Life expectancy at birth for females: The same procedure was followed for estimating the life expectancy at birth for females. Table 6.19 represents the existing and projected life expectancy at birth for females and female population for Punjab and Haryana from 2001 to 2021 on a five-year interval.

This data was used for deriving the population-weighted life expectancy at birth for the females in the Periphery Zone. Table 6.20 demonstrates the working of the data.

After having worked out the life expectancy separately for males and females in the Periphery Zone at a five-year interval, that is, for 2001, 2006, 2011, 2016 and 2021 the figures for intervening years were obtained through interpolation. Table 6.21 presents the results obtained.

TABLE 6.18

Population-Weighted Life Expectancy of Males in the Periphery Zone, 2001-20

Year	*State*	*Male population (in 000)*	*Life expectancy at birth*	*Male population (000) × Life expectancy at birth*	*Population weighted life expectancy of males in Punjab and Haryana*	*Population-weighted life expectancy of Periphery Zone*
2001	Punjab	12985	× 67.7	879084.5	1633654.1/	67.1
	Haryana	+ 11364	× 66.4	754569.6	24349	
	Total	24349		1633654.1		
2006	Punjab	13956	× 68.7	958777.2	1812144.4/	68.3
	Haryana	+ 12568	× 67.9	853367.2	26524	
	Total	26524		1812144.4		
2011	Punjab	14886	× 69.7	1037554.2	1985204.8/	69.3
	Haryana	+ 13754	× 68.9	947650.6	28640	
	Total	28640		1985204.8		
2016	Punjab	15718	× 70.7	1111262.6	2152213.4/	70.3
	Haryana	+ 14892	× 69.9	1040950.8	30610	
	Total	30610		2152213.4		
2021	Punjab	16432	× 71.5	1174888	2305317.6/	71.2
	Haryana	+ 15944	× 70.9	1130429.6	32376	
	Total	32376		2305317.6		

Source : Calculated from the data made available by *Population Projections for India and States, 2001-26*, Report of the Technical Group on Population Projections by the National Commission on Population, May 2006, Census of India, Registrar General and Census Commissioner, India, New Delhi.

TABLE 6.19

Projected Life Expectancy and Female Population for Punjab and Haryana, 2001-21

Years	*Life expectancy at birth (in years)*		*Female population (in 000)*	
	Punjab	*Haryana*	*Punjab*	*Haryana*
2001	70.4	68.3	11374	9781
2006	71.6	69.8	12104	10746
2011	72.8	71.3	12792	11685
2016	73.8	72.5	13394	12586
2021	74.8	73.7	13891	13418

Source : *Population Projections for India and States, 2001-26,* Report of the Technical Group on Population Projections by the National Commission on Population, May 2006, Census of India, Registrar General and Census Commissioner, India, New Delhi.

With the birth rate falling regularly and death rate having reached saturation point, the future population growth in the Periphery Zone will be influenced more by the factor of net-migration (Table 6.22). Hence, computation of net-migration is one of the essentials for projecting its population.

Net-Migration: This is the outcome of the difference between the volume of in-migration and that of out-migration. Since the data on existing number of net-migrants was not available, it was generated by : (i) deriving their number, separately for males and females by working out the difference between actual and natural growth rates of population during 1981-91 and 1991-2001, (ii) projecting their numbers by 2011 and 2021 by using extrapolation technique, and (iii) estimating their number for various years by interpolating the estimates for 2001 and 2021.

The actual working is demonstrated below for estimating male-net-migrants during 1981-91.

TABLE 6.20

Population-Weighted Life Expectancy of Females in the Periphery Zone, 2001-20

Year	*State*	*Female population (in 000)*	*Life expectancy at birth (in years)*	*Female population (000) × Life expectancy at birth*	*Population-weighted life expectancy of Female in Punjab and Haryana*	*Population-weighted life expectancy of Periphery Zone (in years)*
2001	Punjab	11374	× 70.4	800729.6	1468771.9/	69.4
	Haryana	+ 9781	× 68.3	668042.3	21155	
	Total	21155		1468772		
2006	Punjab	12104	× 71.6	866646.4	1616717.2/	70.7
	Haryana	+ 10746	× 69.8	750070.8	22850	
	Total	22850		1616717		
2011	Punjab	12792	× 72.8	931257.6	1764398.1/	72.1
	Haryana	+ 11685	× 71.3	833140.5	24477	
	Total	24477		1764398		
2016	Punjab	13394	× 73.8	988477.2	1885858/	73.2
	Haryana	+ 12586	× 72.5	912485	25980	
	Total	25980		1900962		
2021	Punjab	13891	× 74.8	1039047	2027953.4/	74.3
	Haryana	+ 13418	× 73.7	988906.6	27309	
	Total	27309		2027953		

Source : Calculated from the data made available by *Population Projections for India and States, 2001-26*, Report of the Technical Group on Population Projections by the National Commission on Population, May 2006, Census of India, Registrar General and Census Commissioner, India, New Delhi.

TABLE 6.21

Estimated Life Expectancy at Birth for Males and Female in Periphery Zone, 2001-20

Year	*Males (Years)*	*Females (Years)*
2001	67.1	69.4
2002	67.3	69.7
2003	67.6	69.9
2004	67.8	70.2
2005	68.1	70.4
2006	68.3	70.7
2007	68.5	71.0
2008	68.7	71.3
2009	68.9	71.5
2010	69.1	71.8
2011	69.3	72.1
2012	69.5	72.2
2013	69.7	72.3
2014	69.9	72.4
2015	70.1	72.5
2016	70.3	73.2
2017	70.5	73.4
2018	70.7	73.7
2019	70.8	73.9
2020	71.0	74.2

Source : Calculated from the data made available by *Population Projections for India and States, 2001-26*, Report of the Technical Group on Population Projections by the National Commission on Population, May 2006, Census of India, Registrar General and Census Commissioner, India, New Delhi.

Table 6.22

Population Classified by Sex in Periphery Zone and Birth and Death Rates in Punjab and Haryana during 1981-2001

Year	*Males*	*Females*	*Birth Rate*		*Death Rate*	
			Punjab	*Haryana*	*Punjab*	*Haryana*
1981	229140	187389	30.3	36.5	9.4	11.3
1991	363885	298326	27.7	33.1	7.8	8.2
2001	572228	464965	21.6	26.9	7.4	7.5

Source : Different Issues of *Primary Census Abstract, Punjab and Haryana, 1981 to 2001*, Census of India, and Sample Registration System, Bulletins, Registrar General of India, New Delhi.

Growth of male population during 1981-91 = (Male population in 1991/ Male population in 1981 – 1) × 100
= (363885/229140 –1) × 100
= 58.80 per cent

Growth of male population due to natural increase = 22.80 per cent (Birth rate being 31.9 and death rate 9.1)

Growth of male population due to net-migrants = (58.80 – 22.80) per cent
= 36.0 per cent

Male net-migrants during 1981-91 = (Male population in 1981 × 36.0)/100
= (229140 × 36.0)/100
= 82490

Same way male net-migrants during 1991-2001 were worked out as 135547. Likewise, the female net-migrants were derived as 68209 during 1981-91 and 106950 during 1991-2001.

Male net-migrants for 2011 (Male_NM2011): After having computed figures for male net-migrants for 1991 and 2001, as also for female net-migrants for the same years, it is possible to work out net-migrants (both male and females for 2001-11 and 2011-21. This is demonstrated below:

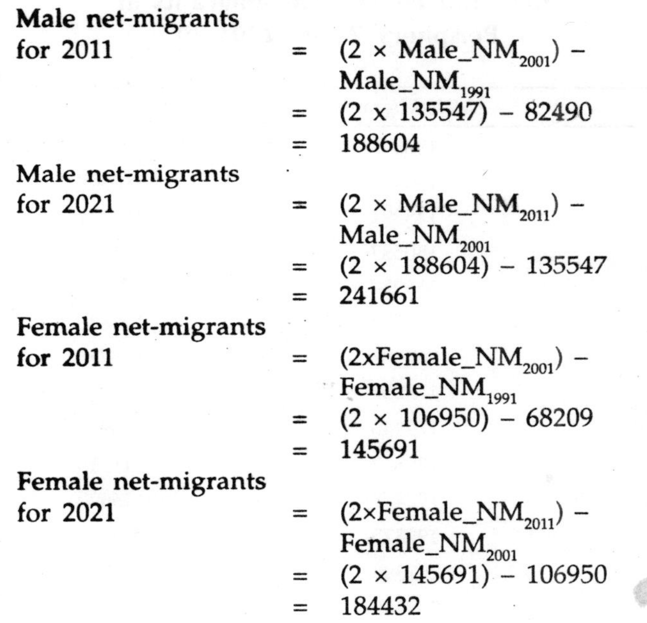

Male net-migrants for 2011 $= (2 \times \text{Male\_NM}_{2001}) - \text{Male\_NM}_{1991}$

$= (2 \times 135547) - 82490$

$= 188604$

Male net-migrants for 2021 $= (2 \times \text{Male\_NM}_{2011}) - \text{Male\_NM}_{2001}$

$= (2 \times 188604) - 135547$

$= 241661$

Female net-migrants for 2011 $= (2 \times \text{Female\_NM}_{2001}) - \text{Female\_NM}_{1991}$

$= (2 \times 106950) - 68209$

$= 145691$

Female net-migrants for 2021 $= (2 \times \text{Female\_NM}_{2011}) - \text{Female\_NM}_{2001}$

$= (2 \times 145691) - 106950$

$= 184432$

Above figures are summarized in Table 6.23.

TABLE 6.23

Number of Net-Migrants Classified by Sex for the Periphery Zone, 1981

Sex	*1981-91*	*1991-2001*	*2001-11*	*2011-21*
Male	82490	135547	188604	241661
Female	68209	106950	145691	184432

Source : Calculated from the data made available by *Sample Registration System, Bulletins*, Registrar General of India, New Delhi and different volumes of the Census of India, *Migration Tables of Punjab and Haryana*, Directorate of Punjab and Haryana.

The decade-wise data obtained on the number of net-migrants was interpolated on yearly basis for each of the sex up to 2020. Table 6.24 depicts the calculations arrived at.

TABLE 6.24
Male and Female Net-Migrants in Periphery Zone, 2001-20

Year	*Male Migrants*	*Female Migrants*
2001	135547	106950
2002	140384	110308
2003	145394	113771
2004	150583	117343
2005	155957	121027
2006	161522	124826
2007	167287	128745
2008	173257	132787
2009	179440	136956
2010	185843	141256
2011	192475	145690
2012	197375	149167
2013	202398	152726
2014	207549	156370
2015	212831	160101
2016	218247	163921
2017	223802	167832
2018	229498	171836
2019	235338	175936
2020	241328	180133

Source : Calculated from the data made available by *Sample Registration System, Bulletins,* Registrar General of India, New Delhi and different volumes of the Census of India, *Migration Tables of Punjab and Haryana,* Directorate of Punjab and Haryana.

Distribution of migrants by age and sex: Another migration-related requirement of the Cohort Component technique is the distribution of migrants by age for each sex. Such data was also not available for the Periphery Zone. Again an assumption was made that the age-structure of migrants would be the same as that of Punjab and Haryana in 2001. The age-structure of migrants was derived from the population-weighted data of Punjab and Haryana.

Compounding the difficulty was the fact that the age-structure of the net-migrants was not available even for Punjab and Haryana. An additional assumption was made that the net-migrants would have the same age-structure as that of the total migrants classified on the basis of sex. Hence, to begin with, the age-sex structure of net-migrants was constructed in congruency with that of migrants in Punjab and Haryana.

Table 6.25 presents data on age-sex structure of Punjab and Haryana as recorded by the Census of India, 2001.

Still further, another difficulty had to be coped with. The cohort Componet technique requires age-data at an interval of five years, such as 0-4, 5-9, 30-34, 35-39, 70-74 and 75-79. The Census data, however, lumps all the migrants below 15 years into one group of 0-14 and those 60 and above into a single group of 60+ years. This called for invoking another assumption, stating that the proportion of migrants in the missing age groups would be the same as their share in total population.

Table 6.26 provides data generated at five-year interval, as per the requirement of the Cohort Component Technique.

The percentage share of male migrants in the age group of 0-14 years as per the 2001 Census was 21.72 per cent. It was divided into three constituent age groups of 0-4, 5-9 and 10-14 years. The procedure followed is demonstrated in Table 6.27.

Similar procedure was followed for deriving male migrants in the 40-44 to 55-59 and 60-64 to 80+ years age groups in Punjab and Haryana. The proportion of female migrants in these age groups was also worked out, following the same procedure.

To meet yet another requirement of the Cohort Component technique is to have the age-sex structure of the migrants on yearly basis, up to the year for which projections are to be made. This was done with the help of available data for Punjab and Haryana for the years 1991 and 2001. Table 6.28

TABLE 6.25
Migrants Classified by Age and Sex for Punjab and Haryana, 2001

Age groups	*Punjab 2001*		*Haryana 2001*		*Punjab + Haryana*		*Per cent of male migrants*	*Per cent of female migrants*
	Males	*Females*	*Males*	*Females*	*Males*	*Females*		
	1	2	3	4	1+3	2+4		
0-14	672969	559785	430022	375837	1102991	935622	21.72	8.01
15-19	287325	256569	206654	299421	493979	555990	9.73	4.76
20-24	296784	629660	219922	701767	516706	1331427	10.18	11.39
25-29	260661	752393	207738	748983	468399	1501376	9.23	12.85
30-34	233568	745590	186296	685048	419864	1430638	8.27	12.24
35-39	240379	710340	184590	621446	424969	1331786	8.37	11.40
40-59	631104	1632796	454457	1294976	1085561	2927772	21.38	25.05
60+	336951	916116	210479	731473	547430	1647589	10.78	14.10
Age not stated	11101	15347	6278	9106	17379	24453	0.34	0.21
All Ages	2970842	6218596	2106436	5468057	5077278	11686653	100.0	100.0

Source : Census of India, 2001, Migration Tables.

TABLE 6.26

Migrants Classified by Age (at 5 year interval) for Punjab and Haryana, 2001

Age group (in years)	Punjab (in 000)		Haryana (in 000)		Punjab + Haryana (in 000)		Per cent of migrants (in 000)	
	Males	Females	Males	Females	Males	Females	Males	Females
	1	2	3	4	1+3	2+4		
0-4	1292	1047	1342	1135	2634	2182	6.88	2.52
5-9	1413	1166	1392	1168	2805	2334	7.32	2.70
10-14	1481	1249	1399	1172	2880	2421	7.52	2.79
					+ 8319	+6937		
40-44	766	681	603	522	1369	1203	7.43	8.80
45-49	634	540	475	395	1109	935	6.02	6.84
50-54	489	410	350	293	839	703	4.55	5.15
55-59	364	339	258	243	622	582	3.38	4.26
					+3939	+3423		
60-64	312	326	225	241	537	567	3.15	4.57
65-69	286	286	209	216	495	502	2.91	4.04
70-74	259	233	186	170	445	403	2.61	3.24
75-79	145	115	88	53	233	168	1.38	1.35
80+	78	77	47	35	125	112	0.73	0.90
					+1835	+1752		

Source : Census of India, 2001, Migration Tables.

TABLE 6.27

Derivation of Percentage of Male Migrants in 0-4, 5-9 and 10-14 Age Groups for Punjab and Haryana

Age groups	*Male population of Punjab and Haryana together*	*Number of male migrants*	*Percentage of male migrants*
0-4	2634	(Male population in 0-4 years/total of male population for 0-14 years) x total migrants in 0-14 years = (2634/8319) x 21.72 =	6.88
5-9	2805	(Male population in 5-9 years/ total of male population for 0-14 years) x total migrants in 0-14 years = (2805/8319) x 21.72 =	7.32
10-14	2880	(Male population in 10-14 years/ total of male population for 0-14 years) x total migrants in 0-14 years = (2880/8319) x 21.72 =	7.52
0-14	+8319	2880	21.72

Source : Calculations from the data made available by Census of India, 2001, Migration Tables.

presents the comparative picture of the age-sex structure of the migrants in Punjab and Haryana in 1991 and 2001.

To meet another requirement of the Cohort Component technique, the data presented in the Table below was extrapolated for the years 2001 and 2021. Using the data on age-sex structure of migrants in 2001, 2011 and 2021, year-wise proportion of migrants was derived on a yearly basis. Table 6.29 and 6.30 depict this series of data separately for male and female migrants.

Table 6.29 and 6.30, which were based on data for Punjab and Haryana together, as detailed above, were adopted as such for projecting the population of the Periphery Zone on a yearly basis for the period 2001-20 in Table 6.31.

TABLE 6.28

Migrants Classified by Age and Sex in Punjab and Haryana in 1991 and 2001

Age group (in years)	*Per cent share of male migrants 1991*	*Per cent share of female migrants 1991*	*Per cent share of male migrants 2001*	*Per cent share of female migrants 2001*
0-4	7.14	2.32	6.88	2.52
5-9	7.30	2.37	7.32	2.70
10-14	7.10	2.27	7.52	2.79
15-19	8.00	4.95	9.73	4.76
20-24	8.68	13.25	10.18	11.39
25-29	8.67	14.16	9.23	12.85
30-34	8.23	12.26	8.27	12.24
35-39	8.31	10.25	8.37	11.40
40-44	7.18	8.26	7.43	8.80
45-49	6.83	6.85	6.02	6.84
50-54	5.82	5.21	4.55	5.15
55-59	3.84	4.29	3.38	4.26
60-64	4.16	4.35	3.15	4.57
65-69	2.93	3.81	2.91	4.04
70-74	2.80	2.61	2.61	3.24
75-79	1.32	1.14	1.73	1.60
80+	1.71	1.64	0.73	0.90
Total	100.0	100.0	100.0	100.0

Source : Census of India, 1991 and 2001, Migration Tables.

POPULATION PROJECTIONS : A COMPARATIVE VIEW

A stage has been reached where we can have a comparative view of the results obtained by use of different techniques. Table 6.32 gives the output for the years 2001 to 2020. The growth differential technique gives the higher figure of 2.14 million as the projected population of the Periphery

TABLE 6.29

Year-wise Percentage Distribution of Male Migrants by Age, 2001-2020

Age Groups	2001	2002	2003	2004	2005	2006	2007	2008	2009	2010
(1)	(2)	(3)	(4)	(5)	(6)	(7)	(8)	(9)	(10)	(11)
0-4	6.9	6.8	6.8	6.8	6.8	6.7	6.7	6.7	6.7	6.6
5-9	7.3	7.3	7.3	7.3	7.3	7.3	7.3	7.3	7.3	7.4
10-14	7.5	7.6	7.6	7.7	7.7	7.7	7.8	7.9	7.9	7.9
15-19	9.7	9.9	10.1	10.3	10.5	10.6	10.9	11.1	11.2	11.4
20-24	10.2	10.3	10.5	10.6	10.8	11	11.1	11.3	11.4	11.6
25-29	9.2	9.3	9.4	9.4	9.5	9.5	9.6	9.6	9.7	9.8
30-34	8.3	8.3	8.3	8.3	8.3	8.3	8.3	8.3	8.3	8.3
35-39	8.4	8.4	8.4	8.4	8.4	8.4	8.4	8.4	8.4	8.4
40-44	7.4	7.5	7.5	7.5	7.5	7.6	7.6	7.6	7.6	7.7
45-49	6	5.9	5.8	5.8	5.7	5.6	5.5	5.4	5.3	5.3
50-54	4.6	4.4	4.3	4.2	4	3.9	3.7	3.6	3.5	3.3
55-59	3.4	3.3	3.3	3.2	3.2	3.2	3.1	3	3	2.9
60-64	3.2	3.1	2.9	2.8	2.7	2.6	2.5	2.4	2.3	2.2
65-69	2.9	2.9	2.9	2.9	2.9	2.9	2.9	2.9	2.9	2.9
70-74	2.6	2.6	2.6	2.5	2.5	2.5	2.5	2.5	2.5	2.4
75-79	1.7	1.8	1.8	1.9	1.9	2	2	2	2.1	2.1
80+	0.7	0.6	0.5	0.4	0.3	0.2	0.1	0	-0.1	-0.2
All	100	100	100	100	100	100	100	100	100	100

TABLE 6.29 (Contd.)

Age Groups	2011	2012	2013	2014	2015	2016	2017	2018	2019	2020
(1)	(12)	(13)	(14)	(15)	(16)	(17)	(18)	(19)	(20)	(21)
0-4	6.6	6.6	6.6	6.5	6.5	6.5	6.4	6.4	6.4	6.4
5-9	7.4	7.4	7.4	7.4	7.4	7.4	7.4	7.4	7.4	7.4
10-14	8	8	8.1	8.1	8.1	8.2	8.2	8.3	8.3	8.4
15-19	11.5	11.7	11.8	12.1	12.2	12.4	12.6	12.7	13	13.2
20-24	11.7	11.9	12	12.2	12.4	12.5	12.7	12.8	13	13.2
25-29	9.8	9.9	9.9	10	10.1	10.1	10.2	10.2	10.3	10.3
30-34	8.3	8.3	8.3	8.3	8.3	8.3	8.3	8.3	8.4	8.4
35-39	8.4	8.4	8.4	8.4	8.5	8.5	8.5	8.5	8.5	8.5
40-44	7.7	7.7	7.8	7.8	7.8	7.8	7.8	7.9	7.9	7.9
45-49	5.2	5.1	5	4.9	4.8	4.7	4.7	4.6	4.5	4.4
50-54	3.2	3.1	2.9	2.8	2.7	2.5	2.4	2.3	2.1	2
55-59	2.9	2.8	2.8	2.8	2.7	2.7	2.6	2.6	2.5	2.5
60-64	2.1	2	1.9	1.8	1.7	1.6	1.5	1.3	1.2	1.1
65-69	2.9	2.9	2.9	2.9	2.9	2.9	2.9	2.9	2.9	2.9
70-74	2.4	2.4	2.4	2.3	2.3	2.3	2.3	2.3	2.2	2.2
75-79	2.2	2.2	2.3	2.3	2.3	2.4	2.4	2.5	2.5	2.5
80+	-0.3	-0.4	-0.5	-0.6	-0.7	-0.8	-0.9	-1	-1.1	-1.3
All	100	100	100	100	100	100	100	100	100	100

Source : Calculations from the data made available by Census of India, 2001, Migration Tables.

TABLE 6.30

Year-wise Percentage Distribution of Female Migrants by Age, 2001-2020

Age Groups	*2001*	*2002*	*2003*	*2004*	*2005*	*2006*	*2007*	*2008*	*2009*	*2010*
(1)	*(2)*	*(3)*	*(4)*	*(5)*	*(6)*	*(7)*	*(8)*	*(9)*	*(10)*	*(11)*
0-4	2.5	2.5	2.5	2.6	2.6	2.6	2.6	2.7	2.7	2.7
5-9	2.7	2.8	2.8	2.8	2.8	2.9	2.9	2.9	2.9	3
10-14	2.8	2.8	2.9	3	3	3.1	3.2	3.2	3.2	3.3
15-19	4.8	4.8	4.8	4.7	4.7	4.7	4.7	4.7	4.6	4.6
20-24	11.4	11.2	11.1	10.7	10.6	10.4	10.2	10	9.8	9.6
25-29	12.8	12.7	12.5	12.3	12.3	12.1	12	11.8	11.7	11.6
30-34	12.2	12.2	12.2	12.2	12.2	12.2	12.2	12.2	12.2	12.2
35-39	11.4	11.5	11.6	11.8	11.9	12	12.1	12.2	12.3	12.5
40-44	8.8	8.9	8.9	9	9	9.1	9.1	9.2	9.3	9.3
45-49	6.8	6.8	6.8	6.8	6.8	6.8	6.8	6.8	6.8	6.8
50-54	5.2	5.2	5.2	5.2	5.2	5.2	5.1	5.1	5.1	5.1
55-59	4.3	4.3	4.3	4.3	4.3	4.3	4.3	4.3	4.3	4.3
60-64	4.6	4.6	4.6	4.7	4.7	4.7	4.7	4.8	4.8	4.8
65-69	4	4	4.1	4.1	4.1	4.1	4.2	4.2	4.2	4.2
70-74	3.2	3.3	3.3	3.4	3.5	3.5	3.6	3.7	3.8	3.8
75-79	1.6	1.6	1.7	1.7	1.7	1.8	1.9	1.9	2	2
80+	0.9	0.8	0.7	0.7	0.6	0.5	0.4	0.3	0.3	0.2
All	100	100	100	100	100	100	100	100	100	100

TABLE 6.30 (*Contd.*)

Age Groups	*2011*	*2012*	*2013*	*2014*	*2015*	*2016*	*2017*	*2018*	*2019*	*2020*
(1)	*(12)*	*(13)*	*(14)*	*(15)*	*(16)*	*(17)*	*(18)*	*(19)*	*(20)*	*(21)*
0-4	2.7	2.7	2.8	2.8	2.8	2.8	2.8	2.9	2.9	2.9
5-9	3	3.1	3.1	3.2	3.2	3.2	3.3	3.3	3.3	3.4
10-14	3.3	3.4	3.5	3.5	3.6	3.6	3.7	3.7	3.8	3.8
15-19	4.6	4.6	4.5	4.5	4.5	4.5	4.4	4.4	4.4	4.4
20-24	9.4	9.2	9	8.9	8.5	8.5	8.3	8.1	7.9	7.7
25-29	11.4	11.3	11.1	11	10.8	10.8	10.6	10.5	10.3	10.2
30-34	12.2	12.2	12.2	12.2	12.2	12.2	12.2	12.2	12.2	12.2
35-39	12.6	12.7	12.8	12.9	13.1	13.2	13.3	13.4	13.5	13.7
40-44	9.4	9.4	9.5	9.5	9.6	9.6	9.7	9.8	9.8	9.9
45-49	6.8	6.8	6.8	6.8	6.8	6.8	6.8	6.8	6.8	6.8
50-54	5.1	5.1	5.1	5.1	5.1	5.1	5.1	5	5	5
55-59	4.2	4.2	4.2	4.2	4.2	4.2	4.2	4.2	4.2	4.2
60-64	4.8	4.8	4.9	4.9	4.9	4.9	4.9	5	5	5
65-69	4.3	4.3	4.3	4.3	4.4	4.4	4.4	4.4	4.5	4.5
70-74	4	4	4	4.1	4.2	4.2	4.3	4.4	4.4	4.4
75-79	2.1	2.2	2.2	2.2	2.3	2.3	2.3	2.3	2.5	2.5
80+	0.1	0	0	-0.1	-0.2	-0.3	-0.3	-0.4	-0.5	-0.6
All	100	100	100	100	100	100	100	100	100	100

Source : Calculations from the data made available by Census of India, 2001, Migration Tables.

TABLE 6.31

Projected Population of the Periphery Zone by Cohort Component Technique: 2001-2020

Year	*Population (in Lakhs)*
2001	104
2002	108
2003	112
2004	116
2005	120
2006	124
2007	128
2008	133
2009	137
2010	142
2011	146
2012	151
2013	155
2014	160
2015	165
2016	169
2017	174
2018	179
2019	184
2020	189

Source : Projection outputs.

Zone in 2020. While the extrapolation technique yields a figure obtained by the Ratio and Cohort Component, also the techniques are very close to each other. These can be averaged to get at most acceptable population projections for the Periphery Zone. Table 6.32 and Figures 6.1 and 6.2 summarize the picture:

TABLE 6.32

Projected Population of Periphery Zone by Different Techniques : Ratio, Growth Differential, Extrapolation and Cohort Component Methods, 2001-2020 (in Million)

Year	*Ratio Method*	*Growth differential*	*Extrapolation*	*Cohort Component*	*Average*
2001	1.04 (actual)	1.04	1.04	1.04	1.04
2002	1.07	1.08	1.07	1.08	1.08
2003	1.11	1.12	1..10	1.12	1.11
2004	1.15	1.17	1.14	1.16	1.16
2005	1.19	1.22	117	1.20	1.20
2006	1.23	1.27	1.21	1.24	1.24
2007	1.28	1.32	1.25	1.28	1.28
2008	1.32	1.37	1.29	1.33	1.33
2009	1.37	1.43	1.33	1.37	1.38
2010	1.41	1.49	1.37	1.42	1.42
2011	1.46	1.54	1.41	1.46	1.47
2012	1.51	1.60	1.44	1.51	1.52
2013	1.55	1.67	1.48	1.55	1.56
2014	1.59	1.73	1.51	1.60	1.61
2015	1.64	1.80	1.55	1.65	1.66
2016	1.68	1.86	1.59	1.69	1.71
2017	1.73	1.93	1.62	1.74	1.76
2018	1.78	2.00	1.66	1.79	1.81
2019	1.82	2.07	1.70	1.84	1.86
2020	1.88	2.14	1.74	1.89	1.91

Source : Project outputs.

AGE STRUCTURE

Table 6.33 shows that the Periphery Zone will experience aging of population due to reduced levels of fertility. The median age of the total population will increase from 23 to 33 years. The population in the age group of 0-14 years will drastically come down from 34 per cent to 20 per cent, a

Fig. 6.1

Chandigarh Periphery Zone Population Projections : 2001-2020 (By Some Selected Methods)

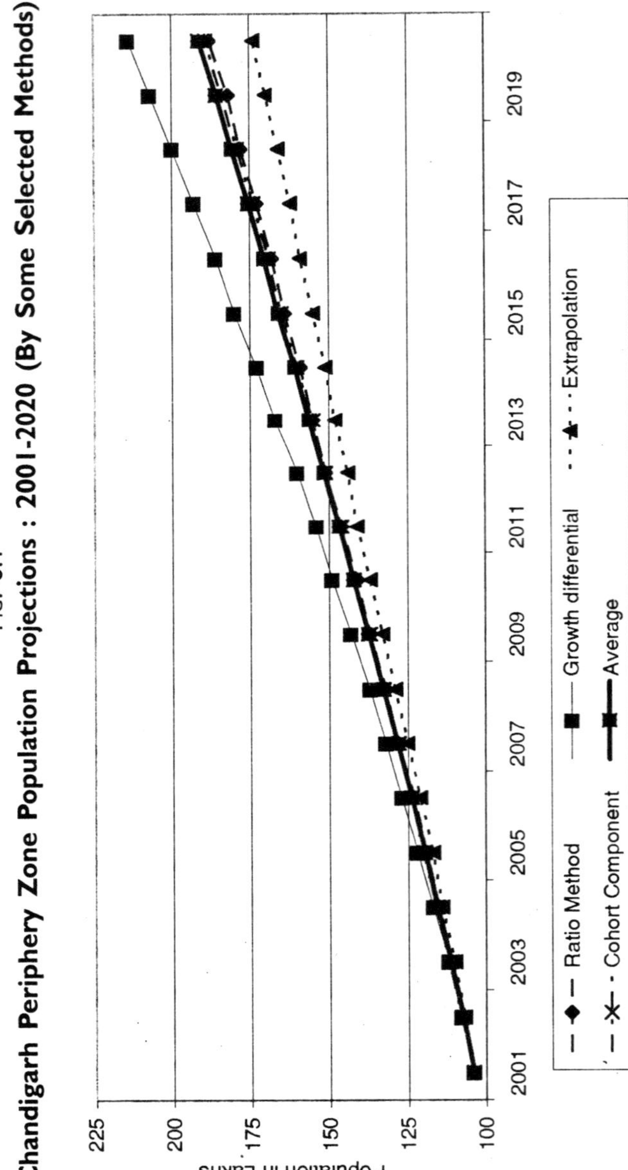

Source : Projection outputs.

FIG. 6.2

Chandigarh Periphery Zone Population Projections : 2001-2020
(Average of Extrapolation, Growth Differential, Ratio and Component Techniques)

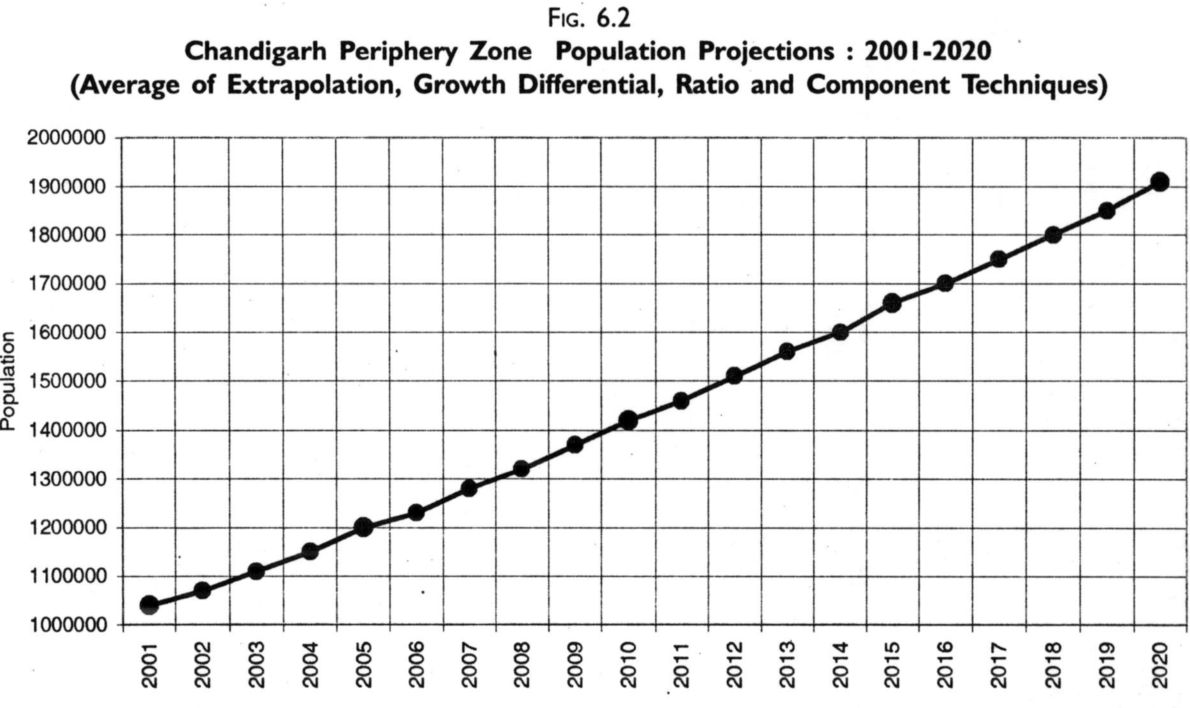

Source : Projection outputs.

decline by 14 per cent points (Table 6.33). On the other hand, the share of population in the age group of 50 years and more will increase from 14 to 22 per cent, an increase of 8 per cent points However, there will be marginal increase in the population in the age group of 15-49 years from 53 to 58 per cent. The population in the working age group of 15-64 years would increase from 61 in 2001 to 73 per cent in 2020 (Figure 6.3).

TABLE 6.33

Population of the Periphery Zone by Age Groups on Yearly Basis, 2001-2020

Year	*Population 0-14 (in per cent)*	*Population 15-64 (in per cent)*	*Population 65+ (in per cent)*	*Median age (in years)*
2001	33.49	61.10	5.41	23
2002	32.32	62.13	5.55	24
2003	31.18	63.14	5.68	24
2004	30.08	64.12	5.80	25
2005	29.04	65.06	5.90	25
2006	28.06	65.95	5.99	26
2007	27.19	66.74	6.07	26
2008	26.36	67.50	6.14	27
2009	25.63	68.16	6.21	27
2010	24.91	68.80	6.29	28
2011	24.25	69.38	6.36	28
2012	23.61	69.95	6.45	29
2013	23.02	70.44	6.54	29
2014	22.48	70.88	6.64	30
2015	22.00	71.24	6.76	31
2016	21.53	71.58	6.89	31
2017	21.04	71.91	7.05	32
2018	20.57	72.22	7.22	32
2019	20.11	72.49	7.40	33
2020	19.67	72.73	7.60	33

Source : Projection outputs.

Fig. 6.3

Age-Structure of Population in the Periphery Zone Classified by Sex, 2001-2020

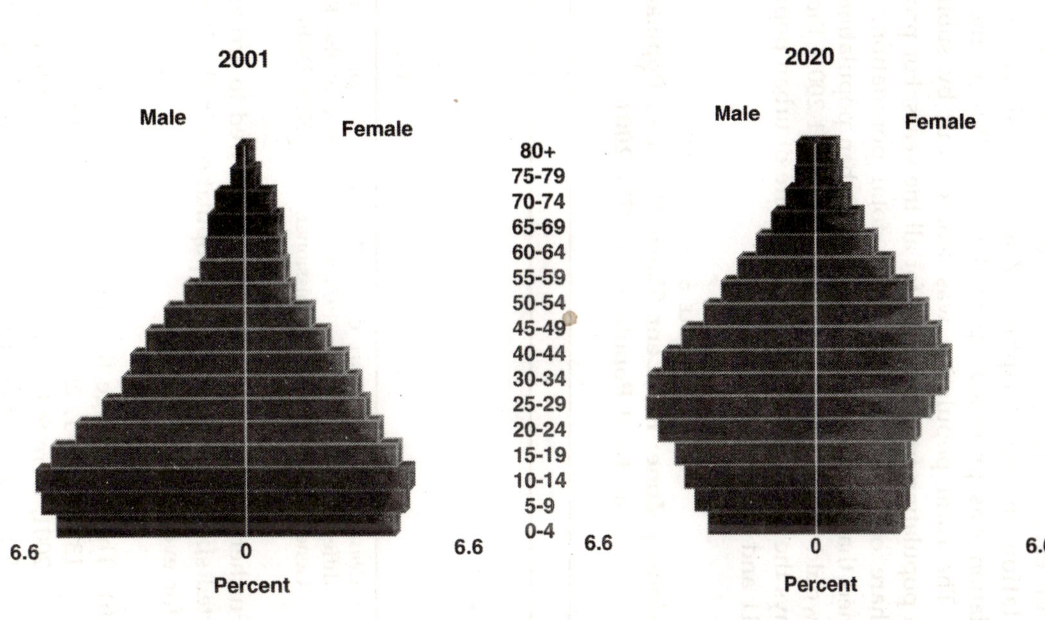

• Source : Projection outputs.

POPULATION PROJECTIONS FOR RURAL AND URBAN AREAS

For estimating the rural and urban segments of the population in the Periphery Zone, the share of urban population was projected up to the year 2020 on the yearly basis. The rural population was worked out by subtracting urban population from the total for all the years. For projecting the share of urban population in total population, it was assumed that the rate of change of the urban population up to 2020 would be the same as it was during 1971-2001. Table 6.34 displays the data used for projecting share of urban population in 2011 and 2021.

TABLE 6.34

Periphery Zone: Per Cent Share of Urban Population in Total Population : 1971-2001

Year	*Per cent Share*
1971	13.8
1981	25.7
1991	35.5
2001	44.8

Source : *Census of India, Primary Census Abstracts of Punjab and Haryana,* different volumes from 1971 to 2001, Office of the Registrar General and Census Commissioner, India, New Delhi.

Further, the following steps were followed to arrive at the projected size of urban and rural populations in the Periphery Zone for every year till 2020:

(i) The percentage figures for urban population, that is 13.8 in 1971, 25.7 in 1981, 35.5 in 1991 and 44.8 in 2001, were fed in computer and a trend line obtained for findings the projected percentage figure for 2011. The computer yielded the following equation to work this out:

$P_{2011} = 10.277 \times 5 + 4.255$
$= 55.24$

In other words, 55.24 is the projected percentage of urban population in the Periphery Zone in 2011.

(ii) Likewise, by using the percentage of urban population figures for all the census years from 1971

TABLE 6.35

Periphery Zone: Projected Total, Urban and Rural Populations, 2001-2020

Year	*Projected total population (in million)*	*Projected urban population (in million)*	*Projected rural population (in million)*
2001	1.04 (actual)	0.47 (actual)	0.57 (actual)
2002	1.08	0.49	0.59
2003	1.11	0.52	0.59
2004	1.16	0.56	0.60
2005	1.20	0.59	0.61
2006	1.24	0.62	0.62
2007	1.28	0.66	0.62
2008	1.33	0.70	0.63
2009	1.38	0.74	0.64
2010	1.42	0.77	0.65
2011	1.47	0.82	0.65
2012	1.52	0.86	0.66
2013	1.56	0.90	0.66
2014	1.61	0.94	0.67
2015	1.66	0.99	0.67
2016	1.71	1.04	0.67
2017	1.76	1.09	0.67
2018	1.81	1.14	0.67
2019	1.86	1.17	0.69
2020	1.91	1.24	0.67

Source : Projection outputs.

Fig. 6.4

Periphery Zone: Projected Total, Urban and Rural Populations, 2001-2020

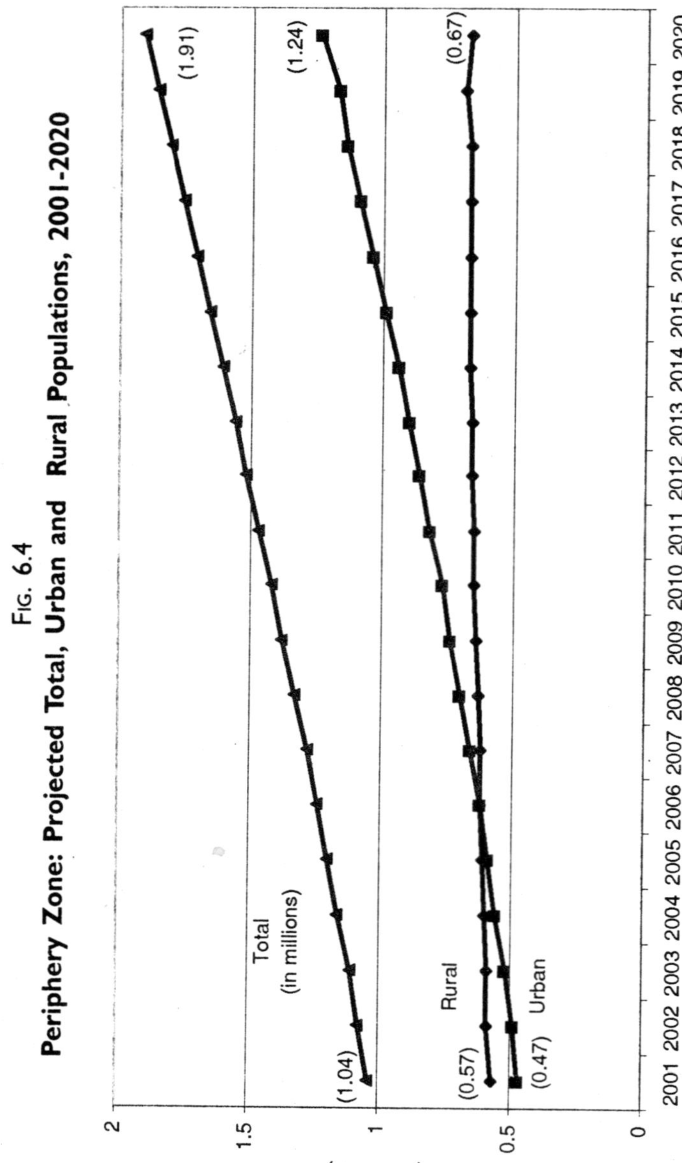

Source : Projectiton outputs. Figures in parenthesis are population in million.

to 2011, another trend was obtained for the year 2021. It gave the figure of 65.9, as percentage of urban population in the Periphery Zone in 2021.

(iii) By using the interpolation technique, figures for percentage of urban population in every year from 2001 to 2020 were arrived at.

(iv) As a corollary, the percentage of rural population in every case would be 100 minus the percentage of urban population.

(v) The percentage figures for urban and rural populations were applied to the already projected total population, and thereby the size of urban and rural population was calculated for every year.

(vi) Table 6.35 presents the results obtained.

Evidently, the size of the urban population in the Periphery Zone will increase from 0.47 million in 2001 to 1.24 million in 2020. This will enlarge the share of urban population in the total from 45 per cent in 2001 to 65 per cent in 2020. This rise by 20 per cent points in as many years is phenomenal indeed (Figure 6.4).

CONCLUSION

The working of various techniques to arrive at the projected population of the Periphery Zone brings out the paucity of requisite data especially for operationalising the Cohort Component technique. This technique seems to be yielding the most reliable results.

The population in the Periphery Zone is expected to increase from 1.03 million in 2001 to 1.91 million in 2020, a rise by 85 per cent in 20 years at an annual compound growth rate of 3.1 per cent. The zone would be crowded almost two times with the density rising from 756 to 1402 persons per square kilometer by then.

With the fall in the total fertility rate from 2.77 in 2000 to 1.8 in 2020, and with attainment of replacement level of 2.1 in 2009, the population growth in the Periphery Zone will be a product mainly of net-in-migration. Life expectancy in the Periphery Zone is expected to increase from 67.1 in 2001 to 69.4

years in 2020 for the male population and from 71 to 74.2 years in case of female population during the same period. The emerging scenario on fertility and mortality is indicative of the ageing of its population. The median age of the total population is expected to rise from 23 to 33 years during 2001 and 2020.

While planning the city all efforts were made to retain rural character in its surroundings. This was, however, not to be. The Periphery Zone would become urban majority in 2006 when more than half of the population would be residing in urban areas. Its urban population will increase 2.7 fold from 464,491 in 2001 to 1,238,826 in 2020. The rural population will increase from 572,590 in 2001 to 671,174 in 2020. The share of rural population would, however, decrease from 55.2 per cent in 2001 to 35.1 per cent in 2020.

It is worth considering that in the coming decades the massive increase in the population of the Chandigarh Periphery Zone is likely to be propelled more by in-migration than by natural increase, taking into account the dramatic fall in fertility rates and saturation level having been reached in the case of death rate. At the same time, the huge addition to its population numbers is likely to have implications for overall infrastructural development. It is also necessary to figure out whether the region will be able to offer enough employment opportunities for the huge workforce anticipated. The three concerned governments in the Periphery Zone need to work in coordination to meet the challenges of the evolving scenario.

It is evident that the Periphery Zone Control Act, which was enacted with the intent to control the population growth in the zone by placing restrictions on the change of land use has failed in achieving its objective. The present projections give an idea of the likely scene as it would emerge in 2020. These can provide a base for strategizing the needs of the tricity and its periphery in the years to come, especially in terms of rationalization of spatial organizations and conservation of what is left of its natural environment.

7

Summary and Conclusions

The present study is an exercise in futuristic geography that sought to foresee the likely metamorphosis of the landscape of the Chandigarh Periphery Zone by 2020. It is based on the premise that landscape dynamics largely center around rational, public and private, human decisions pertaining to organization of space. Accordingly, the emergent scenario has been projected along the parameters of population and land use with an understanding that one would impact upon the other. The main objectives of the study were to:

(i) assess the effectiveness of the Chandigarh Periphery Control Act in retaining the rural character of the Periphery Zone, as visualized;

(ii) look into the nature and extent of the violations of the Act, and to examine their impact on the landscape;

(iii) project the population of the Periphery Zone on a yearly basis, in terms of rural-urban components, age composition and workforce size; and

(iv) visualize the spatial scene of the Periphery Zone in 2020.

The study becomes critical in the light of the fact that the study area is more of a 'naturalized' or an 'officially instituted zone' rather than a 'natural' zone. This Periphery Zone was delineated soon after the conception of Chandigarh, to be preserved essentially as a rural tract. The intention was to provide a green envelope to the city of Chandigarh and protect it from the unsavory appearance of an urban sprawl. To achieve this end, an elaborate set of rules was framed under the title of the Punjab New Capital (Periphery) Control Act, 1952 and amended in 1962, to expand the jurisdiction of the Periphery Zone from the original of 8 kilometers to 16 kilometers radius from the boundary of the then Chandigarh Project site. Envisaged by planners as a belt that would remain more or less static in terms of land use and population change, it defied plan projections and stipulations alike to exhibit an untrammeled transformation. How and why this occurred and what future course this transformation would take are questions germane to the present study. It was in the light of these questions that the following hypotheses were framed.

(i) Under the prevailing populist political culture and indifferent commitment of the bureaucracy, the Periphery Control Act is likely to be violated and the intended rural character of the Periphery Zone would be difficult to sustain.

(ii) The clause of the Periphery Control Act, under which once a village is upgraded to a town or merged by the government into an existing town goes beyond the purview of the Act, is likely to be exploited the most.

(iii) Villages in contiguity with Chandigarh or other existing towns in Punjab and Haryana sub-zones are more susceptible to acquisition of their land for urban use.

(iv) Attracted by employment opportunities, higher wages and better environment available in Chandigarh and its adjunct planned towns of S.A.S. Nagar (Mohali) and Panchkula, and finding cost of living higher in these places, many migrants would seek residence in their neighbouring villages. This would manifest itself in explosive population growth of these villages.

(v) The demand generated for diverse kinds of physical infrastructure in the form of road and rail transport networks, water treatment, sewage disposal, educational institutions, health centres and recreation sites would put pressure on the land in the Periphery Zone thereby squeezing the area under cultivation, cultivable wasteland and forest, and bringing these under the urban carpet.

The requirements of the research theme guided the nature of methodology employed. Both secondary and primary sources were tapped for the requisite data. Individual villages and towns were the basic units for data analysis. Population as well as land use data was collected from the different volumes of Census of India, District Census Handbooks and Village and Town Directories, 1971 to 2001. Methods appropriate for projecting the population of smaller areas were used. These included ratio, growth differential, compound annual growth rate, extrapolation, and cohort component techniques.

In addition, data on the change of land use was obtained from Land Acquisition Offices of the Governments of Chandigarh, Punjab and Haryana. Information on the extent of land use violations was procured from the Departments of Haryana Urban Development Authority (HUDA), Panchkula, Punjab Urban Planning and Development Authority (PUDA), S.A.S. Nagar (Mohali) and Department of Town Planning, Chandigarh. The land use details of different towns were gathered from the Town and Country Planning Departments of the concerned governments in the Periphery Zone. The minutes of the meeting of the Coordination Committee, which deals with issues of common interest to the three sub-zones-Chandigarh, Punjab and Haryana, were sourced from the secretariat of the Union Territory of Chandigarh. To understand ground realities, villages on sample basis, located on the main roads radiating from Chandigarh, as also at a distance from these were visited personally. In the process, detailed interviews with the local community leaders, corporate houses, land developers and property dealers were conducted to understand the underlying dynamics of change. Discussions on the likely scenario of the Periphery Zone were held with the officials involved in the planning process.

What emerged through data analysis and field visits was the glaring fact that the violation of the Chandigarh Periphery Control Act was initiated by the government itself. Ignoring all protestations by Corbusier, who had conceptualized the Periphery Zone, the Government of India acquired vast rural land to lay out the Chandimandir Military Cantonment. The Hindustan Machine Tools Factory, a Government of India enterprise, was also set-up in its proximity around the same time.

The next blow was dealt in 1966 with the trifurcation of the state of Punjab. Henceforth, while the Periphery Zone would remain the 16 kilometers belt around the city, its administrative control would get distributed over the three governments of Punjab, Haryana and Union Territory of Chandigarh. This unforeseen situation gave a free hand to the governments of Punjab and Haryana to carry out changes they desired by manipulating the provisions of the Act. Thus while the blueprint for the city remained sacrosanct, this privilege could not be extended to its periphery.

The perspective on the Periphery Zone changed from environmental to commercial, the approach from preservation to utilization and the landscape from rural to urban. The existence of three independent administrations that took land use decisions in their individual and often competitive interests in place of common one, largely contributed to this scenario.

The race to reap maximum advantage from Chandigarh began with the creation of S.A.S. Nagar (Mohali) and Panchkula towns, one after the other adjacent to the city of Chandigarh. Neither the emergence of S.A.S. Nagar (Mohali) and Panchkula, nor the setting up of the cantonment conformed to the original conception of the Chandigarh Periphery Zone. Obviously, the main constraints to the management of the Periphery Zone were essentially political rather than technical.

This process perhaps took seed in the plan for the city itself which did not cater for the residential needs of the informal sector comprising construction workers, personal service providers, rickshaw-pullers and others of the kind, nor their low levels of affordability that would disable them from raising houses within the city. They were constrained to settle in the villages and towns of the Periphery Zone. Moreover, the impact of Chandigarh as a growth pole that would bring buoyancy in its surroundings was also underestimated. It is in fact inconceivable that the periphery of a dynamic city like Chandigarh could escape such an effect. This is now an irreversible process. Chandigarh, along with the satellite towns of S.A.S. Nagar (Mohali) and Panchkula has assumed the form of an extended compact urban conglomerate with its collective impact on the periphery Zone. The violation of the Periphery Control Act was inevitable

The truth is that politicians, planners and people at large have all contributed alike to the defiling of the Periphery Zone. Whereas the role of the first and the last is more visible in the Punjab Sub-zone, planning bodies themselves have been more active in the case of Haryana and Chandigarh Sub-zone. As a result, the land use and population change in the Haryana and Chandigarh Sub-zones is better structured and organized than in the Punjab Sub-zone

A notable feature of population dynamics within the rural periphery was a rapid movement of villages from lower size class categories to higher ones. There wasn't a single village having a population of at least 5,000 persons in 1971; however, by 2001, there were 16 such villages. What came as a surprise was the lack of any relationship between the population size and growth rate of villages. Contrary to expectation, smaller the size of the village higher was its compound annual growth rate. This is explained by the initial presence of the relatively small villages in close proximity of Chandigarh. The city was superimposed on an agriculturally backward area with low density of population.

Indeed the factors of distance and matters of connectivity were most critical in determining the growth rate of individual villages. The hypothesis that a large share of migrants would seek residence in the neighbouring villages of Chandigarh, S.A.S. Nagar (Mohali) and Panchkula, due to availability of employment opportunities, higher wages and better environment *vis-à-vis* higher cost of living in these cities, stands validated. The rural population in the 0-4 kilometers distance annule measured from Chandigarh recorded a compound annual growth rate of as much as 5 per cent during 1971-2001. The comparable figures for the 4-8, 8-12 and 12-16 kilometers annules were 3.0, 2.3 and 2.1 per cent respectively. Thus, the growth rate of villages decreased with an increase in the distance from Chandigarh.

The scene differed at the sub-zonal level. Since all the villages in the Chandigarh Sub-zone were located within the 0-4 kilometers distance annule, the growth rate of the rural population at 6 per cent in its case was the highest among that of all sub-zones. The Haryana Sub-zone recorded a growth rate of 3.3 per cent while its different distance annules did not display a consistent pattern. The presence of the Panchkula Urban Estate in contiguity with Chandigarh disturbed the expected pattern. In the case of Punjab Sub-zone, the growth rate is high in the 0-4 kilometers distance annule, moderate in 4-8 and 8-12 kilometers distance annules and comparatively low in 12-16 kilometers distance annule. At the sub-zone level, the role of distance and land use get mixed up in influencing surface trends.

Despite the merger of several fast growing villages in neighbouring towns or their urban status, the rural population in the Periphery Zone recorded a compound annual growth rate of 3 per cent during 1971-2001. The rate of natural increase averaged 2 per cent. Evidently, one-third of the increase in rural population could be attributed to the factor of migration. In-migration was of higher order in villages within Chandigarh Union Territory. This was the outcome of a twin process: migrants to Chandigarh settling in these villages and some Chandigarh residents raising residence in these villages. In addition, villages in proximity of Derra Bassi, Kharar, Zirakpur, Pinjore and Kalka towns, and those situated along the National Highway-22 connecting Chandigarh-Pinjore-Kalka and those finding a location close to the Haryana-Himachal Pradesh border also attracted in-migrants in large numbers. These sites had the locational advantage of being in proximity to Chandigarh, S.A.S. Nagar (Mohali) and Panchkula, as also of better connectivity conducive for commuting. Private developers also found these localities lucrative for raising residential colonies legally or illegally.

Out-migration, on the other hand, was typical of villages located at a distance from Chandigarh, especially in the Punjab Sub-zone. Low agricultural productivity associated with undulating topography, soil erosion and inadequate irrigation had impelled out-migration. It was directed largely to villages located in the proximity of Chandigarh, S.A.S. Nagar (Mohali) and Panchkula. A redistribution of population within the Periphery Zone is, thus, indicated.

Over the years, towns in the Periphery Zone grew in their number, population size and physical spread. The hypothesis that the process of upgradation of a village into town or its merger into the existing towns through acquisition is likely to be exploited the most, stands validated. The state governments discovered this system as an easy way of circumventing the Act. At the time of inception, the Periphery Zone had only four towns, the number of which increased to 12 by 2001. The rapid pace of urbanization herein could be attributed to the emergence of new towns and physical expansion of the existing ones onto the adjacent villages besides the rapid increase of population in all towns without exception. The Punjab Sub-zone witnessed the emergence of six new towns and Haryana of two towns since the enactment of the Periphery Control Act. Consequently, the urban area increased from hardly 10 square kilometers to no less than 140 square kilometers during this period. This impressive transformation of the Periphery Zone from rural to urban could be attributed to the dynamism and magnetism of Chandigarh as also to the incapacity and indifference of the governments to administer the Periphery Control Act.

The growth behaviour of towns in the Periphery Zone has been opposite to that of Chandigarh. In the initial years, the city was having a shadow effect on the growth of towns in the proximity but its own growth rate was rapid, the compound annual urban growth rate being 7.5 and 5.8 per cent during 1961-1981 respectively. The scenario got reversed since 1981. The compound annual urban growth rate of Periphery Zone was almost 2.5 times of that of the city during 1981-2001; the two rates being 3.2 and 7.6 per cent. The city was now exercising a spread rather than backwash effect. New towns that emerged were of great variety: S.A.S. Nagar (Mohali) being an industrial town, Panchkula a service centre, and Chandimandir a cantonment.

The factor of escalating land values and rents in Chandigarh is critical to the expansion of towns in its vicinity. Initially these towns absorbed the intensifying pressure on housing in Chandigarh. The state governments of Punjab and Haryana were also keen to capitalize on the proximity of their territory contiguous to the City Beautiful, famous for its environmental beauty and quality of life. This was not without some positive impact on the Periphery Zone as it was kept reasonably free of unauthorized developments. The main adverse effect of S.A.S. Nagar (Mohali) and Panchkula has been the squeeze of the agricultural land and imposition of industrial landscape around. Such satellite towns depend heavily on Chandigarh for education, health and recreational facilities.

Contrary to what was envisaged the Periphery Zone will gradually lose its rural character to get urbanized at an astonishing pace. The urban population in the Periphery Zone is expected to increase from 0.46 million in 2001 to 1.24 million in 2020, an increase of 167 per cent in 20 years at an annual compound growth rate of 5.03 per cent. This will account for nearly two-thirds of the total population of the Periphery Zone. The share of the rural population in the meanwhile will decrease from 55 per cent in 2001 to 35 per cent in 2020. The combined population of all urban centres would cross the one million mark by the year 2016. The existing towns would grow physically bringing, more and more villages within their municipal limits. The overgrown villages in the Periphery Zone would acquire the status of urban centres.

Such an urban scenario of the Periphery Zone would be a critical element of its management. The Periphery Zone, under the tripartite control of Punjab, Haryana and Chandigarh governments is already facing the problem of coordination among these administrating bodies. After the enactment of the 74th Constitutional Amendment in 1992, these towns are under the purview of elected civic bodies, such as municipalities or *nagar panchayats* on a regular basis. This makes the task of coordination still more difficult, and might complicate the already mismanaged urbanization process. The involvement of internationally reputed institutions for managing Greater Mohali Development Plan might give a direction to the process of urbanization in the Punjab Sub-zone but then the other two sub-zones would remain uncovered.

A significant change in the land use pattern of the Periphery Zone was a natural outcome owing to the demand generated for diverse kinds of physical infrastructure in the form of road and rail transport networks, water treatment, sewage disposal, education and health institutions and recreation sites. The two most noticeable features in the land use change in the Periphery Zone were the decrease in the forest area and increase in the share of land not available for cultivation. The forest cover got denuded by six per cent points and 'land not available for cultivation' increased by 7 per cent points during 1971-2001. The forest cover was completely wiped away from 42 out of 50 villages where it existed in 1971. This phenomenon was more typical of the villages falling in the Punjab and Chandigarh Sub-zones. The decline in the net sown area and cultivable wasteland was marginal during 1971-2001.

The process of urbanization in the Periphery Zone was concomitant with a gradual transformation of the agricultural land into urban use. The premise that villages in contiguity with Chandigarh or other existing towns in Punjab and Haryana Sub-zones are more susceptible to acquisition of their land for urban use stands validated. During 1991-2001 itself, as many as 20 villages were merged into the adjacent towns and five had their status upgraded as towns.

The villages located adjacent to S.A.S. Nagar (Mohali) and Panchkula townships have lost a large chunk of their land to large scale construction activities herein. All kind of land, cultivated, cultivable or forest here is under heavy onslaught of encroachment. Virtually the same is true of villages located around other towns in the Periphery Zone. A lot of fertile agricultural land has been lost to residential colonies, farm houses, commercial establishments, godowns and other such uses in many a village.

The metamorphosis of the rural land into urban use was most conspicuous in villages located along the Chandigarh-

Rupnagar, Chandigarh-Kharar-Landran-Banur belt, Chandigarh-Kalka and Chandigarh-Zirakpur-Derra Bassi highway. This development comprised of both large scale authorized and unauthorized constructions. The illegal structures outnumbered the legal ones. The Government of Haryana detected as many as 8243 unauthorized structures in its sub-zone. Only 38 among these could be authorized by some possible manipulation of the provisions of the Periphery Act.

For reasons more than one, the Punjab Sub-zone was witness to more frequent violations of the kind. It enjoys contiguity with the Chandigarh Union Territory on three sides of north, west and south. It is well connected through direct roads, and is relatively well-off economically speaking. Unlike in Haryana Sub-zone, violations here were getting regularized periodically. This was not without its snowballing effect. Unauthorized structures were raised in other villages also in the hope that these would be legalized sooner or later. One of the convenient ways of authorizing them was to bring them in the fold of the extended territorial jurisdiction of the existing towns. While reprieving, no distinction was made with regard to the nature of violations whether these were in residential localities, commercial belts or industrial area or on forest or agricultural land. This led to regularizations of thousands of illegal structures overnight most of which were substandard. Working behind the scene was the lobby of a motley group of stakeholders, politicians, bureaucrats, land developers and others. They gained more by keeping the land market fragmented and dealings non-transparent. While some thrived on this bargain, the Periphery Zone was losing its green hue to grey.

By comparison, the land use changes in Haryana Sub-zone were comparatively more on planned lines. These were primarily in the form of land use acquisition for extension of the Panchkula town. This is not to deny the mushrooming of several unauthorized structures along the main highways in Haryana Sub-zone. In Chandigarh Sub-zone, acquisition of agricultural land for carving out new sectors or for relocation of slum localities has been the most noticeable feature.

Recently, the process of urban development and associated land use changes have assumed a faster pace in the Periphery Zone in response to buoyancy of economy and increasing investment in housing, education, health, recreation, transport, trade and industry, among others. The hypothesis that the intended rural character of the Periphery Zone is difficult to sustain and is likely to be violated under the prevailing populist political culture and indifferent commitment of the bureaucracy stands validated. Farmland owners in connivance with land colonizers and Departments of Punjab Urban Planning and Development Authority (PUDA) and Haryana Urban Development Authority (HUDA), are making land use decisions in the context of a lucrative economic environment and urbanizing landscape. The last few years have witnessed increased state-level involvement in the name of countering the negative impacts of haphazard urban growth. The urban setting has consumed almost 130 km^2 of rural land since the inception of the zone; 1991-2001 decade alone accounted for 87 km^2. This process is intensifying under the impact of not only Chandigarh but also of its adjunct fully planned towns of S.A.S. Nagar (Mohali) and Panchkula. The provisions of the Periphery Control Act are being circumvented and the original green and serene landscape of the Periphery Zone has been swept under the carpet of urban sprawl.

The Periphery Zone is being gradually transformed from rural to urban; thereby making 'the Periphery a peripheral issue'. This is the price to be paid for urban-led growth strategy. The Act which was enacted with an intent to control the population growth in the Zone by placing restrictions on the change of land use has failed dismally in achieving its objective.

The demographic dynamism of the Periphery Zone has been no less vigorous than the land use transformation. There has been a phenomenal increase in its population from 276,538 to 1,037,041 within a span of three decades, 1971-2001. The population of the Periphery Zone is projected to almost double itself to 1.91 million in 2020. This gives an increase of 85 per cent in 20 years at an average annual compound growth rate of 3.1 per cent. This would be accompanied by a rise in population density from 756 to 1402 persons per square kilometers. Life expectancy in the Periphery Zone is expected to increase from 67.1 in 2001 to 69.4 years in 2020 for the male population and from 71 to 74.2 years in case of female population. Emerging scenario on fertility and mortality is indicative of ageing of its population. The median age of the total population is expected to rise from 23 to 33 years during 2001-20.

The population growth in the Periphery Zone is likely to be propelled more by in-migration than by natural increase taking into account the dramatic fall in the fertility rate and saturation level having been achieved in mortality rate. The proportion of population in the school-going age of 5-14 years is expected to decline from 23 to 14 per cent. The future population growth in the zone is likely to be concentrated in the working age group of 15-59 years. With a projected fall in the total fertility rate from 2.77 in 2000 to 1.8 in 2020, and with attainment of replacement level of 2.1 per cent in 2009, the future population growth in the Periphery Zone will gradually be a product mainly of net in-migration. It is a moot point whether the Periphery Zone will continue offering the requisite and lucrative employment opportunities to the growing size of labour force. Nonetheless the administration of the three governments in the Periphery Zone need to spruce up their act and get ready for infrastructure development and its maintenance on a massive level.

The social infrastructure, including housing, transport, communication, electricity, water supply, sewage, schools, hospitals and other community support services is to be planned for in advance, in particular. This is possible only if the three main stakeholders, that is, the Government of Punjab, Haryana and Chandigarh coordinate their activities towards the accomplishment of this objective. This requires envisioning of the desired future landscape of the Periphery Zone, preparation of a Master Plan, and its committed implementation. Accomplishments of all this may call for a special institutional framework. One possible way is to render statutory status to the Coordination Committee already in function, and to convert Chandigarh and its Periphery Zone into a composite planning unit on the pattern of the National Capital Region.

The present study stimulates a number of research questions for future research. It would be worthwhile to compare the development experience of the Periphery Zone to that of the peripheries of other planned state capitals like Bhubaneshwar at the national level and Islamabad at the International level. This would help in understanding whether or not the urbanization of the periphery is inevitable. Secondly, the impact of the government policies in the form of delineating Free Enterprise Zone or involving corporate sector in land development calls for a critical hard look . Similarly, the likely fall out of the proposed Special Economic Zone at S.A.S. Nagar (Mohali) should be subjected to a detailed prognosis. Finally, in the context of the emerging scenario of Chandigarh, S.A.S. Nagar (Mohali) and Panchkula having assumed the form of an extended urban conglomerate, it may be worthwhile to go in for a New Periphery Zone around the tricity. What should be its physical limits and which criteria should be adopted to define it? Only a research exercise can provide an authentic answer. After all, the present Periphery, through the spatial diffusion of the urbanization process, has already become a part of the Core.

Here a task for an analogous research exercise in the spirit of Futuristic Geography gets defined as to how things are going to take shape by 2050 in the new periphery of the present 'Core-Periphery' fusion.

Bibliography

Anklesaria, Sarosh, 2001. "Chandigarh: Vision and Reality". *Architectural Week*, Eugene, http://www.architectureweek.com/2001/0822/culture_1-1.html.

Anthony, Harry A., 1966. "Le Corbusier: His Ideas for Cities". *American Institute of Planners Journal*, 32, No. 5.

Antoniou, J., 2003. "Chandigarh: Once the Future City-Place". *Architectural Review*, March http://findarticles.com/p/articles/mi_m3575/is_ 1273_213/ai_99215199.

Appleyard, Reginald, eds., 1999. *Migration and Development*. Offprint of the Special Issue of International Migration 37 (1). Switzerland: United Nations Population Fund and International Organization for Migration.

Ashford, Lori S., 2006. "How HIV and AIDS Affect Populations". *BRIDGE*, Population Reference Bureau, Washington, DC. http://www.prb.org/pdf06/HowHIVAIDSAffectsPopulations.pdf.

Baga, S.S., 1985. "Examining Corbusier's City Beautiful". *Journal of Indian Institute of Architects*, 15.

Bala, R., 1986. *Trends in Urbanization in India, 1901-81*. Jaipur: Rawat Publishers.

Batra, B.R., 2002. "Chandigarh : Fringe Area Development—Issues and Planning and Development Considerations". *Urban and Regional Planning Reforms*, Institute of Town Planners, India.

Bhat, Mari P.N., 2001. "Indian Demographic Scenario". Institute of Economic Growth. Delhi, Population Research Centre.

Bhat, Mari P.N. 1996. "Contours of Fertility Decline in India: A District Level Study Based on the 1991 Census", in K. Srinivasan, eds. *Population Policy and Reproductive Health.* New Delhi: Hindustan Publishers.

———, 1998. "Demographic Estimates for Post-Independence India: A New Integration". *Demography India,* 27, No. 1, 23-57.

Bhat, Mari P.N. and F. Zavier, 1999. "Findings of National Family Health Survey, Regional Analysis". *Economic and Political Weekly* 34, Nos. 42-43, 3008-33.

Bhat, Mari P.N. and S.I. Rajan, 1990. "Demographic Transition in Kerala Revisited". *Economic and Political Weekly,* 34, Nos. 35-36, 1957-80.

Bhatnagar, V.S., 1996. *Chandigarh: The City Beautiful, Environmental Profile of a Modern Indian City*. New Delhi: A.P.H. Publishing Corporation.

Bhatti, Surinder Singh, 1990. "Chandigarh and the Context of Le Corbusier's Statute of the Land". Unpublished Doctoral Dissertation. Chandigarh: Panjab University.

Bhogal, H.S., 2002. "Chandigarh Fringe Area Development—Planning, Development and Management of Chandigarh Periphery—Fringe Area in Punjab Sub-Region". *Urban and Regional Planning Reforms,* Institute of Town Planners, India.

Bichsel, Ulrich, 1986. *Periphery and Flux: Chandigarh, Chandigarh Villages.* Bern : Geographisches Institutder Universitat.

Bijlani, H.U., 1977. *Urban Problems.* New Delhi: Navchetan Press.

Bose, A., 1978. *India's Urbanization, 1901-2001.* New Delhi: Tata McGraw Hill Publishing Co.

Bose, A.N., 1980. "Meeting the food requirements in 2000 A.D". in Government of India, ed. *Futurology.* Calcutta: Indian Science News Association.

Brockerhoff, Martin, 2000. "An Urbanizing World, 2020 Vision for Food, Agriculture, and the Environment". International Food Policy Research Institute, Focus No. 3, Brief 02. http://www.ifpri.org/2020/focus/focus03/focus03_02.asp (accessed July 25, 2006).

Broek, J.O.M., 1973. *Geography of Mankind.* New York: McGraw-Hill.

Chandigarh Administration, 2005. *Statistical Abstract, Chandigarh—2005*, Chandigarh: Directorate of Economics and Statistics.

———, 2006. *The Official Website of Chandigarh Administration, Chandigarh the City Beautiful.* http://chandigarh.nic.in/ (accessed on September 1, 2006).

Chandigarh College of Architecture, 2002. *Chandigarh Aesthetic Legislation: Documentation of Urban Controls in Chandigarh (1951-2001), Chandigarh.* Chandigarh: College of Architecture, Sector 12.

Chowdhury, U.E., 1965. "Le Corbusier in Chandigarh: Creator and Generator". *Architectural Design,* 135, October.

Cohen, Barney, 2005. "Urbanization in Developing Countries: Current Trends, Future Projections, and the Key Challenges for Sustainability". *Technology in Society,* 28, 63-80. http://www7.nationalacademies.org/DBASSE/Cities_Transformed_World_TechnologyInSociety_Article.pdf.

Cohen, S.E., 1994. "Greenbelts in London and Jerusalem". *The Geographical Review,* 84, Issue 1. http://www.geography.uoregon.edu/cohen/ research.htm.

Constella Futures Group, 2006. Spectrum. http://www.demonetasia.org/links/ linkssoftware.htm (accessed July 10, 2006)

Corbusier, i.e., 1953. "Chandigarh—The New Capital of Punjab". *The Architect and the Building News,* 204, November.

Corbusier, i.e. 1961. "Chandigarh: The Secretariat, the Assembly Building, the Civic Centre". *Architectural Design* 31, February.

Davis, P.K., 1951. *The Population of India and Pakistan.* New Jersey : Princeton University Press.

Dayal, P., 2004. "World Urbanization : Trends and Challenges". *Annals of the National Association of Geographers, India, 24,* no. 2, December.

Demeny, Paul and Geoffrey McNill, eds. 2006. *Population and Development.* U.K. : Earthscan Publications Ltd.

Department of Family Welfare, 2000. *National Population Policy 2000.* Department of Family Welfare, New Delhi: Government of India.

Directorate of Census Operations, Haryana, 1971. *Village and Town Directory* X-A, *Village and Town-wise Primary Census Abstract, Part X-B, District Census Handbooks of Ambala District*, Government of Haryana.

Directorate of Census Operations, Haryana, 1991. *Migration Tables, Part VA & VB, D-Series, Series-8, Punjab*, Census of India.

Directorate of Census Operations, Punjab, Haryana and Chandigarh, 1961 to 2001. *General Population Tables and Primary Census Abstract, Census of India.* Chandigarh, Government of Punjab, Haryana and Chandigarh.

Directorate of Census Operations, Punjab, Haryana and Chandigarh, 2001. *Provisional Villages and Town Directory.* Chandigarh, Government of Punjab, Haryana and Chandigarh.

Directorate of Census Operations, Punjab, 1971. *Village and Town Directory Village and Town-wise Primary Census Abstract, District Census Handbooks of Rupnagar, and Patiala Districts*, Government of Punjab.

Directorate of Census Operations, Punjab, 1981. *Census of India, District Census Handbook, Patiala District, Series 17, Punjab*, Government of Punjab.

Directorate of Census Operations, Punjab, 1991. *Migration Tables, Part VA & VB, D-Series, Series-20, Punjab*, Census of India.

Drew, Jane, 1953. "Chandigarh Capital City Project". *Architects' Year Book*, No. 4, London.

Drew, Jane, 1953. "On the Chandigarh Scheme". *MARG*, 6, No. 4, Bombay.

D'Souza, V.S., 1968. *Social Structure of a Planned City: Chandigarh.* Bombay: Orient Longman.

Dubey *et. al.*, 1999. Baseline Socio-Economic Survey of Unauthorized and Rehabilitated Colonies in Union Territory, Chandigarh. Chandigarh: Centre for Research in Rural and Industrial Development.

Dutt, Ashok, K., and George, M. Pomeroy, 2003. "Cities of South Asia" in Brunn, Stanley, D. *et. al.* ed., *Cities of the World, World Regional Urban Development.* New York: Littlefield Publishers, Inc.

Dyson, T., 2001. "The Preliminary Demography of the 2001 Census of India". *Population and Development Review,* 27, No. 2, 341-56.

Dyson, T., Robort Cassen and Leela Visaria, 2004. *Twenty-First Century India: Population, Economy, Human Development, and the Environment,* New Delhi: Oxford University Press.

Dyson, T. and A. Hanchate, 2000. "India's Demographic and Food Prospects, State Level Analysis". *Economic and Political Review,* 35, No. 46, 4021-36.

Ellerfsen, R.A., 1962. "City Hinterland Relationship in India, with Special Reference to the Hinterland of Bombay, Delhi, Madras, Hyderabad and Baroda", in Roy Turner, ed. *India's Urban Future.* New Delhi : Oxford University Press.

Evenson, Norma, 1966. *Chandigarh,* Berkeley, University of California Press.

Fitting, Peter, 2002. "Urban Planning/Utopian Dreaming: Le Corbusier's Chandigarh Today". *Utopian Studies,* 13, Issue 1. http://www. questia.com.

Fry, Maxwell, 1955. "Chandigarh: The Capital of the Punjab". *Builder,* 188, January.

Fry, Maxwell, 1955. "Chandigarh—New Capital City". *Architectural Record* 117, June.

Fry, Maxwell, 1961. "Problems of Chandigarh Architecture". *MARG,* 15, No. 1.

Fry, Maxwell, 1965. "Chandigarh: The Punjab Scene". *Architects' Year Book* II.

Fry, Maxwell, 1955. "Chandigarh: The Capital of East Punjab". *RIBA, 62,* Series 3, No. 3, January.

Gagnon, Giles, 1957. "Chandigarh". *Royal Architectural Institute of Canada Journal,* 34, June.

Gethin, Christopher, 1973. "Chandigarh : A Memorial of Arrogance". *Built Environment,* 2.

Gibbs, J.P., 1961. *Urban Research Methods.* Princeton: Van Nostrand Co.

Gilbert, A. and J. Guglar, 1988. *Urban Agglomeration and Regional Disparities, The Urbanization in the Third World.* New York: Oxford University Press.

Gill, Mehar Singh, 1984. "Growth of Urban Population in Punjab". *Urban India,* 4, No. 4, September, 22-31.

Gill, Rajesh, 1991. *Social Change in Urban Periphery.* New Delhi : Allied Publishers.

Glass, Ruth, 1964. *Urban-Rural Differences in Southern Asia—Some Aspects and Methods of Analysis.* UNESCO Research Centre on Social and Economic Development in Southern Asia. New Delhi: Allied Publishers.

Gosal, G.S. ed., 1999. *Fourth Survey of Research in Geography.* New Delhi: Manak Publications Pvt. ltd.

Gould, Peter, 1971. *Spatial Organisation: The Geographer's View of the World,* New Jersey : Prentice Hall.

Griffiths, P. Z. Matthews and A. Hinde, 2000. "Understanding the Sex Ratio in India: A Simulation Approach". *Demography,* 37, No. 4, 477-88.

Gugler, Josef. ed., 1997. *Cities in the Developing World, Issues, Theory, and Policy.* New York : Oxford University Press.

Guilmoto, C.Z. and S.I. Rajan, 2001. "Spatial Patterns of Fertility Patterns in Indian Districts". *Population and Development Review,* 27, no. 4, 713-38.

Gupta, J.K., 2001. "The Punjab New Capital (Periphery) Control Act, 1952", in *Chandigarh Aesthetic Legislation: Documentation of Urban Controls in Chandigarh (1951-2001), Chandigarh.* Chandigarh: College of Architecture, Sector 12.

Gupta, J.K., 2002. "Imperatives for Chandigarh Periphery Development". *Urban and Regional Planning Reforms.* Institute of Town Planners, India.

Gupta, Sehdev Kumar, 1974. "Chandigarh : A Study of Sociological Issues and Urban Development in India". *Architectural Design, 44,* June.

Hackett, Brain, 1969. "Chandigarh Revisited". *Indian Architect-*II, January.

Haggett, P., 1975. *Geography: A Modern Synthesis.* New York: Harper and Row Publishers.

Hancock, Tom. ed., 1976: *Growth and Change in the Future City Region.* London : Leonard Hill.

Howard, E., 1902. *"Garden Cities of Tomorrow London".* New York : Cornell University. http://www.library.cornell.edu/Reps/DOCS/howard.htm.

IIPS and ORC Macro, 1995. *National Family Health Survey, Punjab, 1992-93 (NFHS-1).* Mumbai : International Institute for Population Sciences.

IIPS and ORC Macro, 1995: *National Family Health Survey, Haryana, 1992-93 (NFHS-1)*. Mumbai : International Institute for Population Sciences.

IIPS and ORC Macro, 2000. *National Family Health Survey, Haryana, 1998-99 (NFHS-2)*. Mumbai : International Institute for Population Sciences.

IIPS and ORC Macro, 2000. *National Family Health Survey, Punjab, 1998-99 (NFHS-2)*. Mumbai : International Institute for Population Sciences.

Imrie, Mary, 1958. "Hong Kong to Chandigarh". *Royal Architectural Institute of Canada Journal*, 35, May.

Indian Council of Social Science Research, 1972. *A Survey of Research in Geography*. Bombay : Popular Prakashan.

Indian Council of Social Science Research, 1983. *A Survey of Research in Geography*. New Delhi. Concept Publishing Company.

Indian Council of Social Science Research, 1984. *A Survey of Research in Geography*. New Delhi. Concept Publishing Company.

Iyengar, M.S., 1972. "Can We Transform into a Post-Industrial Society?" in Alvin Toffler, ed. *The Futurists*. New York: Random House.

Jacob, J.F.R., 2001. "49th National Development Council Meeting, 1st September 2001". Speech of His Excellency Lt. Gen. J.F.R. Jacob, PVSM (Retd.), Governor of Punjab and Administrator Union Territory Chandigarh at, Vigyan Bhavan, New Delhi. http://www.planningcommission.nic.in/plans (accessed February 10, 2006).

Jain, K.S.S., 1964. "Chandigarh—1951 to 1964". *Urban and Rural Planning Thought*, 7, Nos. 3-4.

Jeanneret, Pierre, 1963. "The Changing Face of Chandigarh". *Design Annual*, 7, July.

Jeanneret, Pierre, 1967. "Four Recent Projects from Chandigarh". *Design*, 3, March.

Johnson, James H., 1969. *Trends in Geography: An Introductory Survey*. Oxford : Pergamon Press.

Johnston, R.J., 1985. *The Future of Geography*. London : Methuen Corporation Limited.

Joshi, K.N., C.R.S. Suthar, 2002. "Chandigarh Urban Land Use and Its Impacts on the Environment (A Case Study of Jaipur City)". http://www. gisdevelopment.net/ aars/ 2002/luc/luc005pf.html. (accessed on August 16, 2006).

Kalia Ravi, 1987. *Chandigarh: The Making of An Indian City.* New Delhi: Oxford University Press.

Kandhari, N., 1984. "Demographic Changes in the Inter-State Chandigarh Region: 1951-71 (A Spatial Analysis)". Unpublished Ph.D. Dissertation. Chandigarh: Panjab University.

Kant, Surya, 1988. *Administrative Geography of India.* Jaipur : Rawat Publications.

Kaur, R., 2004. "Urban-Rural Relations in India (A Case Study of the Inter-State Chandigarh Region)". Unpublished Ph.D. Dissertation. Chandigarh: Panjab University.

Kaur, S., 1962. "Regional Integration of a Planned City—Chandigarh, A Case Study". MA Dissertation. Chandigarh: Panjab University.

Khan, Hasan, Uddin and Others, eds. 2010. *Le Corbusier: Chandigarh and the Modern City*, Maping Publishing, Ahmedabad.

Khurana, J.J., 2002. "Chandigarh Fringe Area Development and Control". *Urban and Regional Planning, Reforms*. Institute of Town Planners, India.

Krishan, G. and S.K. Aggarwal, 1970. "Umland of a Planned City: Chandigarh". *National Geographical Journal of India*, 31-46.

Krishan, G., 1990. "Pricing of Water Supply in Indian Cities". *Urban India*, June.

Krishan, G., 1991. "Urban-Rural Relations in India: A Critique". *IASSI Quarterly*, 10, 92-104.

Krishan, G., 1994. *Chandigarh 2020: Projections of Population and Class Structure.* Chandigarh : Chandigarh Administration.

Krishan, G., 1999. *Inner Spaces, Outer Spaces of a Planned City: Thematic Atlas of Chandigarh*. Chandigarh: Chandigarh Administration.

Krishan, G., 2000. "Chandigarh: A Futuristic Perspective" in Allen G. Noble *et. al.* eds. *Geographic and Planning Research Themes for the New Millennium*. New Delhi : Vikas Publishing House Pvt. Ltd.

Krishan, G., 2002. "Has 'Chandigarh Periphery' Become a Peripheral Issue". *Urban and Regional Planning Reform,* Institute of Town Planners, India.

Krishan, G. and M. Shayam, 1978. "Regional Aspects of Urban-Rural Differentials in India, 1971". *The Journal of Developing Areas,* 13, Nos. 1, 11-21.

Krishan, Gopal, 1994. *Chandigarh 2020: Projections of Population and Class Structure.* New Delhi : Swan Publishers.

Kundu, A., 1980. *Measurement of Urban Processes—A Study of Regionalization.* Bombay : Popular Parkashan.

Lal, H., 1987. *City and Urban Fringe: A Case Study of Bareilly.* New Delhi: Concept Publishing Company.

Lamba, N.S., 1961-62. "Chandigarh Project Study". *Journal of Institute of Town Planners India,* Nos. 25-35.

Lutz, Wolfgang, Warren C. Sanderson and Sergei Scherbov, eds. 2004. *The End of World Population Growth in the 21st Century, New Challenges for Human Capital Formation and Sustainable Development.* London: Earthscan.

Lutz, Wolfgang, 1994. The *Future Population of the World: What Can We Assume Today*? London: Earthscan Publications.

Malik, B.K., 2004. "City Planning and Realities—A Case Study of Chandigarh". International Conference on City Futures. USA : University of Illinois, Chicago. http://www.uic.edu/cuppa/cityfutures/papers/webpapers/city futurespapers/session1_3/1_3cityplanning.pdf (accessed on July 9, 2006).

Malik, Yogendra, 1973. "Conflict Over Chandigarh : A Case Study of Inter-State Dispute in India". *Contribution to Asian Studies,* 3.

Mandelbaum, D.G., 1972. *Society in India.* Bombay: Popular Prakashan.

Mayor, Albert, 1967. *The Urgent Future.* New York: McGraw Hill.

Mehta, A.C., 1996. *Population Projections: Sub-National Dimensions.* New Delhi: Commonwealth Publishers.

Mehta, Asoka, 1962. "The Future of Indian Cities: National Issues and Goals" in Roy, Turner, ed. *India's Urban Future.* Berkley : University of California Press.

Misra, Bidyadhar, 1988. *Village Life in India: Past and Present*. New Delhi: Ajanta Publication.

Mukerji, A.B., 1962. "The Upland of Modinagar". *National Geographical Journal of India*, 8, 250-69.

Murthi, N., A.C. Guio, and J. Dreze, 1995. "Mortality, Fertility and Gender Bias in India: A District Level Analysis". *Population and Development Review*, 21, No. 3, 745-82.

Narasimhan, R.L., Robert D. Retherford, Vinod Mishra, Fred Arnold, and T.K. Roy, 1997. "Comparison of Fertility Estimates from India's Sample Registration System and National Family Health Survey". *National Family Health Survey Subject Reports No. 4*. Mumbai : International Institute for Population Sciences. Honolulu : East-West Centre.

National Committee on Science and Technology. 1980. *Short Studies in Future Research*. New Delhi: NCST.

National Institute of Urban Affairs, 1988. *State of India's Urbanization*. New Delhi: National Institute of Urban Affairs.

Nilsson, Sten A., 1973. *The New Capitals of India, Pakistan and Bangladesh*. Translated by Elisabeth Andreasson. Sweden.

Office of the Registrar General, 1991. *Towns and Urban Agglomerations 1991 with their Population 1901-91, Part II-A (ii)-A Series, Table A4*. Census of India. New Delhi: Office of the Registrar General.

———, 1996. *Population Projections for India and States 1996-2016*. Census of India. New Delhi: Office of the Registrar General.

———, 1999b. *SRS Compendium of India's Fertility and Mortality Indicators: 1971-1997 (Based on the Sample Registration System)*. New Delhi : Office of the Registrar General.

———, 2001. *Primary Census Abstract of Chandigarh, Punjab and Haryana*. New Delhi : Office of the Registrar General.

———, 2001a. *Provisional Population Totals, Paper 1 of 2001*. Census of India. New Delhi: Office of the Registrar General.

———, 2002. *Sample Registration System Statistical Report, 2000*. New Delhi : Office of the Registrar General.

———, 2003. *Sample Registration System Statistical Report, 2000, Report no. 5 of 2003*. New Delhi : Office of the Registrar General.

Office of the Registrar General, 2006. *Migration Tables*. New Delhi. Census Commissioner, India.

———, 2006. *Population Projections for India and States 2001-26*, Report of the Technical Group on Population Projections. New Delhi: Census Commissioner, India.

Papillault, R., 2000. "Temporal Dimensions in the Urban Projects of Le Corbusier: The Case of Chandigarh". *Architecture*, France http://www.atelier-rp.org/recherches/chandienglish.htm.

Pathak, P. and D. Mehta, 1995. "Recent Trends in Urbanization and Rural and Urban Migration in India: Some Explanations and Projections". *Urban India*, 15, No. 2, 1-16.

Perez De Arce Rodrigo, 1981. "Chandigarh Re-Urbanization: A Critical Fantasy". *Design*, April-June.

Planning Commission, 2002a. *Approach Paper to the Tenth Five-Year Plan, 2002-07*. New Delhi: Government of India.

Population Foundation of India, 2000. *Population Growth in 21st Century*. New Delhi : Population Foundation of India.

Potter, Robert and Tim Unwin, 1989. *The Geography of Urban-Rural Interaction in Developing Countries*. London: Routledge.

Ramachandran, R., 1989. *Urbanisation and Urban Systems in India*. New Delhi: Oxford University Press.

Randhawa, M.S., 1967. *Landscaping Chandigarh*. Chandigarh : Chandigarh Union Territory Administration.

Randhawa, M.S. (no date). *Brief Review of Work Done in Chandigarh since Nov. 1, 1966*. Chandigarh : Government Press.

———, *Chandigarh*. Chandigarh, n.p.

Rao, M.S.A., 1970. *Urbanisation and Social Change: A Study of a Rural Community on a Metropolitan Fringe*. New Delhi: Orient Longman.

Reddy, V.N.K., 1985. *Problems of Futurology*. New Delhi: Sterling Publications.

Reps, John W., 2002. "Garden Cities of Tomorrow". http://www.library.cornell.edu/Reps/DOCS/howard.htm (accessed on July 12, 2002).

Ribeiro, E.F.N., 1984. *Regional Plan: Inter-State Chandigarh Region, 2001*. Town and Country Planning Organization. Government of India : Ministry of Works and Housing.

Ruch, M., 2002. *Unbuilt Open Space in Chandigarh New Capital City, A Modern Experiment Circumvented by the Tradition.* Pully, Switzerland.

Sandhu, K.S., 2002. "Uncontrolled Periphery of Chandigarh and Mind Boggling Questions". *Urban and Regional Planning, Reforms,* Institute of Town Planners, India.

Sarhadi, Ajit Singh, 1970. *Punjabi Suba: The Story of Struggle.* Delhi : Gurdas Kapur Publishing.

Sarin, Madhu, 1982. *Urban Planning in the Third World: The Chandigarh Experience.* Mansell Publishing Limited.

Schmetzer, M. and P. Wakeley. 1974. "Chandigarh: Twenty Years Later", *Architectural Design,* 44, June.

Scott, Allen J. ed. 2001. *Global City-Regions, Trends, Theory, Policy.* New York: Oxford University Press.

Seth, S.C., 1980. "Relevance of Futuristic Thinking for Socio-Economic Change" in Government of India, ed. *Futurology.* Calcutta : Indian Science News Association.

Shafi, Sayed S., 1989. "Delhi: In the Year 2000" in Dhamija, Ram, ed. *Delhi: The Deepening Crisis.* New Delhi: Sterling.

Sharma, K.L. and D. Gupta, 1991. *Country Town Nexus.* Jaipur : Rawat Publications.

Sharma, Kanchan, 2006. *Role of Collaborative Planning in Environmental Management : Case Study Peripheral Development of Chandigarh.* Unpublished Master of Engineering Dissertation. Chandigarh: Punjab Engineering College.

Sharma, Mohan, N., 2003. "Le Courbusier's Concept of Chandigarh". Hamburger, *Architektursommer 97,* Hamburg. http://www.tu-harburg.de/b/kuehn/ sharma.html.

Sharma, N. 1997. "Containing Exodus from Villages to Cities: A Panacea". *Kurukshetra,* 46, Nos. 1 and 2, 105-107.

Sharma, Pawan Kumar and Komila Parthi, 2001. "Population Projections for a Hill State : Himachal Pradesh". *Population Geography,* 23, Nos. 1 and 2, June-December.

Sharma, Sri Ram (no date). *Administrative Set-up at Chandigarh.* Chandigarh: Institute of Public Administration, Punjab.

Sharma, Swapnil, 2005. *Future of the Periphery in Chandigarh.* Unpublished M. Planning Dissertation. New Delhi: School of Planning and Architecture.

Singer, Milton, 1972. *When a Great Tradition Modernises.* New Delhi: Vikas Publishers.

Singh, D.P., 1998. "Internal Migration in India : 1961-91". *Demography India,* 27, No. 1, 245-61.

Skeldon, R., 1986. "On Migration Patterns in India during the 1970s". *Population and Development Review,* 12, No. 4, 759-79.

Smith, Anthony, 1983. "Communication in the Year 2000" in Ritchie Calder. ed. *The Future of a Troubled World.* London: Heinemann.

Srinivas, M.N., 1974. "Industrialisation and Urbanisation of Rural Areas", in M.S.A. Rao. ed. *Urban Sociology in India.* New Delhi : Orient Longman.

Stohr, W.B., 1981. "Development from Below the Bottom-up and Periphery Inward Development Paradigm", in Stohr W.B. and Taylor. eds. *Developing from Above or Below.* Wiley Chicester.

Sundram, K.V., 1977. *Urban and Regional Planning in India.* New Delhi: Vikas Publishing House.

Town and Country Planning Department. 1982. Inter-State Chandigarh Region, *Ministry of Works and Housing.* New Delhi: Government of India.

Town and Country Planning Department, 2000. *A Report on Inter-State Chandigarh Sub-Region Punjab—2021.* Chandigarh: Government of Punjab.

Turner, Roy, ed. 1962. *India's Urban Future.* Berkeley: University of California Press.

United Nations Population Division, 2005. "World Population Prospects: The 2004 Revision Analysis". United Nations: Department of Economic and Social Affairs. http://www.un.org/esa/population/publications/WPP2004/WPP2004_Volume3.htm (accessed October 16, 2006).

Verma, P.L., 1954. "Chandigarh—The City of Tomorrow". *Nirman,* April-June.

Verma, S.B. and D. Nimbokar, 2002. "Chandigarh Fringe Area—A Critical Analysis". *Urban and Regional Planning Reforms,* Institute of Town Planners, India.

Vimal, B., 1994. The Planned City of Chandigarh: A Geographical Appraisal. Unpublished Ph.D. Dissertation. Chandigarh: Panjab University.

Westfall, Matthew S. and Victoria A. de Villa, 2001. *Urban Indicators for Managing Cities*. Manila: Asian Development Bank.

World Commission on Environment and Development, 1987: *Our Common Future*. New Delhi: Oxford University Press.

Zinkin, Taya, 1954. "India's Most Modern City: Chandigarh". *Journal of the American Institute of Architects*, 62, November.

Index